NIETZSCHE, POLITICS
AND MODERNITY

PHILOSOPHY & SOCIAL CRITICISM

Series Editor: David M. Rasmussen, Boston College

This series will present an interdisciplinary range of theory and critique emphasising the interrelation of continental and Anglo-American scholarship as it affects contemporary discourses. Books in the series are aimed at an international audience, focusing on contemporary debates in philosophy and ethics, politics and social theory, feminism, law, critical theory, postmodernism and hermeneutics.

NIETZSCHE, POLITICS AND MODERNITY

A Critique of Liberal Reason

David Owen

SAGE Publications
London • Thousand Oaks • New Delhi

© David Owen 1995

First published 1995

 SAGE Publications Ltd
6 Bonhill Street
London EC2A 4PU

SAGE Publications Inc
2455 Teller Road
Thousand Oaks, California 91320

SAGE Publications India Pvt Ltd
32, M-Block Market
Greater Kailash - I
New Delhi 110 048

British Library Cataloguing in Publication data

A catalogue record for this book is
available from the British Library

ISBN 0 8039 7766 2
ISBN 0 8039 7767 0 (pbk)

Library of Congress catalog record available

Typeset by Type Study, Scarborough, North Yorkshire
Printed in Great Britain by The Cromwell Press Ltd,
Broughton Gifford, Melksham, Wiltshire

To Sam
for her courage and curiosity

The question which stirs us as we think beyond the grave of our own generation is not the *well-being* human beings will enjoy in the future but what kind of people they will *be.* . . . We do not want to breed well-being in people, but rather those characteristics which we think of as constituting the human greatness and nobility of our nature.

Max Weber

. . . even if the typical character types of liberal democracies *are* bland, calculating, petty, and unheroic, the prevalence of such people may be a reasonable price to pay for political freedom.

Richard Rorty

Contents

Preface

Why Nietzsche now? Reflecting on the contemporary intellectual scene, it appears as if Nietzsche is rapidly becoming as central to cultural debates in our *fin de siècle* as he was to cultural critics at the end of the nineteenth century. Perhaps Nietzsche is a thinker suited to the sense of change which marks a century's end and beginning? Whether this is so or not, there are clear reasons why Nietzsche's thinking is relevant to us. Firstly, analytic philosophy is finally coming around to positions on truth and ethics which are anticipated in Nietzsche's work. Secondly, the influence of continental philosophy inspired in part by Nietzsche has acquired considerable cultural capital in recent years. Finally, and perhaps most importantly, Nietzsche's diagnosis of modernity as nihilism and decadence finds considerable resonance in our contemporary cultural experience and understanding. Moreover, with the decline – no doubt, to be short-lived – of the public authority of Marxist perspectives, Nietzsche provides another voice for those persons concerned by the platitudes of liberal triumphalism which sustains the project of a critical engagement with liberalism in the public political culture of our constitutional-democratic regimes. In arguing for Nietzsche's inclusion within the canon of political theory, this book is a further attempt to press the case for the critical perspective on liberalism which Nietzsche's thought discloses to us.

Yet I remain somewhat surprised that doing this work has become a necessity for me; having apparently settled my accounts with Nietzsche in my previous book, *Maturity and Modernity* (1994), I did not expect to re-enter this arena so soon afterwards and particularly not in such an utterly self-critical vein. That I was not able to lapse into comfortable complacency on this score is largely due to three friends – Keith Ansell-Pearson, Howard Caygill and Daniel Conway – whose work and example provoked and cajoled me into returning to the arena. Without their inspiration and encouragement, this book would not have been written.

The shape of the argument developed here owes much to teaching a third-year course on Rawls and his critics at the University of Central Lancashire and I am grateful to my students for discussion and support. The set text for this course was Mulhall and Swift's *Liberals and Communitarians* (1992) and I draw on this incisive guide throughout the relevant portions of my argument, not least because they frequently express the issues with greater clarity than I can muster. During the period of writing this book, my then colleagues in the Politics and Government group offered continual encouragement. Thanks are due to Keith Faulks, Joe Ravetz, John Barlow,

Rob Hulme and Tony Bamber for providing a sense of community and solidarity despite – and in part because of – the efforts of the management to undermine such non-contractual sentiments. I owe particular thanks to Terry Hopton for helping to make the teaching of political theory so enjoyable and for the sheer stimulation of our ongoing conversations (thanks also to Terry and his wife Joan for giving me a roof over my head as I commute up and down from London to Preston). I would further like to acknowledge John Joughin and Richard Walker for our continuing discussions of philosophy and literature – a topic central to any work on Nietzsche.

I am fortunate in having received support from a number of other people of whom I would like to single out Tom and Judith Osborne, Chris and Jacqui Butler, Simon Court and Joanna Hodge – all of whom have helped to maintain my sanity as I grappled with Nietzsche's thinking. I would also like to mention the support of Ted Benton and Noel O'Sullivan; despite our different theoretical perspectives, both have encouraged me to engage with this project from the outset. At a more specific level, a number of people (apart from those already mentioned) commented on sections of the manuscript and/or sent me copies of their own work on the topics addressed which have influenced my thinking. Particular thanks in this regard to Samantha Ashenden, Martin Hollis, Duncan Large, Paul Patton, Herman Siemans, Charles Turner and any others I have inadvertently omitted. Ziyad Marar and Robert Rojek have been supportive and non-intrusive editors throughout the period of writing and I am grateful for their encouragement and restraint.

Finally, I would like to thank my family for their perpetual support and Samantha Ashenden – to whom this book is dedicated – for the honesty, friendship and love that continues to fill my life with wonder and joy.

Abbreviations

AC   *The Anti-Christ*, trans. R.J. Hollingdale, Harmondsworth: Penguin, 1968.

BGE   *Beyond Good and Evil*, trans. W. Kaufmann, New York: Random House, 1966.

BT   *The Birth of Tragedy*, trans. W. Kaufmann, New York: Random House, 1967.

D   *Daybreak*, trans. R.J. Hollingdale, Cambridge: Cambridge University Press, 1982.

EH   *Ecce Homo*, trans. R.J. Hollingdale and W. Kaufmann, New York: Random House, 1967.

GM   *On the Genealogy of Morals*, trans. R.J. Hollingdale and W. Kaufmann, New York: Random House, 1967.

GS   *The Gay Science*, trans. W. Kaufmann, New York: Random House, 1974.

HAH   *Human, All Too Human*, trans. R.J. Hollingdale, Cambridge: Cambridge University Press, 1986.

HC   'Homer on Competition' in *On the Genealogy of Morality [and other essays]*, edited by K. Ansell-Pearson and trans. C. Diethe, Cambridge: Cambridge University Press, 1994.

TI   *Twilight of the Idols*, trans. R.J. Hollingdale, Harmondsworth: Penguin, 1968.

WP   *The Will to Power*, trans. R.J. Hollingdale and W. Kaufmann, New York: Random House, 1967.

WS   *The Wanderer and His Shadow*, trans. R.J. Hollingdale, Cambridge: Cambridge University Press, 1986.

Z   *Thus Spoke Zarathustra*, trans. R.J. Hollingdale, Harmondsworth: Penguin, 1969.

Introduction

'Mad, bad and dangerous to know': until recently Lady Caroline Lamb's judgement of Byron typified the response of Anglo-American political philosophy to the enigmatic figure of Friedrich Nietzsche. While few denied Nietzsche's significance for modern culture (his impact on writers, poets and thinkers as diverse as Havelock Ellis, W.B. Yeats, Stefan George, George Bernard Shaw, Sigmund Freud, D.H. Lawrence, Thomas Mann, Georg Simmel, Herman Hesse and Martin Heidegger, to name but a few, renders his status as a cultural icon undeniable),[1] the desirability of this influence, particularly within the domain of politics, remained a matter of heated debate and led proponents as much as critics to present Nietzsche as either an apolitical or, even, an anti-political thinker. Today, perhaps, our historical distance from the cultural appropriation of Nietzsche's name by the ideologues of Nazi Germany allows us to pose again the question of Nietzsche as a political thinker; perhaps too, the much heralded demise of Marxism,[2] driven initially by the repressive practices of the 'communist' states and, latterly, by the (apparent) collapse of these states, has created a vacuum within which an alternative critique of liberalism is rendered both possible and desirable. Whatever the status of such speculations, this book seeks to engage with Nietzsche as a political thinker (and to put the case for his inclusion within the canon of political theory) by focusing on the critique of liberal reason articulated in his work.

Recalling Max Weber's ranking of Nietzsche with Marx as the dominant interpreters and critics of modernity,[3] my claim is simply that for liberals in general and liberal political theorists in particular to take themselves seriously requires that they confront Nietzsche's critique. No doubt this claim will appear extravagent and abhorrent to those for whom Nietzsche's thought is irredeemably connected to the horrors of the Second World War. To such persons, I would reply simply that the Nazi and fascist interpretations of Nietzsche's work do not necessarily impugn the writings themselves if we can offer good reasons for rejecting these readings as lacking the virtues of interpretive activity. In the case of these interpretations, a wilful eliding of Nietzsche's critique of the state, his anti-nationalism and his contempt for anti-semitism on the part of his Nazi and fascist readers seems reason enough to dismiss them. 'But don't Nietzsche's ideas have at least an elective affinity with Nazi and fascist ideologies?' No. Indeed, I would argue that perhaps what is most notable about Nazism and fascism is that their most basic assumptions embody the spirit of revenge (*ressentiment*) against which Nietzsche directed his critical faculties.

No doubt my claim concerning Nietzsche's significance will also seem extravagant (if not abhorrent) to political theorists more generally; it is, after all, an extravagant claim. However, since open-mindedness is generally taken to be an intellectual virtue, I hope the reader will feel able to approach this argument for Nietzsche's significance in a spirit of sceptical tolerance, reading it as an attempt not to command submission to Nietzsche's views (how very anti-Nietzschean such an attempt would be will become clear in the course of the argument) but to open up a debate between Nietzsche's philosophy and liberal political thought. Critical thinking often consists of agonistic dialogues and it is such a conception of reason as dialogic contestation which this book seeks to exhibit. At this stage, having made my plea, it seems appropriate to turn to the structure of the argument.

In the opening chapter, I seek to introduce the combatants in this debate by sketching very briefly the main themes of liberalism as a political ideology and Nietzsche's philosophy. In outlining liberalism, I distinguish two kinds of arguments for liberalism which Nietzsche's critique must address: on the one hand, philosophical or metaphysical arguments for liberalism which I connect to Kant and the early Rawls; and, on the other hand, political or 'postmodern' arguments for liberalism which I link to the later Rawls and Rorty. After introducing Nietzsche, I suggest that his critique of the former of these types of argument is articulated through his doctrines of perspectivism, genealogy and will to power, while his critique of the latter type of argument is articulated through his elaboration of an ethics of integrity centred on the ideas of the Overman, *amor fati* and eternal recurrence, and an agonistic conception of politics as well as a critique of the kinds of human beings facilitated by liberalism. I conclude this chapter by exploring the character of political argument.

Chapter 2 takes up the task of explicating Nietzsche's philosophical position by exploring his perspective theory of affects, the idea of genealogy and the thesis of will to power in terms of a critique of the philosophical commitments of liberal reason as these are presented in the Kantian project of epistemology. I argue that Nietzsche provides us with good reasons for adopting a perspectivist account of truth, a genealogical conception of critique and an erotic account of rational subjectivity. This leads us into Chapter 3, in which I explore Nietzsche's genealogy of modernity in terms of the emergence, development and self-overcoming of the philosophical commitments of foundational arguments for liberalism which constitutes the conditions of possibility and affective interests of Nietzsche's own thinking.

Chapter 4 takes up Nietzsche's account of modernity as characterised by nihilism and decadence before considering his reasons for articulating an alternative ethical ideal. Here the focus is placed, firstly, on Nietzsche's account of the collapse of the ascetic ideal and, thus, the metaphysical beliefs which it exemplifies, and, secondly, on connecting Nietzsche's reasons for constructing a counter-ideal to the work of MacIntyre and Taylor. Chapter 5 goes on to address the substance of the ethical account which Nietzsche offers by identifying a schema characterised by an ontological thesis (will to power), an ethical rule (eternal recurrence), an ascetics (self-overcoming) and a *telos* (the Overman and *amor fati*).

The final chapter takes up Nietzsche's critique of liberal political theory directly. Beginning by suggesting the kinds of criticisms which Nietzsche might offer of Rawls' philosophical liberalism, it goes on to sketch a connection between perspectivism, agonism and the cultivation of *virtù*. I then take up a possible line of objection to the connection of perspectivism and agonism by entertaining Rorty's liberal perspectivism, which is found to be unsatisfactory. At this stage, the argument sets up an encounter between Rawls' political liberalism and Nietzsche's political agonism in terms of their capacities to satisfy our theoretical interests, before going on to contrast agonistic and liberal types of politics in terms of the types of human being which they cultivate. I conclude that it is at least plausible that Nietzsche's philosophy and the kind of politics to which it is committed offer greater resources for human flourishing than liberalism.

Notes

1 For a comprehensive view of Nietzsche reception in Germany, see Ascheim (1992).

2 Perhaps I should make clear that I think the much heralded demise of Marxism is something of a damp squid but that the rhetorical effects of this liberal triumphalism are politically worrying.

3 Weber remarked to a student that the probity of the modern scholar could be judged by the extent to which they acknowledge that their work would not be possible without Marx and Nietzsche.

1

Nietzsche *contra* Liberalism

Reflections on the Character of Contests within Political Theory

Perhaps we should begin by recognising that to interpret Nietzsche as a political thinker and, more specifically, as a critic of liberalism draws us inextricably into three ongoing debates; for to offer an interpretation of Nietzsche as a political thinker is to enter into, *firstly*, the contestation within political theory concerning the character of politics, *secondly*, the dispute between interpretations of Nietzsche's philosophy as political, apolitical or anti-political and, *thirdly*, the debate between different readings of Nietzsche as a political theorist. Each of these agonistic encounters provides a context for the argument developed in this book, however, while the second and third of these contests call on Nietzsche's readers to enter the Nietzschean *agon* (and this book as a whole is an engagement in these debates), the first and most general of these topics – what is politics? – requires our attention if we are to recognise the significance of the challenge which Nietzsche poses to contemporary political theory and, in particular, to liberal varieties thereof. In other words, it is this question which we must address if we are to account for why we should even concern ourselves with Nietzsche's thought. In this context, the concern of this chapter will be initially to provide a brief introduction to the contestants before focusing on the question of the character of political arguments in order to illuminate the nature of the stakes involved in this contest (stakes which we will see include our notion of the character of political contests). Since liberalism is the target of Nietzsche's ire, it seems appropriate to begin by attempting to specify the features of this political tradition.

An Introduction to Liberalism

Liberalism is an ongoing tradition within political theory whose success can be seen in the simple fact that much of our current political vocabulary is drawn from this source. However, liberalism is not a homogeneous tradition; indeed, John Dunn refers to contemporary liberalism as 'an array of shreds and tatters of past ideological improvisation and highly intermittent political illumination' (1985: 10). Given the diversity of views exhibited within this ideological tradition, we can best characterise liberalism as a family of political arguments and evaluations within which different members of the family do not necessarily exhibit identical features. For example, while liberals are typically committed to the idea of individuals as free and equal persons, they often disagree about the character of freedom (positive or negative?) and of equality (legal or social?) as well as their relative priority (is the commitment to freedom grounded in the belief in equality or *vice versa*?). Again, while liberals are generally committed to the idea of individual diversity – 'each person has his own unique conception of what makes life worth living and is entitled to pursue that conception to the best of his ability' (Mendus, 1989: 75) – and, concomitantly, to the idea of toleration, justifications of this commitment appeal to different grounds, most notably scepticism, neutrality and autonomy. Given the plurality of positions within the liberal tradition, I will not try to specify the 'core consensus' of liberalism but will simply set out a number of recurring features within the heterogeneous identity of liberalism, some of which must be held if the claim of an argument to be liberal is to be intelligible to us.

Perhaps the most widely held and internally contested features within the liberal tradition are the two already cited: the commitment to individuals as free and equal persons and the commitment to toleration based on the recognition of individual diversity. To what other features are these related? I will treat them in turn. Historically, the commitment to *individual freedom and equality* acts as a critical limit on the domain of *political authority*. This aspect of liberalism combines an idea of the *natural* or *primary* character of individual freedom and equality and the *constructed* or *secondary* character of political authority with a recognition of the *necessity* of political authority to guarantee and secure the widest possible range of human freedom compatible with equal freedom for all. Closely connected to this feature of liberalism are three further features. Firstly, a conception of *sovereignty* (political authority) as the product of a (real or counterfactual) *contract* between individuals which grounds the *legitimacy* of sovereignty in the free *consent* of individuals. Secondly, a conception of *universal human rights* (such as life, liberty and property) which are enshrined in the social contract and which mark the boundaries of legitimate action on the part of the sovereign. Thirdly, a distinction between *public* and *private* spheres: the public *political* sphere in which the actions of the subject as a *citizen* are regulated by political authority; and the private *nonpolitical* sphere in which the actions of the subject as a *private individual* are not regulated by political authority and in which individuals are free to pursue and revise the diverse conceptions of the good which they hold. At the same time, the commitment to toleration and individual diversity has exhibited itself historically as a commitment to *pluralism* and *democracy* in which the *formal* character of the features already noted may find expression in the equal freedom of persons to express their moral commitments and to participate in the process of political decision-making. The liberal commitment to freedom, equality and diversity is frequently linked to a commitment to the *neutrality* of the state and an emphasis on the *procedural* character of law-making and the *formal* character of law in constitutional democracies.

However, while most liberals are committed to most of these features of liberalism, we should re-emphasise that there is considerable disagreement about the character and the significance of these features which is reflected in the different arguments offered as justifications of liberalism both in terms of what is being argued for and in terms of the structuring of the argument. Despite this variety, we can introduce a formal distinction between two *types* of argument which is immanent to the current development of the liberal tradition, namely, a distinction between 'philosophical liberalism' and 'political liberalism'.[1] This distinction can be formulated in a fairly straightforward way (although we should note that this does not entail that the distinction is necessarily sustainable): *philosophical liberalism* involves the claim that the political principles of liberalism require a comprehensive philosophical foundation (about, for example, the nature of the self and the form of society) which secures the normative force of these principles by revealing their rationality, while *political liberalism* suggests that arguments for liberalism do not require the backing of a comprehensive philosophical doctrine but can be developed in terms of the political judgements implicit in the public political culture of constitutional-democratic regimes, that is, in terms of the features which 'we' (the community formed within 'our' tradition) want from a political argument (and, indeed, a polity), where these 'interests' are revealed in the character of our public political culture.

Even if we adopt this distinction though, there are still a bewildering plurality of liberal arguments and, consequently, in order to make the task of this text manageable, I will focus on a single form of argument for liberalism from each of the frameworks of philosophical liberalism and political liberalism. On the one hand, with respect to philosophical liberalism, I will be concerned with Kantian versions of liberalism of which John Rawls' *A Theory of Justice* (1971) is the most influential recent example. My reasons for addressing this form of argument for liberalism are twofold: firstly, Kant's liberalism is Nietzsche's main political target and he expends considerable energies in attacking its philosophical underpinnings; and, secondly, Rawls' *A Theory of Justice* is widely regarded as the most important work of political philosophy of recent decades. On the other hand, with respect to political liberalism, I will take up arguments for liberalism of the sort developed by Richard Rorty and by John Rawls in his work after *A Theory of Justice* which seeks to eschew reliance on philosophical claims. My reasons for focusing on this line of argument are also twofold: firstly, since Rorty is often taken to be some kind of 'happy Nietzschean' (and his own comments support this characterisation), my claim that Nietzsche is a vigorous critic of liberalism must take up the challenge Rorty offers, namely, that the most important elements of Nietzsche are compatible with liberalism; and, secondly, since the *different* arguments presented by Rorty and Rawls represent the most widely known and currently influential versions of a post-philosophical defence of liberalism, if Nietzsche's criticisms of this style of argument are plausible, we may have good reasons for rejecting liberalism as a project which no longer meets our interests. In this context, to clarify what it is about these positions that I will claim Nietzsche attacks, let us turn to the features of these arguments.

Philosophical liberalism of the kind offered by Kant and the early Rawls may be characterised by three common features: a particular conception of the person, a form of asocial individualism and a commitment to universalism.[2] Let us address these features in turn. Firstly, there is a metaphysical conception of the person which treats individuals as antecedently individuated subjects, that is, as full persons prior to their contingent social relations with others and their particular conceptions of the good. Essentially characterised by the formal capacity for autonomous rational reflection (consciousness) and action (willing), these transcendental subjects are not constituted by their social roles or conceptions of the good but are always already independent of, and prior to, these roles and conceptions. Integral to this metaphysical conception of the person as transcendental subject are the subject/object and appearance/reality distinctions, and, following from these dualisms, the reason/affect and reason/history distinctions. This metaphysical conception of the person receives political expression in the thesis of asocial individualism in which society is conceived as a contract between antecedentally individuated subjects, given expression as a state, for the purposes of achieving goods of co-operation between persons such as security for the pursuit of their individual interests and, most particularly, their interest in autonomy, conceived of as either submitting to the categorical imperative (Kant) or framing and revising conceptions of the good (Rawls). The universalism of this conception of the relation between the individual and society and its expression in the liberal state flows from the metaphysical conception of the person, since what makes this conception 'metaphysical' is the claim that it applies universally to all human beings or, rather, defines what it is essentially to be a human being.

Political liberalism, by contrast, claims to make no such statements about the essence of human beings but, rather, attempts to justify liberalism *either* from within the resources of the public political culture of our constitutional-democratic regimes on the grounds that these resources are the only relevant considerations (Rorty) *or* by arguing that, in the context of pluralism (i.e., lack of agreement on conceptions of the good), a liberal political theory gives us more of what we want from a political theory than any other account because its commitment to persons as free and equal citizens elaborates a politics which best satisfies (or reconciles) our interests in autonomy and community (Rawls).

In other words, if Nietzsche's critique of liberalism is to be cogent, it must provide us with good reasons to set aside both philosophical justifications of liberalism and political justifications of liberalism. The task of this book is to make plausible the claim that Nietzsche achieves both of these goals by undermining the foundationalism characteristic of philosophical liberalism and by presenting a political theory and an understanding of politics which better satisfy our relevant interests than political liberalism and liberal politics. At this stage, however, let us turn to the introduction to Nietzsche.

An Introduction to Friedrich Nietzsche

Born in Saxony on 15 October 1844, Friedrich Nietzsche was educated in Naumburg from 1852 to 1858, before moving to the famous Protestant school Schulpforta, where he received a classical education and founded an artistic society, 'Germania'. In 1864, he entered the University of Bonn, where he became a protégé of the philologist Ritschl, with whom he moved to the University of Leipzig in the following year; here Nietzsche first came into contact with the philosophy of Schopenhauer. In 1868 Nietzsche met Richard Wagner for the first time, while in 1869, at the age of 24, he was nominated Professor of Classical Philology at the University of Basel, where he became friends with the historian Jacob Burckhardt. Nietzsche's academic career received its first significant setback in 1872 when he published *The Birth of Tragedy out of the Spirit of Music*, which was greeted with harsh reviews. Between 1872 and 1878, when he finally resigned from the university on grounds of ill-health, Nietzsche published his *Untimely Meditations* and the first book of *Human, All Too Human*, in which he moved away from the influences of Schopenhauer and, in particular, Wagner towards a 'historical philosophy'. In the next four years, this development continued as Nietzsche completed *Human, All Too Human*, *Daybreak* and *The Gay Science*. These works were followed, in the period from 1882 to 1889, by a series of historical and philosophical reflections on morality, notably *Beyond Good and Evil* and *On the Genealogy of Morality*, in which Nietzsche developed the ideas of genealogy and will to power in seeking to clarify his enigmatic masterpiece *Thus Spoke Zarathustra*, in which the doctrine of eternal recurrence and the notion of the Overman were presented. In 1889, just as he was beginning to achieve recognition, Nietzsche suffered complete mental collapse (probably brought on by syphilis) and continued to live in this state until his death in 1900. A collection of unpublished notes, *The Will to Power*, appeared first in 1901 and was expanded in the following decade, while in 1908 Nietzsche's 'autobiography', *Ecce Homo*, was published.

Throughout his intellectual career, Nietzsche is concerned with the question of culture and, more specifically, of great culture – a culture which is constitutive of noble human beings. Indeed, I will claim that the central question of Nietzsche's work concerns the possibility of noble human beings in the conditions of modernity; a question which requires both an account of what constitutes nobility and a diagnosis of the modern condition. The specific significance of this question for Nietzsche is tied to his recognition

that nineteenth-century Europe and, in particular, Germany are characterised by a state of cultural exhaustion and a decline into nihilism and
decadence. Consequently, Nietzsche's work is typically divided into three
periods in which it is suggested that he offers different responses to the
question of how to produce cultural renewal and, concomitantly, noble
human beings:

1   the 'Schopenhauer/Wagner' phase, which is specifically tied to *The Birth
    of Tragedy,* the *Untimely Meditations* and other unpublished writings
    from 1872 to 1876; in this period, Nietzsche's hopes of cultural renewal
    are predicated on art and, to a lesser extent, philosophy (particularly
    Wagner's art and Schopenhauer's philosophy);
2   his 'positivist' period which runs from *Human, All Too Human* in 1878 to
    the first four books of *The Gay Science* in 1882; at this juncture,
    Nietzsche looks to science to provide cultural renewal through the
    elaboration of a critical historical philosophy;
3   his mature work, which encompasses *Thus Spoke Zarathustra* and all the
    works published thereafter (the status of the unpublished notes of this
    period – many of which are collected together in *The Will to Power* – is a
    matter of considerable controversy[3]); in this period Nietzsche develops
    an artistic ethics and agonistic politics through which he claims great
    culture and nobility can be reconstituted.

In this book, our focus will be on Nietzsche's mature work, although I will
draw on earlier work as and when it seems appropriate to do so.[4] Since my
concern is specifically with Nietzsche's critique of liberal reason, I will
highlight the features of this mature work which contrast with the liberal
sensibility by setting out, firstly, his critique of the dualisms which sustain the
metaphysical conception of the person characteristic of philosophical
liberalism and, secondly, his critique of liberalism as a political doctrine.
The former of these interests will involve focusing on Nietzsche's *philosophical* critique of the metaphysical commitments of philosophical liberalism by attending to his perspective theory of affects, his notion of genealogy
and his thesis of will to power, as well as examining his related *historical*
critique of the metaphysical commitments of philosophical liberalism by
attending to his diagnosis of modernity in terms of nihilism and decadence.
The latter interest will entail analysing the ethics and politics which
Nietzsche counterposes to liberalism by examining, firstly, his notions of
eternal recurrence, *amor fati* and the Overman and, secondly, his commitment to an agonal form of culture and politics in the service of the
production of noble human beings.

In conclusion, then, the purpose of this counter-posing of Nietzsche and
liberalism is both to reveal Nietzsche as a significant political theorist and to
articulate a critique of liberalism. However, before we engage in this task, it
is as well to reflect briefly on what is involved in such political arguments,
that is, to muse on the character of political contests.

The Concept of Politics and the Character of Political Argument

What is politics? The simplicity of this question is deceptive, concealing a wealth of difficulties. Of course, it is a commonplace to note that politics is a contested concept, competing conceptions of which differ as to the extent of the political domain and the character of political activity. In this respect, we might say that politics is a typical political concept since it appears to be a characteristic of concepts commonly termed political (such as freedom, equality and justice) that they are contested or, at the very least, recognised as being contestable. How, then, should we proceed in attempting to capture the sense of the concept of politics? One route is suggested by our reference to politics as a political concept, and we can draw out the significance of this reference by attending to some examples of how we use the concept of politics. Consider the following uses: 'family politics' and 'the politics of the family'.

What do we mean by 'politics' when we refer to 'family politics'? One use of the concept of politics in the deployment of this phrase is to refer to the political features of family relations. This usage involves an interest in identifying and ranking the political features of familial relations. In this context, our arguments about the character of family politics are typically of two sorts. On the one hand, we may agree on the identity of the political features of familial relations but disagree about their relative significance. For example, we may agree on the political character of financial and sexual relations within the family but disagree as to the ranking of these political features of familial relations. On the other hand, more seriously, we may disagree about what count as the political features of familial relations. For example, we may disagree as to whether or not sexual relations are properly characterised as political features of familial relations.[5]

In the second type of usage, namely, 'the politics of the family', the concept of politics can be used to refer to the activity of political reflection on the character of the family. In the context of this usage, our political arguments about the character of the family are also typically of two sorts. On the one hand, we may agree about the characteristics of the family but disagree about the relative significance of these characteristics. For example, we may agree that families involve relations between spouses and relations between parents and children but disagree as to the relative importance of these features in constituting a family (and such disagreements might have significant policy implications, for example, in terms of family support legislation). On the other hand, again more seriously, we may disagree about what count as the characteristics of a family. For example, we might disagree about whether or not a one-parent household can properly be characterised as a family (consider newspaper reports on the 'breakdown' of *the* family).

What is the significance of these examples? Their relevance becomes clear if we note that 'family politics' can refer to the political features of familial relations (are they political? to what degree?), while 'the politics of the family' can refer to political judgements about the character of the family (what are the characteristics of a family? how are they ranked?). Thus, we might comment that the first usage points to politics as a concern with identifying and ranking political relations, while the second usage points to politics as a reflective activity concerned with identifying and ranking the character of particular forms of human relations such as family relations. The curious implication of these two uses of the concept of politics is that it would appear to make sense to talk about the politics of politics, in which our political arguments about political relations are again of two types. On the one hand, we may agree about what count as political relations but disagree as to their relative significance. For example, we might agree that economic relations and sexual relations are political but disagree about their order of rank (consider some of the debates between socialist feminists and feminist socialists). On the other hand, we may disagree about what count as political relations. For example, we may disagree about whether or not economic relations are properly characterised as political (consider the debate between socialists and libertarians).[6]

These reflections on our ordinary uses of the concept of politics suggest two conclusions. Firstly, they suggest that politics as a reflective activity involves identifying and ranking what counts as political. In other words, we are led to the conclusion that the concept of politics is *reflexive* in that it contains within itself the idea of the politics of politics: the concept of politics involves – as an integral part of its grammar – the recognition that the activity of politics involves political judgements about what count as criteria of politics and how these criteria are to be ranked. Secondly, our reflections seem to imply that politics is a *contestable* concept, that politics may involve arguing about what counts as politics. In other words, we are drawn to the conclusion that the character of the concept of politics is, at least in principle, open to contestation.[7] If this second conclusion is correct, it would suggest that the practice of thinking and theorising about politics is not simply about suggesting modes of political action (e.g., through specifying political principles and programmes) but also, and perhaps more fundamentally, about the activity of *arguing for* a particular understanding of the character of politics.

Is this brief reflection on the concept of politics sufficient? Perhaps not. We might, after all, admit the reflexive character of the concept of politics without committing ourselves to the claim that politics is a contestable concept. In other words, it is not immediately apparent that the reflexive character of politics need entail its contestability; we might accept its reflexivity but still reasonably argue that it is possible to specify the core of the concept.[8] The issue which arises at this stage concerns the relation between the *concept* of politics and the various competing *conceptions* thereof (e.g., liberal, republican and socialist notions of politics). Consequently, to submit the question 'what is politics?' to more rigorous scrutiny, let's consider three models of concept/conception relations which, for purposes of identification, I will call Rawls' model, Feyerabend's model and Wittgenstein's model.

1   *Rawls' model.* In his classic work *A Theory of Justice*, John Rawls deploys the distinction between concept and conception with respect to the concept of justice when he comments thus: 'It seems natural to think of the concept of justice as being specified by the role which these different sets of principles, these different conceptions, have in common' (1971: 5–6).[9] On this account, the concept of politics is the kernel of the various conceptions of politics; it is as if we were able to draw a Venn diagram of the conceptions of politics, a circle marking the boundaries of sense of each conception and the space where all the possible circles overlap delimiting the sense of the concept.[10] Thus, while politicians contest the meaning of politics by offering different conceptions, the political philosopher is able to elucidate the common ground on which these contests take place; the concept of politics is not contestable, merely in need of philosophical elucidation – the meaning of 'politics' is given by the boundary which can be drawn around it. Yet, despite Rawls' claim that this relation between concept and conception seems natural, it is not particularly self-evident. Against the self-evidence of Rawls' model of the concept as the common ground of conceptions, I will consider two other models of the relation between concepts and conceptions which seem just as intuitively satisfying.

2   *Feyerabend's model.* According to this second model, the distinction between concept and conception is spurious; different conceptions are incommensurable concepts which are referred to by the same label for purely contingent reasons. The argument for such a claim could proceed by analogy with those arguments developed by Thomas Kuhn and radicalised by Paul Feyerabend with respect to science – arguments which abound with political metaphors such as 'revolution' (Kuhn) and 'anarchism' (Feyerabend) – in seeking to show that political ideologies, like scientific paradigms, involve such different conceptions of the world that they lack any common ground at all and are, consequently, radically untranslatable. Let us note that far from being 'unnatural' or 'counter-intuitive', this model allows us to make sense of certain typical features of political life such as 'ideological conversion' in which the movement from one ideological position to another is typically described not in terms of the suasive force of reasons but in terms of revelation, of suddenly seeing the world differently so that one's old ideological views no longer seem to 'fit' (while, of course, one's new ones do).[11] On this model, different conceptions are different concepts; thus the concept of politics is not essentially contestable because there are just different concept(ion)s of politics. Politics is not a political concept because there is no common ground on which the contestation of the concept could take place, there are just different concepts.[12]

3   *Wittgenstein's model.* On the account offered by this third model, the distinction between concept and conception is pertinent but the concept is not necessarily the element *common* to all conceptions. While different conceptions are not incommensurable, this does not entail that, for example, the common ground between liberal and socialist conceptions of politics is necessarily the same common ground as that between liberal and

republican conceptions of politics. To admit common ground between conceptions is not to admit the *commonality* of common grounds. To clarify this model, we can reflect on Wittgenstein's example of games (which he uses to make a similar point):

> Consider for example the proceedings that we call 'games'. I mean board-games, card-games, ball-games, Olympic games, and so on. What is common to them all? – Don't say: 'There *must* be something common, or they would not be called "games"' – but *look and see* whether there is any thing common to all. – For if you look at them you will not see something that is common to *all*, but similarities, relationships, and a whole series of them at that. To repeat: don't think, but look! Look for example at board-games with their multifarious relationships. Now pass to card-games; here you find many correspondences with the first group, but many common features drop out and others appear. When we pass next to ball-games, much that is common is retained, but much is lost. – Are they all 'amusing'? Compare chess with noughts and crosses. Or is there always winning and losing, or competition between players? Think of patience. In ball-games there is winning and losing; but when a child throws his ball against a wall and catches it again, this feature has disappeared. Look at the parts played by skill and luck; and at the difference between skill in chess and skill in tennis. Think now of games like ring-a-ring-a-roses; here is the element of amusement, but how many other characteristic features have disappeared! And we can go on through the many, many other groups of games in the same way; can see how similarities crop up and disappear. (1958: §66)

As with games, so with politics. Of course, this does *not* rule out the possibility that all the conceptions of politics which are used at any given time and place do share a common core, only that it is not necessary that they do so for us to make sense of the concept. Wittgenstein uses the notion of 'family resemblances' to capture this characteristic of concept/conception relations:

> I can think of no better expression to characterise these similarities than 'family resemblances'; for the various resemblances between members of a family: build, features, colours of eyes, gait, temperament, etc., etc. overlap in the same way. – 'And I shall say: "games" form a family'. (1958: §67)

Of course, taking Wittgenstein's metaphor literally for a moment, we can argue about both whether some family resemblances are more salient than others (perhaps because they are more frequent or persist more strongly across generations) and whether some family resemblances are family resemblances at all. Thus, with respect to games, we might argue about both whether certain games are more significant exemplars of what a game is than others and whether some 'games' are really games at all (is Russian roulette a game?). Concomitantly, with respect to politics, we can argue about both whether certain types of politics are more significant exemplars of the character of politics than others and whether certain kinds of 'politics' are appropriately judged to be politics at all. In this way, Wittgenstein's model allows us to see that politics is a contestable concept in the same way as any other concept.

But don't we tend to mean something stronger than this when we talk about contestable concepts? I think that we do but that this 'stronger' claim has to do with the degree of reflexivity embedded in the grammar of the concept (that is, the degree of reflexivity which characterises the activity designated by the concept). For example, when we engage in playing games, our activity as game-players is not typically characterised by arguments about what we mean by 'games', that is, if we engage in such an argument we are seen as having stopped playing whatever games we are engaged in. This does not mean that we could not invent a game which consisted, at least in part, of arguing about what a game is, but it does mean that we don't typically take such activity to be *internal* to the activity of playing a game. By contrast, to engage in the activity of politics does entail, at least in part, arguing about the character of political activity, about both which activities may be appropriately judged to be political and which activities are the 'paradigmatic' exemplars of political activity. Such arguments *are* internal to political activity. This does not entail *either* that the concept of politics is contested, since we may only have a single conception of politics, *or* that, if it is contested, the concept of politics does not exhibit a common core between competing conceptions, since they may share the same criteria for judging an activity political but rank these criteria differently, *but* it does entail that it is still intelligible to talk about the concept of politics whether or not particular conceptions of politics share any common criteria at all on the model of family resemblances. On this model, the concept of politics is the site on which (and for control of which) conceptions of politics contest with each other.

Consequently, Wittgenstein's model may be seen to take up a position between the 'common core' model provided by Rawls and the collapse of the concept/conception distinction articulated by Feyerabend which allows us to make sense of our 'common-sense' understanding of the reflexive and contestable character of politics. This may itself be an argument in favour of this third model, but let us consider another related reason for adopting it by reconsidering all three models with respect to the history of the concept of politics.

On the one hand, Rawls offers a vision of competing conceptions but stabilises this competition through the idea of the concept as the necessary common core of conceptions. On this model, the concept is the uncontested core which, since it is common to all possible conceptions, is radically ahistorical. Yet the ascription of an ahistorical core to concepts doesn't seem to fit very well with our historical accounts of conceptual change (for example, compare Aristotle's conception of politics with Machiavelli's conception and with Rawls' conception). On the other hand, Feyerabend's model also appears to offer a vision of competing conceptions but radicalises this competition through the collapsing of the concept/conception distinction. On this model, there are just different concept(ion)s which, since they are untranslatable, can hardly be said to be competing. Yet this ascription of utter incommensurability doesn't seem to mesh well with our sense that when we – as liberals, socialists and republicans – are engaged in politics, we are engaged in the 'same' activity even if we have competing conceptions of this activity (where the notion of 'sameness' is used here in the sense that a chess player and a draughts player can say 'We're engaged in the same activity, namely, playing board-games'). Here the 'history' of the concept of politics is not a Rawlsian picture of unbroken and flawless continuity but an 'anti-history', a series of radically discontinuous events. By contrast, Wittgenstein's model offers a logically coherent vision of competing conceptions which does not present the concept as the common core but as a family such that any given conceptions exhibit at least some of a set of historically and culturally constituted family resemblances. On this understanding, politics is a contestable concept because both the ranking of its criteria and these criteria themselves are open, at least in principle, to being contested in the course of political activity. The history of the concept of politics is the history of such contestations: the history of politics is a fractured but never broken history of struggle over the uses of this concept. I would suggest that this philosophical understanding of concept/conception relations fits our best understanding of the history of the concept of politics.

At this juncture, it might seem that the lack of historical and logical sense of Rawls' and Feyerabend's models respectively seems to provide us with reasons for rejecting them; even if I have not established this case, it has hopefully acquired at least a *prima facie* plausibility. However, the significance of these models of concept/conception relations does not lie merely in the different answers they give to the question of whether or not politics is a contestable concept but also in the distinct understandings of the activity of politics and, concomitantly, the character of political arguments which these answers disclose.

1   *Rawls' model.* On this account of the concept of politics as the common core of competing conceptions of politics, the activity of politics is revealed as an activity of competition which is made possible (and limited) by a consensual core. This *liberal* understanding discloses an understanding of political activity as analogous to playing a game, whereby this activity presupposes that the participants share a common understanding both of the value of the activity and of what counts as 'doing' this activity (its domain, rules, norms, etc.). In this context, the rationality of political argument consists in its recognition of the core political consensus which both makes possible and limits the content of this argument, whereby this recognition is predicated on a common recognition of the core features of rationality which both render possible and limit the form of argument as such. In other words, on this model of concept/conception relations, the possibility of rational political argument is based on a core consensus about what counts as being political and what counts as being rational. It is the job of the political philosopher to establish and clarify the features of the consensual core presupposed in the activity of politics and to develop a normative political philosophy out of this consensus. This position is exemplified with respect to the concept of justice by Rawls' *A Theory of Justice*.

2   *Feyerabend's model.* On this account of the concept(ion)s of politics, it makes no sense to speak of *the* activity of politics nor to speak of rational

political argument since there are only incommensurable concept(ion)s of politics and of rationality.

3   *Wittgenstein's model.* On this model of the concept of politics as the site of the possible contestation of different conceptions as to what count as, and how to rank, the criteria of politics, an *agonistic* understanding of the activity of politics is disclosed which specifies the activity of politics as involving the possible contestation of the character of politics *without* presupposing an essential consensus that renders possible and limits the contest of conceptions. Within this understanding, political argument presupposes neither a core agreement on what counts as political nor a shared sense of what counts as rational; on the contrary, political contests are perceived as involving, at least potentially, a contestation of *either* the ranking of criteria *or* the criteria themselves of both politics and rationality. In other words, the rules governing the form of the debate and the parameters limiting the content of the debate are not necessarily set in advance as the conditions of possibility of debate but may themselves be part of what is being contested in the course of political argument; the conceptual form and content of the debate may be immanent to its development, not prior to its inception. It is the job of the political philosopher to elucidate the character of such contests.

At this juncture, I will set aside the position which I have called 'Feyerabend's model'. This is partly because I know of no one who holds this position (what would it mean to hold this position?), which has now served its purpose in the narration of this argument, and partly because my real concern is with the dispute between the *liberal* and *agonistic* understandings of politics as a form of human activity. Let us begin by reflecting on the objection to Rawls' model which we made above, namely, that it presents an ahistorical understanding of concepts. Two replies to this objection are open to the liberal thinker.

Firstly, it may be claimed that attention to history reveals a myriad of conceptions of politics, for example, but that we are simply wrong to characterise this history in terms of conceptual change, it is just that philosophy has not yet identified or clarified the common core of these conceptions. We need not infer that the *apparent* lack of a common core entails the *real* lack of such a core. Consequently, the liberal can hold on to this model of concept/conception relations despite the appearance of inadequacy. The problem posed by this claim is that it is not clear when, if ever, the liberal quest for an ahistorical common core is to be recognised as fruitless – what would count as evidence that this research programme is misguided? A liberal who held this 'philosophical' or 'metaphysical' position would be analogous to a member of the Flat Earth Society who maintains his or her claim by refusing to specify what would or could count as evidence against it. The only way which I can think of whereby a liberal could sustain this claim would be to appeal to the idea of liberalism as a political paradigm which is predicated on the 'philosophical' claim that a concept is the core of all possible conceptions but that this claim cannot be subject to criticism by other political paradigms which embody distinct models of concept/ conception relations because these paradigms are simply incommensurable with each other. However, making this claim would commit the liberal (at least at a meta-level) to Feyerabend's model of concept/conception relations, which it rightly rejects as incoherent.

Secondly, the liberal could weaken the claim he or she is making and argue that the concept is not the common core of all *possible* conceptions but simply of all *current* conceptions with a given cultural space (e.g., Western liberal democracies). On this understanding, the concept marks an 'overlapping consensus' between the different conceptions within a culture. We might question the empirical truth of this claim in the context of contemporary multiculturalism and, even if we admit the liberal's claim, it is not apparent why we should adopt a liberal understanding of politics and political argument. In what sense does liberalism offer us the 'best' model? Consider firstly that a state of 'overlapping consensus' does not constitute an objection to Wittgenstein's model or the agonistic understanding of politics which it discloses because this model does not claim that the various existing conceptions of politics do not have a common core, only that they do not need a common core for us to talk about the concept of politics; it does not claim that the concept of politics is *contested*, only that it is *contestable*. Of course, the 'political' liberal might claim that it is precisely because we exist in a culture characterised by 'overlapping consensus' that the liberal understanding of politics and political argument is more appropriate, but this claim seems weak both since this state of affairs is historically and culturally contingent, and thus subject to the possibility of changes which a liberal understanding would not equip us to deal with, and because the weakening of the liberal claim which restricts it to a given cultural space raises the question of how, if at all, politics between cultural communities characterised by different 'concepts' is to take place (e.g., Western liberal democracies and the People's Republic of China). Moreover, both of these points suggest that to maintain its understanding of politics, liberalism *must* be committed to maintaining (and deepening) the 'overlapping consensus' which secures its understanding of politics and this position entails *imposing* a liberal understanding of political activity and argument on any groups whose conceptions of politics do not fall within the bounds of this consensus by *excluding* them from political activity and argument unless and until they revise their conceptions.[13] To justify this 'illiberal' liberal position would require an argument about the desirability of liberalism. How might such an argument be presented? Well, the liberal might argue for the desirability of consensus (on the grounds, for example, that it secures the freedom to pursue our individual conceptions of the good), but this argument must *either* presuppose a consensus about the value and character of consensus (which presupposition seems to be implicit in the form of liberal rationality), and thus rig the argument in a way which raises the very problem being addressed,[14] *or* engage in a contest with those groups who do not share its commitment to, or conception of, the value and character of consensus, and thereby undermine their own position by admitting the agonistic under-standing of politics.

These critical reflections on liberalism support the contention that an understanding of politics as agonistic offers the most appropriate model for thinking about this activity and, specifically, about the character of political argument. But why have we engaged in this discussion which makes no apparent reference to Nietzsche, who is after all the subject of our concerns? The claims which have been developed in this section are important to this book for two reasons. Firstly, they are significant because the purpose of this book is to present Nietzsche's argument with liberalism, his contestation of its claims and character, and consequently it is necessary to demonstrate that the sense of this argument does not depend on a liberal understanding of what counts as a political argument. If this were not the case, it would be unclear why we should consider this utterly illiberal thinker. Secondly, and perhaps more importantly, the support for an agonistic understanding of politics offered here underpins the claim as to why we should engage with Nietzsche as a political thinker, because it is precisely as a thinker who presents politics as an agonistic activity that Nietzsche demands our atten-tion. Whatever conclusions we may reach about the cogency of Nietzsche's critique of liberal reason or the alternative conceptions of philosophy and politics which his work discloses, the beating heart of Nietzsche's thought is an attempt to displace a liberal vision of politics with an agonistic under-standing of this activity. It will undoubtedly be the case that much of what Nietzsche says about truth, reason, democracy, equality and feminism, to mention but a few significant examples, will be deeply offensive to a liberal sensibility, *but* it is important to make clear that such utterances cannot simply be dismissed as 'not playing the game' or falling outside of our supposed 'overlapping consensus'. Even, or perhaps especially, at his most hyperbolic or rhetorically outrageous, Nietzsche demands our attention precisely because he engages with our contemporary concern with the limits of liberalism, with our worry that a liberal understanding of politics is not only incapable of coping with the realities of the world in which we live but puts blinkers on our political imaginations and impoverishes our sense of what it is to be a human being.

Conclusion

The aim of this chapter has been twofold. Firstly, to introduce the reader to the family features of liberalism and to the figure of Friedrich Nietzsche by offering brief sketches of both participants in the dispute. Secondly, to examine various accounts of politics and political argument in order to heighten our awareness of the stakes involved in this contest by contrasting liberal and agonistic visions of political activity and to underscore the reasons for addressing Nietzsche as a political thinker who can contribute to our current concerns. Of course, it has not yet been demonstrated that

Nietzsche exhibits the agonistic understanding which I have ascribed to him; this task will engage the remainder of this book.

Notes

1 I borrow this distinction from John Rawls.

2 I borrow these three points from Mulhall and Swift's *Liberals and Communitarians* (1992).

3 See Bernd Magnus' article, 'The Use and Abuse of *The Will to Power*' (1988).

4 For an account which presents an overview of Nietzsche's politics in the three different periods, see Keith Ansell-Pearson, *An Introduction to Nietzsche as a Political Thinker* (1994).

5 Consider, for example, the ongoing debate between liberalism and socialism on the political character of economic relations.

6 I am grateful to Terry Hopton and Stephen Mulhall for comments on an earlier draft of this argument. Both pointed out several confusions which I hope (but am not sure) have now been rectified.

7 Interestingly, this point suggests that one criterion for judging political regimes could be their openness to the contestation of the ideas of the political they exhibit.

8 Thanks to Terry Hopton for clarifying this point to me.

9 It should be noted that Rawls draws this idea of concept/conception relations from Hart's *The Concept of Law* (1961).

10 Note Rawls' conclusion to *A Theory of Justice*, in which he argues that his account of justice is universal (1971: 87).

11 We should note incidentally that a Wittgensteinian account of this phenomenon could be developed under the idea of 'aspect change'. For an account of this topic, see Stephen Mulhall's *On Being in the World* (1990).

12 Note that Putnam (1981: 113–24) has argued neatly for the incoherence of this view and that it cannot actually maintain a notion of 'fit' at all.

13 We can note here John Major's recent speeches to the effect that now the IRA have given up violence, they can at last engage in politics, as if they haven't been engaged in politics all along.

14 Stephen Mulhall and Adam Swift (1992: 220–6) point out that Rawls' 'political liberalism', as expressed in 'The Idea of Overlapping Consensus' (1987), involves a distinction between the political and non-political (with priority being assigned to the former) which appears to require philosophical liberalism if it is to be sustained.

2

Truth and *Eros*

A Critique of the Philosophical Commitments of Liberal Reason

Fundamental innovation: in place of epistemology, a perspective theory of affects. (cited in Strong, 1988: 295)

The world seen from within, the world described and defined according to its 'intelligible character' – it would be 'will to power' and nothing else. (BGE §36)

What are the conditions of possibility of knowledge? What is the form of critique? What is the character of human subjectivity? The centrality of these questions to philosophical inquiry is illustrated by the variety of responses they elicit; these questions are sites of contest on which different philosophies wrestle with each other and Nietzsche's philosophy exhibits an active engagement in this intellectual *agon*. It is in this context that we can grasp Nietzsche's philosophical critique of liberal reason as a contestation of its commitments to the project of epistemology, an ahistorical understanding of critique and a disembedded and disembodied conception of rational subjectivity. In articulating this critique, Nietzsche seeks to show both that each of these liberal commitments is incoherent and that alternatives which avoid the contradictions of liberal philosophy are readily available in the form of a perspective theory of affects, genealogy as an historical mode of immanent critique and the hypothesis of will to power.[1]

The stakes of this contest are high. On the one hand, liberal commitments are deeply entrenched within Western culture and these commitments entail a portrait of Nietzsche's thinking as relativist (perspectivism and genealogy) and irrational (the doctrine of will to power). On the one hand, Nietzsche argues that these commitments are constitutive of the condition of nihilism which, he claims, characterises our modernity. The cogency of Nietzsche's argument on this score will be taken up in the following chapters; however, the concern of this chapter is to initiate our analysis of the encounter between Nietzsche and liberalism by attending to his critique of the philosophical character of liberal reason. In order to facilitate this task, we will focus in turn on the possibility of knowledge, the idea of critique and the character of subjectivity.

The Critique of Epistemology

In articulating his critique of epistemology, Nietzsche focuses his attention on Kant's attempt to provide secure foundations for knowledge. This section will sketch the context within which Kant's epistemological project emerges by referring to the philosophical claims of Descartes and Hume before offering a brief outline of Kant's account. Following this account, the discussion will explicate Nietzsche's critique of epistemology as setting the stage for the appearance of his perspective theory of affects.

How can we provide secure foundations for knowledge? For Descartes, writing against the scepticism which characterised the work of thinkers such as Montaigne, securing the foundations of knowledge required the identification of that which resisted sceptical doubt, that which we could know with certainty, namely, that which is presupposed by the activity of doubting – a subject who doubts. This claim is summarised in Descartes's famous formulation 'I think, therefore I am' (*cognito ergo sum*)[2] and he argues that 'clear and distinct ideas' such as this are necessarily true:

> . . . having noticed that there is nothing at all in this, *I think, therefore I am*, which assures me that I am speaking the truth, except that I see very clearly that in order to think one must exist, I judged that I could take it to be a general rule that all things we conceive very clearly and very distinctly are all true. (1968: 54)

In elaborating this argument, Descartes suggests that the identity of 'clear and distinct ideas' (ideas which we feel intuitively to be certain) with true ideas (ideas which are certain) requires only the assumption that God exists and is a perfect being:

> . . . the rule which I stated above that I held, namely, that the things we grasp very clearly and very distinctly are all true, is assured only because God is or exists, and because he is a perfect Being, and because everything that is in us comes from him; whence it follows that our ideas and notions, being real things and coming from God, in so far as they are clear and distinct, cannot to this extent be other than true. (1968: 58)

Descartes's position requires the assumption that God is perfect to identify the intuitive certainty of clear and distinct ideas with the certainty of true ideas because if God is not perfect in the senses of being all-knowing and utterly truthful, it would follow that the clear and distinct ideas he provides might be either accidentally or deliberately misleading. Consequently, Descartes requires a proof of God's existence and perfection to secure the foundations for knowledge which he claims to establish.

In *Discourse on Method*, Descartes offers an argument for a perfect being which claims that since man is an imperfect being, the idea of perfection cannot be internally generated but must proceed from a perfect being. Descartes suggests that whereas one could accept that one's ideas about 'the sky, the earth, light, heat and a thousand others' can be located in the 'dependencies of my nature, in as much as it had some perfection', this is not the case with the idea of perfection, and, consequently, concludes:

> . . . it remained that must have been put into me by a being whose nature was truly more perfect than mine and which even had in itself all the perfections of which I could have any idea, that is to say, in a single word, which was God. (1968: 55)

This argument is reiterated in the 'Third Meditation' of Descartes's *Meditations* and he begins the 'Fourth Meditation' by offering the following summation of this case:

> And when I consider that I doubt, that is to say, that I am an incomplete and dependent being, the idea of a complete and independent being, that is to say of God, presents itself to my mind with such distinctness and clearness, and, from the fact alone that this idea of is found in me, or that I, who possess this idea, am or exist, I conclude so evidently that God exists, and that my existence depends entirely on him in each moment of my life, that I do not think that the human mind can know anything with more clearness and certainty. (1968: 132)

The problem with the somewhat scholastic argument of this 'causal' proof[3] is that it seems to predicate the existence of God on a clear and distinct idea of God which is predicated in turn of the fact of my existence demonstrated by Descartes's phrase 'I think, therefore I am', yet the very purpose of this putative proof of God's existence was to establish that our clear and distinct ideas are true and, in particular, to establish the truth of 'I think, therefore I am'. In other words, Descartes offers a circular argument; he grounds his proof in what the proof was constructed to ground. Consequently, if this were Descartes's only argument for the existence of God, we would be justified in setting aside his attempt to provide certain foundations for knowledge without further ado. However, in the 'Fifth Meditation', Descartes offers a separate 'ontological' proof of God's existence which he suggests would serve even if all his preceding arguments were invalidated and which he insists does not depend on the fact that he possesses an idea of God but simply on the idea of God considered formally.

Descartes's ontological argument begins by noting that we commonly distinguish between existence and essence yet claims that

> when I think about it more attentively, it becomes manifest that existence can no more be separated from the essence of God than the fact that the sum of its three angles is equal to two right-angles can be separated from the essence of a triangle or than the idea of a mountain can be separated from the idea of a valley; so that there is no less contradiction in conceiving of a God, that is to say, a supremely perfect being, who lacks existence, that is to say, who lacks some particular perfection, than in conceiving of a mountain without a valley. (1968: 145)

Descartes considers the obvious objection to this argument that the conceptual relationship between the ideas 'mountain' and 'valley' does not imply the existence of mountains and valleys, only that one could not exist without the other. However, he claims that this rebuttal does not apply to the idea of God because 'I am not free to conceive a God without existence, that is, a supremely perfect being devoid of a supreme perfection' (1968: 145). Thus Descartes hangs his argument on the identification of existence as a predicate of perfection. However, as Gassendi pointed out, and Kant reiterated, existence is not a predicate but the condition of predication:

> . . . something which does not exist has neither perfection nor imperfection; and what exists and has various perfections, does not have existence as one particular perfection among them – rather, existence is that by which both it and its perfection exist, and without which, we can neither say that it has perfections, nor that the perfections are had. (Gassendi cited in Williams, 1978: 155)

Consequently, we may judge that Descartes's 'ontological' proof of God's existence is no more successful than his 'causal' proof.

In the context of the failure of Descartes's attempt to provide certain foundations for knowledge by identifying pieces of certain knowledge, scepticism re-emerges in a more virulent form. Whereas Montaigne articulates a pragmatic scepticism in the service of ethics, Hume presents a philosophical scepticism in the service of empiricism. Three features of Hume's thought call for our attention in this context. Firstly, Hume rejects the rationalist claim that we can have knowledge about the world prior to experience of the world and presents a model of mind as a passive material upon which sensory experience makes impressions which he terms 'perceptions of mind' (it is these impressions which we know directly, not the external world). Secondly, Hume goes on to argue that we cannot ground knowledge of the external world on sensory experience, we cannot move with any surety from the 'inner world' of impressions to the 'outer world' of objects (how can I know that an impression always 'corresponds' to an object which causes it?). Thirdly, Hume attempts to demonstrate the truth of this second claim (and thus secure the first) by showing that the idea of necessity integral to the concept of causality cannot be drawn from experience. He performs this task by offering both a *logical* critique of the idea of necessity (the problem of induction) and a *psychological* account of our attachment to the idea of causality.

The purpose of Hume's critique of necessity, then, is to secure his scepticism concerning the possibility of any *a priori* knowledge about matters of fact, that is, about the nature of the world, and thus to affirm his contention that our knowledge of the world is a matter of experience which cannot itself provide secure foundations for 'objective' knowledge. We can broach this topic by noting that Hume is asking three related questions.

1 *What is the nature of all our reasoning concerning matters of fact?* Responding to this question, Hume argues that this type of reasoning is 'founded on the relation of cause and effect' (1975: 32, §28) and he defines cause as '*an object, followed by another, and where all objects similar to the first are followed by objects similar to the second. Or in other words where, if the first object had not been, the second never had existed*' (1975: 76, §60).

2 *What is the foundation of all our reasonings and conclusions concerning relations of cause and effect?* Hume's answer to this question is given in one word 'Experience', and he seeks to demonstrate this case by the following kind of argument: '*[T]hat the sun will not rise tomorrow* is no less intelligible a proposition and implies no more contradiction than the

affirmation, *that it will rise*', since if the former proposition did imply a contradiction 'it could never be distinctly conceived by the mind' (1975: 26, §21). Hume's contention is that 'whatever is intelligible, and can be distinctly conceived, implies no contradiction, and can never be proved false by any demonstrative argument or abstract reasoning *a priori*' (1975: 35, §30). In other words, Hume's argument is the entirely reasonable one that logical ideas cannot provide knowledge of facts.

3 *What is the foundation of all conclusions from experience?* It is with his final question in Hume's sceptical delving that his conclusions become utterly scandalous. Let us separate the two related issues involved in Hume's response to this question. Hume is addressing the question of how we can glean knowledge from experience in the sense of being said to 'know' that, for example, the sun will rise tomorrow. But this question has deep consequences because it implies a second question, namely, how can I know that similar impressions (on the passive material of the mind) are caused by similar objects, or, to put this point another way, how can I know that the cause of any given impression is always the effect of the same object? Unless some principle of 'necessary connection' is uncovered, Hume's scepticism will threaten to undermine the basis for knowledge as such. This is precisely what Hume's logical critique of necessity accomplishes, so let us now state this critique. Suppose I assert that the sun will rise in the east tomorrow, I might base this claim on the fact that the sun has always, in every known instance, risen in the east but it is open to the logical objection that because an event X has always occurred in form Y on N number of occasions (where N is a finite number), this does not entail that X will occur in form Y on the N + 1th occasion. To support my case against the sceptic, I might refer to the laws of physics and assert that X *must* take form Y because this process is the causal effect of event Z according to scientific law. However, simply because the laws of physics have always held on N number of occasions does not entail that they must hold on the N + 1th occasion. Finally, I might throw open my arms and appeal to the regularity of nature by claiming, as Hume admits, that if nature were not regular we would have no concept of cause and effect (these ideas would be unintelligible to us), but this appeal is open to precisely the same objection as my previous two claims: the constant conjunction of events does not imply the necessity of this conjunction.

Of course, in launching this attack on the possibility of foundations for knowledge, Hume is left with a psychological question: 'why, if we have no reason to hold to the idea of necessity, do we believe in it so strongly?' Hume's response is devastating for human vanity: 'All inferences from experience . . . are effects of custom, not of reasoning' (1975: 43, §36). Of course, this conclusion implies a distinction between custom and reason (which, as we will see later, Nietzsche holds to be unsustainable); however, for the moment let us focus on Kant's reception of Hume, for it is the radical scepticism of Hume's arguments which Kant credits with waking him from his dogmatic slumber. Hume's denial that we can have sure knowledge of an external world and his relegation of causality to a habit contingent on the character of human psychology construct a challenge which Kant determines to take up and it is with Kant's attempt to overcome Hume's scandalous conclusions that the project of epistemology comes of age.

Kant's project is ambitious: on the one hand, he attempts to hang on to the empiricist idea concerning the contingent character of what we perceive (phenomena) and, on the other hand, he wants to maintain the rationalist claim that we have knowledge of an external world of objects and the necessary relations between them.[4] But how can he have it both ways? Kant proceeds by suggesting an alternative model of mind in which the knowing self is not the passive recipient of experience but the active constitutor of experience:

> Hitherto it has been assumed that our knowledge must conform to objects. But all attempts to extend our knowledge of objects by establishing something in regard to them a priori, by means of concepts, have, on this assumption, ended in failure. We must therefore make trial whether we may not have more success in the tasks of metaphysics if we suppose that objects must conform to knowledge. (1966: 75)

By viewing the mind as actively 'synthesising' what is perceived (phenomena) *both* in terms of the 'intuitions' of time and space (so that we perceive phenomena as ordered in space and time) *and* in terms of 'concepts' such as substance and causality (so that we understand phenomena as objects which have necessary relations with one another), Kant hopes to overcome the impossible position into which Hume seems to place the attempt to provide foundations for knowledge. However, to examine Kant's attempt requires that we begin our discussion by considering Kant's reasons for proposing this alternative model of mind, and we can start with his identification of a problem in the empiricist model of consciousness.

The point which Kant emphasises is that we experience sense-data as all of a piece, our sensory experience possesses a unity insofar as it is ordered in terms of space and time, and Kant suggests that this cannot be accounted for in terms of the empiricist model of mind as the passive recipient of discrete atoms of sense-data. Kant's point is that since space and time are not experienced as sense-data, we can have no 'impression' of them, and, consequently, since 'ideas' correspond to 'impressions', it is unclear how (if the empiricist model of mind were true) we could possess any idea of space or of time. This is Kant's point when he claims that empiricism confuses a succession of apprehensions (or impressions) with an apprehension of succession and which legitimates his proposal of a different model of mind.

Recall that if Kant is to rebut Hume's scepticism, what is required is that he offer an account of how it is both that we experience the world as a spatio-temporal unity and that we understand our experience of sensations in terms of objects and their relations. To make possible such an account Kant introduces the idea of synthetic *a priori* judgements. Hume had distinguished two types of true statement: on the one hand, 'relations of ideas' (truths of reason) which we would now describe as analytic, *a priori* statements of logical necessity, that is, statements in which the concept of the predicate is contained within the concept of the subject (e.g., 'A = A' or '*x* cannot be identical to both *y* and *z*, if *y* is not identical to *z*'), *and*, on the other hand, 'matters of fact and real experience' (truths of fact) which we would now label as synthetic, *a posteriori* statements of empirical contingency such as 'I see the sky as blue' (the statement 'the sky is blue' would also be of this type if we could justify the movement from inner to outer realm). There is no room in this division for statements that are *a priori* (knowable by reason independently of experience) and synthetic (the concept of the predicate is not contained in the concept of the subject); yet it is precisely this type of statement (e.g., 'the sum of the three angles of a triangle is equal to the sum of two right angles' or 'all causes are effects') which are necessary if Kant is to sustain the rationalist claim that we can have knowledge of an external world of objects and the necessary relations between them, that is, if he is to account for the possibility of experiencing the world as a spatio-temporal unity and understanding the world in terms of objects and their relations. Consequently, since Kant wants to provide secure foundations for (scientific) knowledge, his question becomes 'how are synthetic *a priori* judgements possible?'

In *The Critique of Pure Reason*, Kant addresses this question by distinguishing three faculties of the knowing self: sense (our capacity to have sensations), understanding (our capacity to impose concepts on our sensations) and reason (our capacity to apply concepts to themselves). For Kant, these faculties are not formless; on the contrary, each has its own structure and it is the structures of the faculties of sense and understanding which are imposed on all possible experience. Thus, it is the transcendental structure of the faculty of sense which synthesises sensory experience in terms of space and time, while it is the transcendental structure of the faculty of understanding which synthesises sensory experience into independent objects and the causal relations between them. Thus, Kant argues, synthetic *a priori* judgements are possible because they are the products of the constitutive activity of the knowing self as transcendental subject: the self as 'transcendental' because this activity is both necessary and universal, it attends all possible experience; the self as 'subject' because it is the unity of the self (transcendental structures of consciousness) which *produces* the unity of the world as object. Of course, the transcendental self cannot be identified with the empirical self; on the contrary, precisely because it imposes space and time on our experiential world, it cannot be a part of this world. To resolve this issue, Kant introduces a distinction between the real (noumenal) world and the apparent (phenomenal) world; the latter is the world as we experience it, the former is the world as it is in-itself wherein 'resides' the transcendental (noumenal) self.

With this account, Kant reconfigures the project of epistemology into the enterprise we recognise today as

> that branch of philosophy concerned either to ground knowledge in a realm that is 'objective,' that is, not affected by the act of knowing, or to establish 'objectively' that this aim is impossible in at least certain realms of human experience. In both cases the aim of epistemology is to delineate a realm secure from the phenomenal

vagaries of the knower. . . . Of necessity, epistemology must either seek to establish a knowing self that transcends the vagaries of phenomenal life or it must despair of attaining knowledge at all. (Strong, 1988: 295)

It is this epistemological enterprise which Nietzsche seeks to undermine, not in order to argue that knowledge is impossible but in order to suggest that the conception of the activity of knowing exhibited by this enterprise is fatally flawed. This critique of epistemology is articulated through an attack on the idea of the knowing self as transcendental subject.

For Nietzsche, the conception of the self as transcendental subject exhibits a *reification* of the self which is typical of the idiosyncrasies of metaphysical philosophers: 'they [philosophers] think they are doing a thing *honour* when they dehistoricize it, *sub specie aeterni* – when they make a mummy of it' (TI ' "Reason" in Philosophy' §1). This activity of reification is characterised by two features: a *separation* of the self as subject (knower) from the world as object (known), which locates the activity (knowing) as an operation authored and performed by the subject, *and* a *separation* of the transcendental (real) self from the empirical (apparent) self, which abstracts the self from the embedded and embodied conditions of human subjectivity, that is, abstracts the self from all contingency. Each of these elements is integral to Kant's account: on the one hand, the subject/object distinction allows Kant to claim that the unity of the known (world) is a consequent of the unity of the knower (self) and, on the other hand, the appearance/reality distinction allows Kant to specify the constitutive activity of the self as 'universal and necessary' rather than particular and contingent. On Nietzsche's account, the typicality of this reification of the self which he identifies in Kant's notion of the transcendental subject is not least due to the seductions of language. On the one hand, the subject/object distinction is simply a transference of the subject/predicate distinction which character-ises the grammar of our language onto the structure of the world: 'The inference here is in accordance with the habit of grammar: "thinking is an activity, to every activity pertains one who acts, consequently" ' (BGE §17). At root, Nietzsche argues that the projection of the subject/predicate distinction onto the world is a product of 'the great fateful error that the will is something that *produces an effect*' (TI ' "Reason" in Philosophy' §5). On the other hand, the appearance/reality distinction is rendered possible through our 'mistaking the first for last' by putting 'the "highest concepts", that is the most general, the emptiest concepts, the last fumes of evaporating reality, at the beginning *as* the beginning' and concluding that 'all supreme concepts that which is, the unconditioned, the good, the true, the perfect – all that cannot have become, *must* therefore be *causa sui*' (TI ' "Reason" in Philosophy' §4). In *Beyond Good and Evil*, Nietzsche deploys a certain degree of caustic wit in characterising the reasoning of philosophers on this topic:

How could something originate in its antithesis? Truth in error, for example? Or will to truth in will to deception? Or the unselfish act in self-interest? Or the pure radiant gaze of the sage in covetousness? Such origination is impossible; he who dreams of it is a fool, indeed, worse than a fool; the things of highest value must have another origin *of their own* – they cannot be derivable from this transitory, seductive, deceptive, mean little world, from this confusion of desire and illusion! In the womb of being, rather, in the intransitory, in the hidden god, in the "thing-in-itself" – *that* is where their cause must lie and nowhere else!' – This mode of judgement constitutes the typical prejudice by which metaphysicians of all ages can be recognized. (BGE §2)

At this juncture, however, our concern is not with how the subject/object and appearance/reality distinctions become entrenched within our culture – this *genealogical* concern will be addressed in the next chapter; rather, our current focus is on Nietzsche's philosophical critique of these two distinctions which underpin the epistemological enterprise. In both cases, we shall see that Nietzsche suggests that we have good reasons for rejecting the idea that our linguistic grammar mirrors the structure of the world or that our abstract concepts are the names of things-in-themselves.

Nietzsche's critique of the subject/object distinction can be elucidated by adducing an example he deploys in the first essay of *On the Genealogy of Morals*:

> . . . the popular mind separates the lightning from its flash and takes the latter for an *action*, for the operation of a subject called lightning. . . . The popular mind in fact doubles the deed; when it sees the lightning flash, it is the deed of a deed: it posits the same event first as cause and then a second time as its effect. (GM I §13)

In other words, *the event* (lightning/flash) *is taken both as subject-cause* (lightning) *and object-effect* (flash). By bringing this example into evidence, Nietzsche gives us reason to suppose that the subject/predicate distinction does not mirror the structure of the world, that 'there is no "being" behind doing, effecting, becoming; "the doer" is merely a fiction added to the deed – the deed is everything' (GM I §13). We can clarify Nietzsche's position further by noting Yeats' line 'And who can tell the dancer from the dance?', which, by playing on our grammar, draws our attention strikingly to the way in which it separates an activity (dancing) into a subject-cause (dancer) and an object-effect (dance). The rhetorical force of this image underpins Nietzsche's claim that our activity in the world is illegitimately separated into the operations of the self as subject on the world as object. Consequently, whereas Kant claims that the unity of the world which is known is a function of the unity of the self which knows, Nietzsche argues that 'the unity of the known and the unity of the knower are derived from the activity of knowing' (Strong, 1988: 301):

> . . . the unity of the world is a double imputation, first from the unity of the knower derived from the act of knowing and then, in turn, by the transfer of the unity of the knower onto the world. (Strong, 1988: 302)

The project of epistemology, on Nietzsche's account, elides the first moment of this imputation (the positing of the self as subject) by failing to recognise that ways of knowing the world are ways of being-in-the-world which produce our ways of understanding both subject (self) and object (world) and focuses on articulating the second, namely, the constitutive activity of the self as subject and *securing* this 'transfer' by making it the activity of a transcendental self. In other words, the epistemological enterprise does not simply 'forget' the first moment of this imputation by presupposing the subject/object distinction, it also secures the 'transfer of the unity of the knower onto the world' as universal and necessary by presupposing the appearance/reality distinction.

Nietzsche's critique of the appearance/reality distinction is developed in a number of comments in his mature (i.e., post-*Zarathustra*) work, the most sustained account being set out more or less enigmatically in *Twilight of the Idols*, particularly in the section 'How the "Real World" At Last Became a Myth'. We will sketch this account shortly; however, we can begin by reflecting on what it is that Nietzsche is attacking. Maudemarie Clark has recently argued that Nietzsche's critique of the idea of the thing-in-itself which articulates the appearance/reality may be construed as an attack on 'metaphysical realism', namely, the idea that knowledge about how the world is in-itself is independent of our cognitive constitution (i.e., our cognitive capacities and interests). In a sophisticated discussion of theories of truth, Clark distinguishes metaphysical realism from anti-metaphysical realism by arguing that while both recognise that our best theory about the world may be false since we can imagine that beings with greater cognitive capacities could (if they were so minded) discover its falsity and hence that truth is independent of our cognitive capacities (what we have the capacity to know), metaphysical realism also claims that our knowledge of truths may be independent of our cognitive interests (our best standards of rationality), that is, 'the cognitively relevant properties we want from a theory or set of beliefs *other than truth* (e.g., simplicity, comprehensiveness, etc.)' (Clark, 1990: 48).

Clark ascribes this metaphysical realist position to Descartes on the grounds that his attempt to secure knowledge through a proof of the existence (and perfection) of God is only intelligible if he thinks that truth is independent of our cognitive interests ('clearness' and 'distinctness'), that is, if he thinks that a proposition like 'I think, therefore I am' might be both clear and distinct (i.e., satisfy our best standards of rationality) and still be false. Now, in considering this example, Clark's position might seem counter-intuitive since we can reasonably argue that Descartes's statement 'I think, therefore I am' is false (indeed Nietzsche, amongst others, takes up this position)[5] but consider that, in making this case, we have two strategies available to us: firstly, we can argue that Descartes's statement is not clear and distinct (that it does not, for example, follow from his premises) and/or, secondly, we can argue that clarity and distinctiveness are either not the cognitively relevant properties that we want from a theory or not the *only* and/or *most significant* cognitively relevant properties that we want from a theory (note how these strategies recall our discussion of the contestable character of the concept of politics). In both cases, we are involved in claiming that Descartes doesn't give us what we want from a theory, that he doesn't satisfy our cognitive interests (our best standards of rationality).

Thus, we can see that, despite its apparent counter-intuitiveness, if we think through Clark's argument it supports the contention that truth is dependent on our cognitive interests; a position which she describes as anti-metaphysical realism. Before going on to set out Clark's argument for this position (and her ascription of it to Nietzsche) in more detail, we should note that Kant may also be described as a metaphysical realist insofar as he denies that we can have any knowledge of the world-in-itself, that is, the noumenal world. Clark argues that this denial implies metaphysical realism because Kant's position *qua* noumenal reality entails that the truth is independent of both our cognitive capacities and interests (i.e., that any possible theory about the character of the noumenal realm, even one conducted under ideal conditions of inquiry, might still be false), whereas his position *qua* phenomenal reality only implies that the truth may be independent of our cognitive capacities (in that a being with greater observational powers might know truths denied to us) but not that it is independent of our cognitive interests.[6] If this characterisation is right, Kant may be described as a metaphysical realist *qua* noumenal reality and an anti-metaphysical realist *qua* phenomenal reality. At this stage, having briefly outlined Clark's distinction between metaphysical and anti-metaphysical accounts of truth, let us turn to her formal arguments for an anti-metaphysical position. On Clark's account, there are two crucial steps in the argument against metaphysical realism.

The first stage involves the recognition that the metaphysical realist's idea of thinking about truth as independent of all possible activities of knowing is incoherent: 'we can have no conception, or only a contradictory one, of something that would be independent of all knowers, and therefore of all conceptualization, because to conceive of something is to conceive of it as satisfying some description or other, which is to think of it as being conceptualizable in some way or other' (Clark, 1990: 46–7). This is Nietzsche's point when he comments: 'What is "appearance" for me now? Certainly not the opposite of some essence: what could I say about any essence except to name the attributes of its appearance! Certainly not a dead mask that one could place on an unknown x or remove from it!' (GS §54). As this passage makes clear, Nietzsche accepts that we only know things under descriptions (a position he shares with Kant) and that the idea of the 'essence' of a thing as independent of all possible description is contradictory (a position he doesn't think he shares with Kant since he regards Kant as a metaphysical realist because of the idea of the thing-in-itself). He states this point explicitly when noting that the thing-in-itself 'contains a *contradictio in adjecto*' (BGE §16).

The second step involves the recognition that the idea of truth as independent of human knowledge entails the idea of truth as independent of all possible knowledge:

> To conceive of our best theory as false . . . we must assume that possible beings with cognitive capacities superior to our own could in principle discover its falsity. But how are we to conceive of this cognitive superiority? We seem only to have two

choices. Cognitive abilities would certainly be superior to our own if they would give us more of what would satisfy our cognitive interests than our abilities do. To admit this as the only possibility would be to deny that truth is independent of our cognitive interests, to take these interests to be the only standard in terms of which our best theory could be false. The only alternative I can see is to say that abilities are superior to our own if they would allow greater correspondence to things as they are in themselves independently of all possible knowers or conceptualization. Greater correspondence to things as they are in independence of our abilities will not help here, since it is precisely what we are trying to conceptualize. To insist that truth is independent of our cognitive interests, we would therefore need the objectionable concept of the thing-in-itself. (Clark, 1990: 50).

Thus, Clark concludes that while truth is independent of our cognitive capacities, the argument that it is independent of our cognitive interests (our own best standards of rational acceptability) requires the incoherent notion of the thing-in-itself, of the world-in-itself as independent of all possible conceptualisation. Evidence that Nietzsche accepted this second step is provided by the 'historical' account of the appearance/reality distinction given in the section 'How the "Real World" At Last Became a Myth'. In the first three positions sketched, Nietzsche characterises three versions of the appearance/reality distinction:

1 'The real world, attainable to the wise, the pious, the virtuous man – he dwells in it, *he is it*': this is the Platonic view exhibited in the myth of the cave and expressed as Plato's commitment to the 'real world' as eternal ideas or forms accessible only to the philosopher.
2 'The real world, unattainable for moment, but promised to the wise, the pious, the virtuous man ("to the sinner who repents")': this is the Christian conception of the 'real world' as the kingdom of God promised to the faithful.
3 'The real world, unattainable, undemonstrable, cannot be promised, but even when thought of a consolation, a duty, an imperative': this is Kant's position in which the inaccessibility of the world-in-itself does not prevent it from anchoring Kant's moral philosophy, in particular the categorical imperative.

The following three positions sketch the stages of development of Nietzsche's thought:[7]

4 'The real world – unattainable? Unattained, at any rate. And if unattained also *unknown*. Consequently also no consolation, no re-demption, no duty: how could we have a duty to something unknown?': the position of Nietzsche in *Human, All Too Human* when he stresses the utter irrelevance of the existence of the 'real world' but does not deny its existence.
5 'The "real world" – an idea no longer of any use, not even a duty any longer – an idea grown useless, superfluous, *consequently* a refuted idea: let us abolish it!': this is the position of Nietzsche in *The Gay Science* and some sections of *Beyond Good and Evil* when he rejects the idea of the thing-in-itself as a contradiction in terms (note the 'real world' is

enclosed in quotation marks at this juncture) yet still conceives of the empirical world as appearance and of our knowledge as illusory.

6 'We have abolished the real world: what world is left? the apparent world perhaps? . . . But no! *with the real world we have also abolished the apparent world*!': Nietzsche's mature position in which he recognises that rejecting the thing-in-itself entails rejecting the idea that the empirical world is mere appearance and, consequently, rejecting the idea that our human truths are illusions, which, in turn, entails recognising that truth is not independent of our cognitive interests.

The importance of the argument Clark develops lies in its performance of two functions: firstly, it clarifies Nietzsche's critique of the appearance/ reality distinction and, secondly, it illustrates that this critique does not entail abandoning the idea of true knowledge about the world.

In the context of Nietzsche's critique of epistemology, we can therefore conclude that Nietzsche succeeds not only in undermining the subject/object distinction[8] which articulates the imputation from the unity of knowing to the unity of the knower, but also in undermining the appearance/reality distinction which secures the imputation from the unity of the knower to the unity of the known. At the same time, however, Nietzsche's critique of epistemology as a way of thinking about how we can have knowledge of the world does not produce the conclusion that we cannot have knowledge of the world; on the contrary, to reach this conclusion would be to stay within the parameters of the epistemological enterprise. Rather it necessitates a different kind of account of how we can have knowledge of the world. Nietzsche's attempt to provide such an account is developed through the idea of perspectivism.

A Perspective Theory of Affects

Perhaps the most straightforward route into a discussion of Nietzsche's perspectivism is to note Richard Rorty's contention that the epistemological enterprise and its concern to secure foundations of knowledge is 'a product of the choice of perceptual metaphors' (1980: 159), that is, thinking about knowing as somehow being akin to seeing. Bearing this in mind, Nietzsche's perspectivism may be understood as a deployment of the perceptual metaphor against epistemology.[9] To elaborate and elucidate this claim, we will address a passage from the third essay of *On the Genealogy of Morals* in which Nietzsche sets out his position at length:

> Henceforth, my dear philosophers, let us be on guard against the dangerous old conceptual fiction that posited a 'pure, will-less, painless, timeless knowing subject'; let us guard against the snares of such contradictory concepts as 'pure reason,' 'absolute spirituality,' 'knowledge in itself': these always demand that we should think of an eye that is completely unthinkable, an eye turned in no particular direction, in which the active and interpreting forces, through which alone seeing becomes seeing *something*, are supposed to be lacking; these always

demand of the eye an absurdity and a nonsense. There is *only* a perspective seeing, *only* a perspective 'knowing'; and the *more* affects we allow to speak about one thing, the *more* eyes, different eyes, we use to observe one thing, the more complete will our 'concept' of this thing, our 'objectivity', be. But to eliminate the will altogether, to suspend each and every affect, supposing we were capable of this – what would that mean but to *castrate* the intellect? (GM III §12)

For our concerns, this passage exhibits two points of significance. On the one hand, Nietzsche deploys the metaphor of seeing to point to the absurdity of the view from nowhere, the God's-eye view, postulated by epistemology and predicated on the contradictory ideas of the transcendental ego and the thing-in-itself. This leads him to assert the position that all views are from somewhere, our perspectives are always already situated. In other words, as Clark astutely notes:

The crux of the matter is that perspectivism excludes only something contradictory. As creative power is not limited by the inability to make a square triangle, cognitive power is not limited by the inability to have nonperspectival knowledge. (1990: 134)

On the other hand, Nietzsche also specifically attacks the idea of knowledge as disinterested which attends the epistemological enterprise and claims that the activity of knowing is rooted in our affective constitution. Our consciousness is neither disembedded nor disembodied; knowing, like seeing, is an activity which attends the embedded and embodied character of human subjectivity. Consequently, we can conclude that for Nietzsche our cognitive constitution is not separable from our affective constitution, our cognitive interests are not independent of our affective interests: *logos* is entwined with *eros*. Thus, the basic character of perspectivism is that it emphasises the contextual character of our knowledge (beliefs) about the world and claims that the kind of knowledge about the world we have is not independent of our affective interests. At this juncture, before moving to an attempt to elucidate and elaborate the idea of a perspective invoked by Nietzsche, I want briefly to reflect on and rebut the charge of relativism directed at perspectivism.

In taking up this topic, we can distinguish here between a strong version of the charge of relativism, which is rebutted by the critique of the very idea of non-perspectival knowledge, and a weaker version, which is rebutted by Nietzsche's commitment to contextual standards of rationality. The strong version of this charge posits certain transcendental criteria of rationality and claims that any position which does not recognise these universal and necessary features of rationality is relativist.[10] Nietzsche would count as a relativist in this sense if there were any such criteria; however, insofar as Nietzsche's critique of the appearance/reality distinction is cogent, it undermines the very idea of transcendental criteria of rationality deployed to make this charge of relativism intelligible. The weaker version of the claim that perspectivism is relativist suggests simply that perspectivism gives us no criteria for saying that one perspective is better than any other perspective. Yet this claim confuses the fact that perspectivism grants all perspectives equal rights to claim epistemic authority with the idea that it grants them equal authority, but it is precisely in distinguishing claims to epistemic authority (i.e., truth) that our standards of rationality come into play, contextual and affectually grounded though they may be (to repeat the rebuttal of the first charge, that these standards are contextual would be an objection if and only if non-contextual standards were available). Thus we can conclude that perspectivism is not relativist in either a strong or a weak sense. Having rebutted this charge, let's return to the task of clarifying and developing Nietzsche's notion of perspectivism by drawing on some more recent developments in philosophy to reflect on the nature of a perspective.

We can begin by focusing on the metaphor Nietzsche deploys and asking what the characteristics of a perspective are. We can draw these out by thinking of other ways in which we can describe a perspective such as 'seeing from a point of view' and 'a field of vision'. The first of these descriptions helps us to capture the sense of the situatedness of the activity of knowing and, in particular, the sense that our practical (cognitive/affective) interests constitute the 'point of view' from which we 'see'. The second description stresses the sense in which perspective 'seeing' defines a field of visibility bounded by a perceptual horizon; the correlate of this aspect of perspectives would be the sense in which perspective 'knowing' constructs a field of knowledge bounded by an epistemic horizon. This redescription points to a notion of what is visible (knowable) being defined by the perspective. This second feature is emphasised to a greater extent in Nietzsche's other major metaphor for knowing, namely, interpreting. For example, we can note that the activity of interpreting a text involves selecting certain features as significant while downplaying others, and that this activity of picking out significant features is guided by practical interests which constitute our criteria of significance. Thus this metaphor highlights the extent to which different forms of knowing involve different ways of picking out features of the world according to their interests. On this account, for example, Nietzsche's comment that 'physics too is only an interpretation and arrangement of the world (according to our own requirements if I may say so!) and *not* an explanation of the world' (BGE §14) is simply saying, firstly, that the activity of doing physics involves deploying certain criteria of significance (interests) in selecting and arranging features of the world and, secondly, that the truth of this interpretation of the world does not exclude the truth of other interpretations of the world which serve other interests. It is an important feature of perspectivism that it rejects the idea that the truth about the world could be exhausted by any single description of it. However, what we should also note about the discussion thus far is that I have already entered into a slight ambiguity about the notion of perspective insofar as I use it to refer to both a set of beliefs (judgements) about the world and a way of generating beliefs about the world, a style of reasoning[11] (or epistemic horizon) in terms of which we distinguish between true and false. At this juncture, I would like to elucidate the idea of perspective as a set of beliefs about the world; this will also lead to a resolution of ambiguity about the idea of perspective.

Let's start with Quine's notion of a *conceptual scheme* as a web of beliefs or, more formally, a set of sentences held to be true. Quine uses the figure of 'a field of force whose boundary conditions are experience' to clarify the features of a conceptual scheme:

> A conflict with experience at the periphery occasions readjustments in the interior of the field. Truth values have to be redistributed over some of our statements. Reevaluation of some statements entails reevaluation of others, because of their logical interconnections. . . . But the total field is so underdetermined by its boundary conditions, experience, that there is much latitude of choice as to what statements to reevaluate in the light of any single contrary experience. No particular experiences are linked with any particular statements in the interior of the field, except indirectly through considerations of equilibrium affecting the field as a whole. (1961: 42–3).

Within this image, Quine distinguishes (but only as a matter of degree) between core beliefs which are at the centre of the forcefield and more peripheral beliefs which are at the edge. Now what is intuitively appealing about this way of thinking about perspectives is that it points out that a perspective must be treated holistically and it captures our sense of being able to ad hoc our way around potential threats to core beliefs by changing peripheral beliefs (although this process of ad hoc-ing has limits). Thus, for example, Nietzsche refers to the ability of the Greeks to elide the emergence of the notion of guilt predicated on personal responsibility by mobilising the idea of possession by the gods: 'For the longest time these Greeks used their gods precisely so as to ward off the "bad conscience," so as to be able to rejoice in their freedom of soul' (GM II §23). Furthermore, Quine's notion of a conceptual scheme also captures our sense of the sublime, that is, the anxiety of experience that disrupts our beliefs and which Nietzsche regards as providing the impetus to develop our conceptual schemes:

> To trace something unknown back to something known is alleviating, soothing, gratifying and gives moreover a feeling of power. Danger, disquiet, anxiety attend the unknown – the first instinct is to *eliminate* these states. (TI 'The Four Great Errors' §5)

We should note also that Quine's idea of conceptual scheme provides a model not only for thinking about a perspective as a web of beliefs but also for thinking about our worldview as made up of a web of perspectives. This point is important because it highlights the fact that the justification of any belief or perspective always takes place in relation to our other beliefs or perspectives: 'all justification is contextual, dependent on other beliefs [or perspectives] held unchallengeable for the moment but themselves capable of only a similarly contextual justification' (Clark, 1990: 130).

Since I am suggesting the pertinence of Quine's notion of a conceptual scheme for illuminating Nietzsche's notion of perspective, it is probably a good idea in order to sharpen our notion of perspective, to render explicit the distinction between beliefs and perspectives which is implicitly introduced in the preceding comments. In these comments, I have simply treated a perspective as an ensemble of beliefs, that is, as more complex entities than individual beliefs. To this distinction, I would like to add a further clarification by distinguishing between perspectives and complexes of beliefs *per se*; the salient point is this – a perspective is not just a complex of beliefs, it is a complex of beliefs which are rooted in common practical interests. By analogy, we could say that this distinction is rather like that between grouping cars on the motorway in terms of speed or in terms of velocity (speed and direction); a perspective is a complex of beliefs going in the same direction! Having noted this point, let's return to our slight ambiguity about perspective as a complex of affectually bound beliefs about the world and perspective as a way of reasoning about the world.

In *On Certainty*, Wittgenstein is confronted by the same ambiguity. On the one hand, he thinks about a conceptual scheme in terms of a complex of judgements (beliefs):

> We do not learn the practice of making empirical judgements by learning rules: we are taught *judgements* and their connexion with other judgements. A *totality* of judgements is made plausible to us. . . . When we first *believe* anything, what we believe is not a single proposition, it is a whole system of propositions. (1969: §§140–1)

On the other hand, he also conceives of our picture of the world in terms of the epistemic horizon (or style of reasoning) in terms of which we generate beliefs about the world:

> But I did not get my picture of the world by satisfying myself of its correctness; nor do I have it because I am satisfied of its correctness. No: it is the inherited background against which I distinguish between true and false. (1969: §94)

To try to resolve this apparent ambiguity, Wittgenstein offers a metaphor of the river as a way of thinking about our 'picture of the world' as both 'a *totality* of judgements' and 'the inherited background against which I distinguish between true and false'. He elaborates this metaphor as follows:

> It might be imagined that some propositions, of the form of empirical propositions, were hardened and functioned as channels for such empirical propositions as were not hardened but fluid; and that this relation altered with time, in that fluid propositions hardened, and hard ones became fluid. (1969: §96)

We can clarify the point of this metaphor by adducing the following comments: 'the same proposition may get treated at one time as something to test by experience, at another as a rule of testing' (Wittgenstein, 1969: §98) and 'I want to say: We use judgements as principles of judgement' (Wittgenstein, 1969: §124). In other words, Wittgenstein is suggesting that our judgements are constitutive of our principles of judgement (our standards of rationality) and that, at the extreme, judgements (beliefs) may become entrenched to the degree that to doubt them is unintelligible and that these beliefs act as 'foundational' principles for judging other beliefs. In *Beyond Good and Evil*, Nietzsche adopts a similar position:

> . . . 'being conscious' is in no decisive sense the *opposite* of the instinctive – most of a philosopher's conscious thinking is secretly directed and compelled into

definite channels by his instincts. Behind all logic too and its apparent autonomy there stand evaluations. (BGE §3)

This is very much the way, for example, that Nietzsche thinks about Kant's notion of synthetic *a priori* judgements. For Kant these judgements were the product of the constitutive activity of the transcendental ego; however, for Nietzsche these judgements are simply judgements which are deeply entrenched. This is why the important question about synthetic *a priori* judgements for Nietzsche is not how they are possible but why they are necessary; his suggestion being that 'for the purpose of preserving beings such as ourselves, such judgements must be *believed* to be true' (BGE §11).[12] There is one further point about the fact that judgements can act as principles of judgement which, although it is no doubt obvious, we should make explicit, namely, that the kind of judgements which act as our principles of judgement determine the character of our style of reasoning. Thus, for example, Nietzsche's distinction between master and slave moralities shows how different judgements about the relationship of self and world lead to different kinds of moral reasoning.

Using Wittgenstein's river metaphor, then, allows us to show that Nietzsche's use of perspective as an (affectually bound) web of beliefs and as an (affectually rooted) style of reasoning is quite coherent. At this stage, I want to conclude our reflections on the notion of perspective by referring to two further points: firstly, the relation between perspectives and human agency and, secondly, the ranking of perspectives and our 'best' standards of rationality. Following the discussion of these topics, I will briefly summarise the conclusions reached about perspectivism as a way of thinking about knowledge.

I have suggested that perspectives are affectually bound bundles of judgements about the world. We can give grounds for holding most of these judgements about the world in terms of our deeply entrenched judgements, but what of these entrenched judgements, these judgements we cannot intelligibly doubt? If we cannot doubt them, the idea of giving grounds seems bizarre. Here Wittgenstein makes a useful point when he writes:

> 'An empirical proposition can be *tested*' (we say). But how? and through what?
> What *counts* as its test? – 'But is this an adequate test? And, if so, must it not be recognizable as such in logic?' – As if giving grounds did not come to an end sometime. But the end is not an ungrounded presupposition: it is an ungrounded way of acting. (1969: §§109–10)

In other words, our judgements about the world are ultimately rooted in our ways of acting in the world. Wittgenstein repeats this point in a different context when he comments that agreement in language is agreement in judgements which is agreement in form of life (1958: §§240–1). That this is also Nietzsche's position with respect to perspectives emerges in his comments on master and slave moralities in which he ties these perspectives to different forms of agency which characterise the typical experience of noble and slave classes. However, it is not simply a case of our judgements being rooted in agency, it is also the case for Nietzsche that our judgements articulate our agency and different kinds of judgements articulate different kinds of agency. For example, Nietzsche argues not only that master and slave morality as moral perspectives are rooted in different experiences of agency but also that they lead to different forms of ethical agency. Moreover, in the context of his discussion of nihilism, it is through transforming our judgements that Nietzsche seeks to transform our mode of agency into one with less destructive consequences for our experience of being in the world.

The other topic to which I want to refer requires us to reflect briefly back to Nietzsche's claim that our cognitive constitution is not separable from our affective constitution. My point is this: insofar as different perspectives are rooted in different affects and since the different affective interests of perspectives may clash (and Nietzsche suggests that they often do), the ranking of perspectives is a function of the ranking of affects and our 'best' standards of rationality are the product of this ranking of our affective interests. Recalling my concurrence with Clark's argument that Nietzsche thinks of truth as not being independent of our cognitive interests (our best standards of rationality), we are now led to the conclusion that truth is not independent of (the ranking of) our affective interests. Or, as Nietzsche comments: 'Proof by *pleasure* ("by potency") as criterion of truth' (TI 'The Four Great Errors' §5). Thus, for Nietzsche's perspectivism, the question of how we rank our affective interests thus becomes a central question for reflection about rationality and truth.

We will return to these points about perspectives and agency in the next section as part of our discussion of Nietzsche's notion of genealogy and to the comments on the erotic character of rationality and truth in the following section on the doctrine of will to power. For the moment, however, let us conclude by summarising the characterisation of perspectivism and of perspectives elaborated in this section:

1   it is the activity of knowing which articulates the unity of knower and known;
2   this activity is always both a culturally embedded and physically embodied activity;
3   as such our cognitive constitution cannot be separated from our affective constitution (i.e., truth is erotic);
4   different forms of knowing, which we term 'perspectives', involve different affects and the world is always (in principle) open to new perspectives;
5   perspectives are complexes of affectually bound judgements about the world and, seen under a different aspect, styles of reasoning about the world;
6   the justification of perspectives as bundles of judgement is always a contextual activity articulated through our 'best' standards of rationality, which are the product of the affective ranking of perspectives;

7   perspectives are rooted in our ways of acting in the world and articulate our agency;
8   perspectivism does not entail relativism.

Having developed this account of Nietzsche's perspective theory of affects, I want to turn to how this account leads him to the ideas of genealogy and will to power which characterise his philosophical method.

Genealogy as Immanent Critique

The term 'genealogy' is used by Nietzsche to characterise his historical investigations; this notion, more commonly used to describe the tracing of a family tree, is used metaphorically by Nietzsche to capture the sense of his activity. Consider for a moment the book *Roots* in which the author Alex Haley recounts the process of tracing his family history from present-day America back through the 1960s civil rights movement to slavery and finally to nineteenth-century Africa as a story about coming to reflect on his own identity as a black American; grasping the contingent routes through which he has become what he is provides Haley with a context in terms of which to understand his present. Nietzsche's historical reflections are similarly concerned with sketching the contingent routes through we have become what we are (namely, modern individuals) in order to provide a context of meaning within which we can recognise and critically reflect on our modernity. Thus, a provisional understanding of genealogy as a Nietzschean term of art would point to its concern with providing a history of the present in order to facilitate critical reflection on the present.

In taking up the idea of genealogy then, our attention may be said to turn from Nietzsche's account of the possibility and character of knowledge to his understanding of the activity of critique. These are not, of course, unrelated issues; on the contrary, Nietzsche's recognition that our reflective activity is always already both historically and culturally situated and affectively structured entails that the activity of critique must recognise its own contextual and interested character. Consequently, the Kantian activity of critique as specifying transcendental conditions of possibility is transformed into the enterprise of establishing historical conditions of possibility and the affective interests embedded in these conditions of possibility. To put this slightly differently, we might say that Nietzsche's version of critique is concerned with tracing how we have become what we are: what are our conditions of possibility? Another slightly more Wittgensteinian way of putting this point would be to say that genealogy is the activity of rendering visible the judgements and forms of agency constitutive of our form of life through a historical investigation of the emergence and entrenchment of these judgements and forms of agency. Moreover, just as Kant's concern is to specify the possibilities and limits of human reflection and agency, Nietzsche's concern with reflecting on how we have become what we are is also a reflection on how what we are both enables and constrains what we may become. In other words, Nietzsche's concern with reconstructing the historical conditions of possibility of what we are is also directed to how what we are acts as the conditions of possibility for our being otherwise than we are (in passing we can note that it will be one of Nietzsche's major claims that our present provides the conditions of possibility for two very different types of human being – the *Last Man* and the *Overman*). At this stage, to elucidate this genealogical conception of critique further requires that we look at what is involved in the practice of genealogy.

Thus far we have noted that the practice of genealogy involves three related interests: (i) 'what are we?', (ii) 'how have we become what we are?' and (iii) 'given what we are, what can we become?' The first issue to which I want to draw attention concerns the reasons which we might have for asking these questions. My point is simply this: insofar as our engagement in cultural practices involves the deployment of a given cultural self-understanding of what we are (i.e., the capacities which flow from our affective/cognitive constitution), we are only prompted to pose the question 'what are we?', when this self-understanding becomes problematic. Thus, to engage in genealogy as a critical practice of interpretation presupposes a certain dissatisfaction with our current self-understanding. If our self-understanding satisfies our embodied experience of agency in the world, we have no reason to ask this question. The second topic which we should address concerns the question of what is involved in satisfying the interests of genealogy. Here we can distinguish two accounts which are required: firstly, to respond to the question 'what are we?' entails that we offer an account of the *restricted* ontology of human beings in modern culture (i.e., the affective/cognitive interests which characterise the constitution of modern individuals); while, secondly, to answer the questions 'how have we become what we are? and 'given what we are, what can we become?' requires that we relate this restricted ontology to a *general* ontology of human beings (i.e., the architectonic affective/cognitive interest which characterises the constitution of human beings) in order to explain the movement between particular restricted ontologies which characterises the history of humanity. We can develop our understanding of what is involved in this issue by addressing it in terms of one of the points with which we closed our discussion of perspectivism, namely, that judgements and agency articulate each other.

It was suggested in that discussion that, for Nietzsche, we can say that our perspectives are constitutive of our forms of agency and our forms of agency are constitutive of our perspectives. However, while this formulation is clear, it is not entirely precise; we need to refine it. The basic idea expressed here is straightforward:

1   it is through our perspectives that we recognise ourselves (and others) both as selves (and others) and as particular sorts of selves (and others);
2   recognition of ourselves as specific kinds of selves includes recognition of

ourselves as having certain capacities (and not others) for acting in the world and for acting in terms of certain practical interests (and not others);

3   however, the ways in which we act (or are acted on by others) in the world also affects our perspectives (to the extent that we can develop, revise or, even, reject a perspective) and thus the ways in which we recognise ourselves (and others).[13]

We should note that there is no suggestion here that the ways in which we recognise ourselves in the world *determines* how we act in the world or that the ways in which we act *determines* the perspectives we hold; on the contrary, all that is being claimed is that the ways in which we recognise ourselves as agents construct a field of possible ways of acting (and thus rule out other ways of acting) and the ways in which we act construct a field of possible ways of 'seeing' the world and ourselves in it (and thus rule out other ways of knowing).

Perhaps a more traditional way of putting this claim would be to say that the structure of consciousness and the structure of the will are neither given nor independent of each other but are contingent products of their mutual articulation in the worldly conditions of our activity (Nietzsche shares this general position with Marx). Be that as it may, we can now specify the character of this relation more precisely as the following claim: the *actual* ways in which we recognise ourselves and others as particular selves and others opens up a field of *possible* ways of acting on ourselves and others, while the *actual* ways in which we act on ourselves and others (and are acted on by others) opens up a field of *possible* ways of recognising ourselves and others.[14]

Reflecting on this formulation, we can note its implication that in accounting for our conditions of possibility, that is, our contemporary structures of recognition and forms of agency (which he addresses through the idea of the *nihilism* of modernity), Nietzsche must be able both to trace the articulation of structures of recognition and forms of agency *and* to render intelligible the particular patternings of possibility and actuality which are constitutive of our genealogy. In other words, Nietzsche must be able both to *describe* the history of the relations of consciousness and willing and to *account* for this history being *this* history and not another history. In other words, Nietzsche needs an ontological account of human beings if he is to make the fact that our history is as it is intelligible to us. The name of ontological thesis or the principle of intelligibility which articulates this activity of accounting is *will to power*.

Thus, on the account offered in this section, genealogy is a particular interpretive practice in which we engage when our current self-understanding breaks down. As such, genealogy is a practice through which we seek to understand how and why our self-understanding failed and to open the space for the development of a new self-understanding. Integral to this task is the provision of a general ontology of human beings and it is to this ontological account which we now turn.

The Doctrine of Will to Power

If our actual judgements open up a field of possible ways of acting and our actual ways of acting open up a field of possible ways of judging, Nietzsche needs a principle or 'analytic' in terms of which to explicate the patterning of possibility and actuality. An alternative formulation of this point would be to say that if genealogy is to operate as a form of critique it must account for how the specific possibility of our being what we are which is immanent within our cultural practices becomes actual, while other possibilities immanent within these practices don't.[15] This issue is important not just in terms of the coherence and cogency of Nietzsche's notion of genealogy as a form of critique but also in terms of the *political* task which Nietzsche constructs for his work, namely, seeking to enable the actualisation of a particular possibility immanent within our current cultural practices (the Overman) and constrain the actualisation of another possibility (the Last Man). If Nietzsche is to engage in this political endeavour, he needs to understand what it involves and what it entails. In this section, then, I'll be concerned with, firstly, establishing my claim that the principle of intelligibility involved is the idea of will to power and, secondly, elucidating how it is that the notion of will to power can operate to explain cultural change.

We can begin by noting that there is considerable controversy about how to interpret Nietzsche's idea of will to power. Thus, liberal critics typically point to passages in *Beyond Good and Evil* such as section 259 in which Nietzsche comments:

> 'Exploitation' does not pertain to a corrupt or imperfect or primitive society: it pertains to the *essence* of the living thing as a fundamental organic function, it is a consequence of the intrinsic will to power which is precisely the will of life.

Such remarks lead liberal moralists to claim that Nietzsche posits an irrational will to domination at the heart of human existence (and, indeed, all existence), whereas liberals themselves locate a rational commitment to freedom as an integral feature of humanity. There are two versions of this liberal critique. The first version involves a conception of power 'as necessarily external and opposed to the freedom of individuals' (Patton, 1993: 144); consequently, this form of liberalism regards Nietzsche's hypothesis of will to power as a form of *philosophical* irrationalism insofar as it appears to deny the immanent relation of humanity, freedom and reason. For the second version of this critique, 'there is no externality between power and freedom' (Patton, 1993: 144); consequently, this form of liberalism sees Nietzsche's position as a form of *political* irrationalism (along neo-Hobbesian or Social Darwinist lines) insofar as it seems to make desire for self-preservation through power over others a central tenet of existence.[16] There are, however, problems with both of these lines of attack. The first requires the attribution to Nietzsche of a conception of power as external to freedom, which he does not hold; Nietzsche refers to freedom in terms of our capacity to do things (i.e., power).[17] The second entails committing Nietzsche to the Hobbesian claim of the primacy of self-preservation, which he explicitly rejects:[18]

> Physiologists should think again before postulating the drive for self-preservation as the cardinal drive in an organic being. A living thing desires above to *vent* its strength – life as such is will to power – : self-preservation is only one of the indirect and most frequent *consequences* of it. (BGE §13)

If, then, Nietzsche's notion of will to power is not dismissable in the immediate manner which his liberal critics claim, we are still left with the difficulty of accounting for what it is that Nietzsche means by will to power.

An interpretation which rejects the moralism of the liberal dismissal and yet does not seek to elide those comments which lead to this liberal judgement has been offered by Paul Patton. Patton's strategy is to highlight two features of Nietzsche's notion of will to power: firstly, he attends to the conception of power developed by Nietzsche and, secondly, he stresses the significance of consciousness for the character of human will to power. Focusing on Nietzsche's conception of power, Patton points out that it can be distinguished from that which grounds Hobbesian or Social Darwinist conceptions of life on three counts. Firstly, there is 'the fact that for Nietzsche the fundamental principle is not the goal but the process, not the momentary stasis attained by the satisfaction of need or desire but the expenditure of energy itself' (Patton, 1993: 152). Secondly, Nietzsche presents a more general conception of power

> which includes all forms of activity directed at the maintenance or increase of the power of the body in question, as well as forms of activity which might lead to its destruction or its transformation into a different kind of body. (Patton, 1993: 153)

Thirdly, whereas the Hobbesian tradition conceives of power reactively 'as present means to obtain some future apparent good', that is, 'power defined with reference to objects initially outside or beyond a given body, with reference to what that body lacks', Nietzsche presents an active conception of power 'defined only with reference to the activity of which a given body is capable' (Patton, 1993: 153). From these three points, Patton concludes that 'while it is a "primordial fact" that "human life is inextricably caught up in the web of mutually hostile relations to other forms of life" and, thus, in relations of exploitation, this "fact" does not completely constrain the kinds of human being or the forms of agency which are possible' (1993: 154).

The cogency of this interpretation becomes clear when we note that for Nietzsche one of the ways in which humanity is transformed by the operation of will to power is through the development of consciousness, where Nietzsche identifies this development as the result of enclosure within 'the walls of society and of peace' (GM II §16). With this transformation of the human animal into a historical being, that is, a being characterised by consciousness, the character of human will to power is also changed,

> [f]or on this basis, Nietzsche proposes a conception of human agency as governed not simply by the drive to increase power but by the drive to maximize the *feeling* of power. . . . Given the self-conscious, interpretive element in every human act

of will, it follows that mankind is the one animal in which the feeling of power is divorced from any direct relation to quantity of power. (Patton, 1993: 155)

We can draw out this 'self-conscious, interpretive element' by saying that it is with the development of consciousness that the feeling of power becomes mediated through meaning.[19] For a human being to experience his or her *self* as powerful requires that s/he experience being in the world as meaningful. We can note two significant consequences of this conception of human agency. Firstly, it entails that an increased feeling of power may denote a decrease in actual power and *vice versa*. In other words, my way of rendering my experience meaningful may generate an increased feeling of power, yet this mode of account may undermine my actual capacity for autonomous agency; this is essentially Nietzsche's objection to Christianity. Secondly, this interpretation removes any *necessary* relation 'between the expression of the human will to power and hostile forms of exercise of power over others' (Patton, 1993: 156). This latter point does not claim that the expression of human will to power may not take the form of exploitation, only that such an expression would be a contingent rather than necessary form. If how I experience myself as an autonomous agent is 'mediated' by my conceptual scheme, the feeling of power might involve oppressing others but it also might involve the quest for self-mastery.[20]

What can we draw from Patton's interpretation of Nietzsche's doctrine of will to power? I think that the strength of this reading is that it allows us to see how the idea of will to power can function as a principle of intelligibility insofar as it suggests that what mediates between possibility and actuality is the capacity of the distinct possibilities for human being immanent within our cultural practices to increase our feeling of power. An alternative way of putting this point would be to say that the degree to which any given belief about the world is entrenched (and thus the capacity of this judgement to act as a principle of judgement for other less entrenched judgements) is a product of the degree to which it increases our feeling of power, where an integral part of this is the degree to which it renders our experience of the world meaningful. Thus, Nietzsche regards Kant's synthetic *a priori* judgements as among our most deeply entrenched judgements because they are 'the most indispensable to us' (BGE §4), where this indispensability consists in the fact that they increase our feeling of power immeasurably by enabling us to order our experience in terms of space and time, and to understand our experience in terms of objects and their relations.

But does this interpretation succeed in banishing the spectre of irrationalism? At this juncture, let us recall that we concluded our discussion of Nietzsche's notion of truth by suggesting that truth is not independent of our cognitive/affective interests. On this account, our best standards of rationality are a complex of affectually ranked cognitive interests. Now let's note that Nietzsche's doctrine of will to power provides a way of thinking about the affective character of our cognitive constitution, that is, how our cognitive interests are constituted and ranked in terms of their affective character. We can express this point by saying that for Nietzsche *will to power is the affective (or erotic) structure of reason* or, alternatively, *will to power is the architectonic interest of reason*. Thus, far from offering us a species of irrationalism, Nietzsche's hypothesis of will to power represents an attempt to develop concretely his philosophical account of the erotic character of rationality and truth in terms of an ontological account of human beings which locates will to power as the architectonic interest of our affective constitution. On this understanding, freedom, truth and reason are immanently related to each other.

Having set out the basic character of will to power as the affective structure of reason, we can now turn to the question of how this principle of intelligibility operates as a way of explaining cultural change. The basic character of this mode of explanation is straightforward: our beliefs about the world and our ways of acting in the world change as they lose their 'proof of power'. But this statement is all too summary; let's elucidate Nietzsche's position further. One route into Nietzsche's account is to return to the idea of our web of beliefs as a conceptual scheme. In discussing this model, I suggested that its advantage lay in the fact that it fitted our experience of protecting core beliefs by changing peripheral beliefs, although I also claimed that this process of ad hoc-ing, of not inferring, had limits. But these comments elided the question of how these limits are determined.

Consider by analogy Kuhn's (1970) account of the history of science in which a paradigm[21] (conceptual scheme) is established because of its power to explain core questions and in the course of its development generates anomalies which eventually lead to the formulation of new core questions and the revolutionary establishment of a new paradigm which answers these questions. The analogous issue which Kuhn addresses is that of identifying the point at which the build-up of anomalies becomes such that what have been peripheral puzzles become core questions. The response to this question seems to be that it becomes irrational to continue to consign anomalies to the periphery when the scientific community recognises that the capacity of the paradigm to satisfy our cognitive interests is outweighed by the dissatisfactions produced by the accumulated anomalies; the satisfaction or dissatisfaction of these interests may, of course, be dependent on their identity and ranking which is itself often a matter of considerable controversy within the scientific community. In other words, on this reading of Kuhn, the process of scientific change is a product of the communal judgement of the cognitive power of competing paradigms, wherein this judgement is predicated on the identification and ranking of cognitive interests by the scientific community. My suggestion is that Nietzsche's account of cultural change is in some salient ways similar to Kuhn's account of scientific change; this claim can be developed as a series of points.

Firstly, if we consider a perspective (conceptual scheme) as analogous to a paradigm, we can say that the emergence of a perspective is tied to the conditions of agency of the community who organise their subjectivity through these beliefs. Thus, for example, Nietzsche argues that the perspective of Christianity emerges amongst the downtrodden because it provides them with a means of sustaining their sense of their autonomy and value (i.e., feeling of power) by, firstly, distinguishing between the empirical self (mere flesh) and the transcendental self (pure spirit) and, secondly, by inverting the social order of rank (the first shall be last and the meek will inherit the earth).

Secondly, the development of a perspective is tied to its ability to sustain our feeling of power in the context of changes in our experienced reality of ourselves as meaningful subjects and autonomous agents (changes which may themselves be the products of our practices). This may entail replacing peripheral beliefs in order to sustain core beliefs. Thus, Nietzsche suggests that in its initial form the perspective of slave morality involved the belief in the evil character of nobility as a way of explaining the suffering of the good slave, but that with the achievement of hegemony by this form of morality (i.e., the incorporation of the noble into the herd) this belief could no longer explain suffering and, consequently, was displaced by the belief that we are responsible for our own suffering (punishment for sin) in order to maintain the 'proof of power' of the perspective as a whole, that is, its capacity to make meaningful our experience in such a way as to sustain (or increase) our experience of ourselves as autonomous agents. It should be noted that Nietzsche argues that this change was the product of *unintended* consequences of the forms of subjectivity and agency articulated through the perspective of slave morality.

Thirdly, if the core beliefs of a perspective cannot sustain our experienced reality of ourselves as meaningful subjects and autonomous agents despite ad hoc changes to peripheral beliefs, then a perspective may be said to lose its 'proof of power' and be displaced. Thus, for example, Nietzsche remarks of Judaism that, in the context of internal and external threats,

> every hope remained unfulfilled. The old God *could* no longer do what he formerly could. One should let him go. What happened? One altered the conception of him: at this price one retained him. Yaweh the God of 'justice' – *no longer* at one with Israel, an expression of national self-confidence: now only a God bound by conditions. (AC §25)

Similarly, Nietzsche comments of the entrenchment of Socratic dialectics in Greece:

> Rationality was at that time divined as a *saviour*; neither Socrates nor his 'invalids' were free to be rational or not, as they wished – it was *de rigueur*, it was their *last* expedient. The fanaticism with which the whole of Greek thought throws itself at rationality betrays a state of emergency: one was in peril, one had only *one* choice: either to perish or – be *absurdly rational*. (TI 'The Problem of Socrates' §10)

We should note again that this 'paradigm switch' may itself be the product of capacities developed under the aegis of the perspective displaced; thus Nietzsche comments of Christianity that it was undermined by the capacity for truthfulness which it was instrumental in developing (GM III §27).

To these three features of Nietzsche's account of cultural change, we can add a fourth which parallels a point drawn out by MacIntyre in a discussion of paradigm change.[22] MacIntyre points out that an integral feature of the establishment of a new paradigm is the construction of a dramatic narrative which accounts for the overthrow of the preceding paradigm in terms of the capacity of the new paradigm for both explaining the limitations of the preceding paradigm and overcoming these limitations itself. This process of narrative redescription acts as a form of cognitive legitimation. The fourth feature of Nietzsche's account of cultural change is a precise anticipation of MacIntyre's argument. Thus, for example, he comments of the perspective switch in Judaism (which we've already mentioned above) that a crucial element of this process was a rewriting of the history of Israel:

> The entire *history* of Israel was useless: away with it! – These priests perpetrated that miracle of falsification the documentation of which lies before us in a good part of the Bible: with unparalleled disdain of every tradition, every historical reality, they translated their own national past *into religious terms*, that is to say they made of it a stupid salvation-mechanism of guilt towards Yaweh and punishment, piety toward Yaweh and reward. (AC §26)

This dramatic rewriting serves to legitimate the establishment of the new perspective by casting it as able to resolve the affective crises of the previous perspective because it can account for these crises. Another way of putting this point would be this: while one's current perspective is no longer capable of sustaining one's experience of oneself as meaningful in such a way as to maintain (or increase) one's experience of oneself as an autonomous agent, a condition of the 'proof of power' of the new perspective is that it can make this loss of the feeling of power meaningful in such a way as to re-establish our sense of our own powerfulness.

On the basis of this analogy with Kuhn's account of scientific change then, we can grasp the central features of how Nietzsche's notion of will to power acts to account for cultural change by specifying the two elements of *meaning* and *autonomy*. Consequently, we can summarise the core of this account thus: a perspective may require revision or rejection if it ceases to be capable of *either* constituting our experience of the world as meaningful *or* constituting it as meaningful in such a way as to maintain (or increase) our experience of ourselves as autonomous agents.[23] On this note, we can conclude this section by reflecting on the fact that we have established that Nietzsche's notion of genealogy can act as a form of critique insofar as will to power as an ontological account of human beings functions as a principle of intelligibility and explanation. In the next chapter, we will see how Nietzsche puts this philosophical method to work.

The Pathos of Style

Thus far in our discussion of Nietzsche's idea of genealogy, the focus has been placed on its construction and operation as a form of immanent critique; however, Nietzsche also conceptualises the activity of genealogy – and of writing in general – as a form of affective performance which seeks to communicate particular affective dispositions to the reader. This issue is addressed by Nietzsche in terms of a concern with *style* – the tempo, tone and texture of writing or what we may call the 'musicality' of language.[24] This topic is not one typically considered by Anglo-American philosophers in whom the liberal idea of language as a set of conceptual tools for communicating ideas is entrenched; an attitude which elides the affective or expressive dimension of language by marginalising it as extraneous or incidental and, anyway, the proper business of poets rather than philosophers. Yet it is an issue with a history as old as philosophy itself; thus, in the *Phaedrus*, Plato calls for an account of mutual accommodation of speech and soul, a quest which Gadamer argues is taken up in Aristotle's *Rhetoric*:

> . . . the task is to master the faculty of speaking in such an effectively persuasive way that the arguments brought forward are always appropriate to the specific receptivity of the souls to which they are directed. (Gadamer, 1976: 21 cited in Beiner, 1983: 84)

It is in this context that I think we need to situate Nietzsche's concern with style, and since I will be claiming that this aspect of Nietzsche's work is integral to his project of overcoming modern *decadence*, it is appropriate to conclude this chapter by examining Nietzsche's reflection on this topic.

In *Ecce Homo*, Nietzsche offers the following comments on his art of style:

> To communicate a state, an inward tension of pathos, by means of signs, including the tempo of these signs – that is the meaning of every style. . . . *Good* is any style that really communicates an inward state, that makes no mistake about the signs, the tempo of signs, the gestures – all the laws about long periods are concerned with the art of gestures. (EH 'Why I Write Such Good Books' §4)

Nietzsche is not claiming that a style can be good-in-itself, that is, in abstraction from its context; on the contrary, the communication of an inward state requires that there are those capable of experiencing the same pathos.[25] This is an intuitively appealing idea insofar as it fits well with our experience of the affective effects of music, literature and cinema. Consider, for example, the passionate pathos of Rachmaninov's 4th Piano Concerto, the tragic pathos of *King Lear* or the thrilling pathos of virtually all Hitchcock's films. However, we need to examine more closely how Nietzsche thinks about style as a means of communicating affects and in order to do this I am going to focus on the issue of tempo.

In *Beyond Good and Evil*, Nietzsche expands on his remarks about style with particular reference to tempo in claiming that the feature of writing

> which translates worst from one language to another is the tempo of its style, which has its origin in the character of the race, or, expressed more physiologically, in the average tempo of its 'metabolism'. (BGE §28)

Nietzsche elucidates the point he is getting at in this comment by claiming that '[t]he German is virtually incapable of *presto* in his language: thus, it may be fairly concluded, also of many of the most daring and delightful nuances of free, free-spirited thought', and his posing of the following rhetorical question:

> But how could the German language . . . imitate the tempo of Machiavelli, who in his *Principe* lets us breathe the subtle dry air of Florence and cannot help presenting the most serious affairs in a boisterous *allegrissimo*: not perhaps without a malicious artist's sense of the contrast he is risking – thoughts protracted, difficult, hard, dangerous and the tempo of the gallop and the most wanton good humour. (BGE §28, cf. §§246–7)

Consider these comments in the context of Nietzsche's remarks on 'metabolism' and climate by returning to *Ecce Homo*, in which Nietzsche comments:

> The *tempo* of the metabolism is strictly proportionate to the mobility or lameness of the spirit's *feet*; this 'spirit' itself is after all merely an aspect of this metabolism. List the places where men with *esprit* are living or have lived, where wit, subtlety, and malice belong to happiness, where genius found its home almost of necessity: all of them have excellent dry air. (EH 'Why I Am So Clever' §2).

It is not, however, merely the choice of climate and place which is important for one's 'metabolism'; Nietzsche also refers to the choice of nutrition (in the preceding section) and 'the choice of *one's own kind of recreation*' (in the following section). Although Nietzsche is particularly concerned in these reflections with indulging in his favourite activity of attacking 'German-ness' (we should recall that he is himself writing in German) and stressing, somewhat ironically, the importance of finding an appropriate diet, climate and recreational practice for his own thinking, we can see that the broad thrust of his argument is that the most significant features of the average tempo of a '"race's" metabolism' are its conditions of agency (the climatic and other characteristics of the territory which it inhabits) and its forms of agency (its dietary practices and its major recreational practices).[26]

In reflecting on these comments, it's important to note that Nietzsche's appeal to physiology is not an appeal to the natural as distinct from, or in opposition to, the cultural. On the contrary, Nietzsche rejects any strict nature/culture distinction; the physiological and the cultural run into one another. While Nietzsche regards the majority of our physiological features as the species-wide products of the pre-history of humanity[27] rather than as specific to particular historical groups or individuals, precisely because this is the case he may be read as acknowledging that the physiological differences of 'races' are simply the corporeal product of different cultural judgements and conditions of agency. In other words, the 'metabolic' tempo of a 'race' is simply a reference to the physiological characteristics which are the product of the form of life and the conditions of the form of life of the cultural community in question.

But aren't these arguments really just bizarre, implausible and potentially politically dangerous? Perhaps – but reflect briefly on the conceptual character of language. With respect to this issue, Nietzsche argues that the development of language and the development of consciousness are inextricably tied together in the context of the constitution and development of a cultural community (GS §354). This claim leads to the entirely plausible idea that different cultures will develop conceptual vocabularies suited to the forms of agency characteristic of these cultures, where these forms of agency are not utterly independent of the conditions of agency in which a given community finds itself. The obvious example to cite in support of this claim is the plurality of concepts for distinct types of 'snow' exhibited in the conceptual vocabulary of the Inuit, which simply exhibits the fact that the activities and conditions of agency of the Inuit require a much finer conceptual discrimination of the phenomenon 'snow' than the activities of cultures located in more temperate climes. Yet if we are willing to grant that the forms and conditions of agency of a cultural community are integral to the character and range of its language *qua* conceptual vocabulary, why should we be any less willing to grant that they are also integral to the character and range of its language *qua* tempo, texture and tone? Insofar as we are willing to grant the plausibility of this claim, Nietzsche's equation of the average 'metabolism' of a 'race' (the physiological expression of the rhythm of its forms of agency) with the tempo of its typical style (the linguistic expression of the rhythm of its forms of agency) looks at least less immediately bizarre. Consequently, Nietzsche's claim that the German language is virtually incapable of *presto* because of the character of the 'race' is simply the claim that the German form of life (diet and recreation) and conditions of form of life (place and climate) render its linguistic forms and rhythms unsuited to the expression of *presto*. Thus Nietzsche comments ironically:

> But German cuisine quite generally – what doesn't it have on its conscience! Soup *before* the meal . . .; overcooked meats, vegetables cooked with fat and flour; the degeneration of pastries and puddings into paperweights! Add to this the virtually bestial prandial drinking habits of the ancient, and by no means only the *ancient* Germans, and you will understand the origins of the *German spirit* – from distressed intestines. (EH 'Why I Am So Clever' §1)

This point is underscored in the following section when Nietzsche remarks sardonically that '[t]he German climate alone is enough to discourage strong, even inherently heroic, intestines.' (EH 'Why I Am So Clever' §2).

On Nietzsche's account then, the tempo of a language translates least well because it is the physiological tempo of the form of life (and conditions of form of life) of a historical community which is expressed through style.[28] For our immediate concerns, the significance of Nietzsche's discourse on language, tempo and 'race' is that it offers a potentially plausible argument for regarding linguistic styles as tied to physiological states, and, consequently, for thinking of style as a means of affective communication. At this stage, we need to be more specific about how Nietzsche thinks this dimension of communication operates.

It was noted at the beginning of these reflections that Nietzsche's concept of style is relational in the sense that it refers to affective communication between an author and an audience, that is, for the work to have style requires an audience capable of experiencing the affects it seeks to communicate. Nietzsche's remarks about his own 'untimeliness', his lack of an audience contemporary with his work, and the 'posthumous' character of his writing (if read literally) would gesture to the futural character of his styles.[29] However, even if there exists an audience which can, at least in principle, experience the affects embodied in Nietzsche's writing, this does not entail that there will be clarity of affective communication. For the full force of the affective dimension of writing to strike its audience requires certain practices of reading as an art which Nietzsche claims to regard both his German contemporaries (BGE §246) and modern individuals in general (GM 'Preface' §8) as lacking. Now I am not going to address the question of Nietzsche's claimed lack of audience or the inability of his contemporaries to read properly at this stage,[30] rather I want to focus on the practices of reading which Nietzsche recommends for clarity of affective communication.

In the preface to *On the Genealogy of Morals*, Nietzsche uses the metaphor of 'rumination' to capture the activity of reading he seeks to encourage, a metaphor which suggests slowly chewing over the textures, tones and rhythms, a pre-digestive activity which surrenders the full flavours and reduces the risk of indigestion. In *Beyond Good and Evil*, Nietzsche describes this activity in terms of attentiveness to tempo:

> . . . one should lend a refined and patient ear to every *staccato*, every *rubato*, that one should divine the meaning in the sequence of vowels and diphthongs and how delicately and richly they can colour and recolour one another through the order in which they come. (BGE §246).

While, in section §247 of the same text, Nietzsche praises the activity of reading aloud clearly and strongly which he claims characterised the ancient world; here Nietzsche emphasises the role of breathing in the art of recitation as physiological communication.[31] This suggestion that the performance of proclaiming the words, while remaining attentive to texture, tone and tempo, produces an effective reproduction of the physiological affects embedded in style is further supported by the section 'Of Reading and Writing' in *Thus Spoke Zarathustra* in which Zarathustra begins by supporting the Nietzschean notion of affective writing – 'Of all writings I love only what is written with blood. Write with blood: and you will discover that blood is spirit' – before commenting: 'He who writes in blood and aphorisms does not want to be read, he wants to be learned by heart.' Here the phrase 'learned by heart' operates to capture the sense of the incorporation of words and rhythms into the heart as that which regulates the rhythm of blood; the rhythm of writing with blood becomes the rhythm of blood. What these remarks makes clear is that Nietzsche presents a model of the clarity of affective communication as not simply dependent on the affective precision of the writing (which simply expresses the affective pathos characteristic of the author) but also on the reading practices of the audience; in particular, his notion of reading as rumination refers to attentiveness, performance, breath control and learning by heart as integral features of an effective reading practice.[32]

We can conclude this section by noting that insofar as the features of language which Nietzsche highlights are all essential elements of contemporary dramatic training, it does not seem unreasonable to claim that Nietzsche's concern with both style as affective communication and the practices of reading and writing which allow the affective effects of style to speak mostly clearly and directly offers us an understanding of the textuality of philosophy, of the musicality of philosophical writing, to which the discipline should be more attentive. Perhaps more importantly for our concerns, however, is the fact that just as the cognitive dimension of Nietzsche's genealogical writing seeks to articulate the overcoming of *nihilism* by providing a context in which our experience of meaninglessness becomes intelligible (and, consequently, something we can overcome, at least in principle), the affective dimension of Nietzsche's genealogical writing plays a part in his attempt to articulate an overcoming of modern *decadence* by communicating the affective dispositions (heroism and irony) which he regards as necessary to mobilise our volitional resources for this task.

Conclusion

The purpose of this chapter has been to set out Nietzsche's critique of the philosophical character of liberal reason by highlighting his attacks on its commitment to the project of epistemology and, in particular, the conception of the self as transcendental subject integral to this project. This critique is accomplished by focusing on the '*a priori*' judgements of liberal reason, namely, the subject/object and appearance/reality distinctions which, taken together, engender the reason/history and reason/affectivity (truth/*eros*) distinctions. By setting out Nietzsche's perspective theory of affects, his idea of genealogy and the doctrine of will to power, it has been shown that Nietzsche's rejection of these liberal commitments does not entail an irrational relativism but that, on the contrary, his thought expresses an erotic commitment to truth, reason and human freedom. In the following chapters, I'll seek to illustrate Nietzsche's account of how we came to hold the commitments of liberalism and why we must now surrender them if we are to sustain a cogent ethical commitment to the future of humanity.

Notes

1 In some senses, Nietzsche's historial idea of critique parallels that of Marx. For an illuminating comparison, see Love (1986).

2 For Nietzsche's objection to this claim, cf. BGE §19.

3 See Williams' *Descartes* (1978: 130–53) for a fuller explanation of the scholastic principle of cause deployed by Descartes in this argument.

4 I am grateful to Martin Hollis for suggesting this route into explaining Kant's position as clearly as possible and for his helpful comments on this section as a whole.

5 See BGE §19.

6 For a fuller discussion of this issue, cf. Clark (1990: 55–61).

7 I accept Clark on this point, cf. Clark (1990: 112).

8 One problem with Clark's account is that she doesn't address this issue, talking about knowing subject and not activity of knowing; it is perhaps for this reason that she is happy to describe Nietzsche as 'neo-Kantian'.

9 It should be noted that Nietzsche's account also acts against the representationalism which Rorty thinks this perceptual metaphor produces.

10 I think the weakness of those who argue that our concept of rationality involves notions of non-contradiction and identity is that they don't account for how we acquired this concept!

11 I am not using the idea of a style of reasoning in the provocative sense given to it by Hacking (1982).

12 Nietzsche continues: 'although they might of course still be false judgements', which confirms the suggestion made earlier that in BGE he still thinks of truth as illusion.

13 Examples of the development and revision of a perspective would include St Paul's reinterpretation of Christianity (AC §§40–2) and the break between Catholicism and Protestantism. Examples of the rejection and replacement of a perspective would include the priestly revolt in theology in ancient Israel (AC §§25–6) and the Socratic revolt in philosophy in ancient Greece (TI 'The Problem of Socrates', §§5–10); notably, in both cases Nietzsche regards this 'revolution' as a last expedient.

14 Recognition does not have to be conscious, just bodily; cf. GS §354.

15 I use the term 'practice' to refer to an organised complex of judgement and agency.

16 Thus Patton notes that the Hobbesian vision of a war of all against all is often taken to be the end of Nietzsche's desire for the return of noble morality (1993: 144).

17 We can refer to Nietzsche's discussion of promising in GM II as a good example of this position.

18 See also GM II §12 for further evidence of this rejection.

19 Patton does not use this formulation because he does not assign feelings to animals (a perfectly legitimate Wittgensteinian point): however, because Nietzsche does talk about animals in terms of the feeling of power I am highlighting the issue of meaning as the significant difference.

20 Nietzsche ranks forms of will to power – noble and ignoble – in terms of strength, that is, overcoming resistances; however (curiously like the Islamic notion of *jihad*), I will argue that Nietzsche regards self-mastery as a nobler form of will to power than domination of others.

21 I am using 'paradigm' in the sense of disciplinary matrix. We should also note that in using this analogy I am not committed to accepting Kuhn's incommensurability thesis.

22 See his article 'Epistemological Crises, Dramatic Narratives and the Philosophy of Science' (1977).

23 Are these the same if the meaning of an action includes reference to its success or failure?

24 For a fascinating discussion of Nietzsche's work in terms of affective communication, see Henry Staten, *Nietzsche's Voice* (1990).

25 To have ears is equated with being able to experience the pathos in question.

26 For an illuminating discussion of Nietzsche's deployment of bodily metaphors, see Eric Blondel's *Nietzsche: The Body and Culture* (1991).

27 As species-competences?

28 It is not clear to me why in principle this should be any worse than translating concepts.

29 In my discussion of decadence I will argue that this is a rhetorical provocation.

30 See my discussion of authority and exemplarity in Chapter 5.

31 Consider chanting and the difference between aggressive and humorous chanting in football crowds and Vedic chanting for meditation purposes.

32 I wonder if it is our sense of hearing and feeling the texture, tempo and tone of words which seduces us into a representational view of knowledge?

3

On the Genealogy of Modernity

A Critical History of the Philosophical Commitments of Liberal Reason

To begin this chapter, we can note that Nietzsche's critique of the philosophical character of liberal reason is not itself an unsituated or disinterested affair. On the contrary, if we are to grant the virtue of coherence to Nietzsche's philosophical stance, we must recognise the embedded and embodied character of his critical reflections. This recognition has two consequences for Nietzsche's critique of liberal modernity. Firstly, it must be able to account for its own historical conditions of possibility; it must be able to account for how the embedded judgements which make up Nietzsche's philosophical position become possible. Secondly, it must acknowledge the affective interests that it embodies and which motivate and structure its reflective activity; thus, it must offer up its interests to the collective ranking of affects.

The first of these elements involves Nietzsche in providing a critical history of liberal reason and the emergence of the conditions of its demise – a demise which Nietzsche signals with the phrase 'the death of God'. In offering this history Nietzsche seeks to account for the emergence, development and entrenchment of the types of judgement, the structuring dualisms, which characterise liberal reason (subject/object, appearance/reality, truth/*eros*, reason/history) and the forms of agency which sustain this style of reasoning, before illustrating that this 'paradigm' can no longer perform its explanatory and empowering task. As a historical narrative in terms of which our present becomes intelligible, Nietzsche's genealogy is a crucial element in the task of overcoming both the liberal paradigm and the nihilist vacuum its demise engenders, while legitimating an alternative paradigm.

The character of this critical history (and of the alternative paradigm it prefigures and seeks to legitimate) is constituted by its affective interests as these are expressed in Nietzsche's judgement about the most significant characteristics of our modernity, the most important aspects of what we are today. Nietzsche's judgement is that we today are *nihilists*. I will suggest that it is Nietzsche's argument that the condition of nihilism is a product of the overcoming of the liberal will to truth. In this chapter, however, I will not address the specific character of our nihilism (this will be the main task of the following chapter), rather I will focus on Nietzsche's account of how we come to be in this condition – a condition in which Nietzsche's thoughts become possible.

In order to accomplish this task – and in doing so to illustrate the coherence of Nietzsche's critique – I will focus on the three essays which Nietzsche presents in *On the Genealogy of Morals*. In these essays Nietzsche presents a historical account of the philosophical commitments of liberal reason by attending to the emergence, development and demise of a particular style of moral reasoning which he labels 'slave morality' and which he contrasts with another form of moral reasoning which he terms 'noble morality'. In the first essay, ' "Good and Bad", "Good and Evil" ', Nietzsche sketches the character of these two types of moral reasoning by providing an ideal-typical account of their conditions of emergence and, concomitantly, their fundamental judgements. It should be noted in this context that, on Nietzsche's account, slave morality and noble ethics are the ethical correlates of the epistemic positions which he characterises as 'epistemology' and 'perspectivism' respectively precisely because each ethical/ epistemic pair share presuppositions (i.e., fundamental judgements). The second essay, ' "Guilt", "Bad Conscience", and the Like', focuses on accounting for the conditions of possibility of these two forms of morality by posing the question of the emergence of conscience in general and bad conscience in particular. Here Nietzsche's concern is with the production of man as a historical being who is autonomous and supramoral (where 'moral' in this instance refers to the morality of custom). The final essay, 'What is the Meaning of Ascetic Ideals?', focuses on slave morality as a way of providing ascetic ideals, that is to say, rendering suffering meaningful and providing direction to human activity, before going on to examine how the development of slave morality brings about the conditions of its own demise, its self-overcoming. Nietzsche is particularly concerned in this essay with the relation between religion, morality and science articulated through the development of the liberal will to truth.

However, I will not be addressing these essays in the sequence in which Nietzsche places them and perhaps this requires a word of explanation. Since the second essay of *On the Genealogy of Morals* accounts for the conditions of possibility of the forms of morality addressed in the opening essay, I will depart from Nietzsche's sequence and reverse the order of the first two essays before addressing the final essay.[1] A second reason for this strategy concerns the fundamental judgements of liberal reason which we identified in the previous chapter as the subject/object, appearance/reality, reason/affectivity (truth/*eros*) and reason/history distinctions. The suggestion made in the following pages is that the essay on bad conscience accounts for the emergence of the subject/object distinction, the essay on noble and slave moralities elucidates the emergence of the appearance/ reality distinction, the essay on the meaning of ascetic ideals focuses on the emergence of the reason/affectivity or truth/*eros* distinction (and, more implicitly, the reason/history distinction).

We can also read these essays on another related register with respect to liberal political theory. Firstly, whereas philosophical liberalism presupposes a conception of the self as an autonomous subject, the essay on bad conscience focuses on giving a historical account of the production of 'sovereign individuals' who are able to act autonomously, that is, who have the capacity to make and keep promises. Secondly, whereas philosophical liberalism presupposes the idea of the transcendental subject and its attendant conception of autonomy, the essay on noble ethics and slave morality seeks to give a historical account of the contingency of, and practical interests embodied in, this presupposition. Thirdly, whereas philosophical liberalism presupposes the distinction between truth and *eros*, and presents the quest to overcome *eros* in the name of truth as the *telos* of humanity, the essay on ascetic ideals seeks to illuminate the absurdity and auto-destructive character of attempts to legislate moral rules from a disembedded and disembodied God's-eye view, a view from nowhere. Needless to say throughout these essays Nietzsche attempts to show how the emergence and development of our forms of judgement are tied to our forms of agency (and *vice versa*), and how their articulation is intelligible in terms of the idea of will to power.

'"Guilt", "Bad Conscience", and the Like'

My claim with respect to this essay is that Nietzsche seeks to provide an account of the emergence of the subject/object distinction and, concomitantly, the idea of the self as a free subject by offering a speculative account of how man is constituted as an animal with the capacity to make promises and, thus, to be held accountable for his actions – or, to put it differently, how man becomes a being with a conscience. Integral to this account is a distinction between two ways of thinking about accountability: a *tragic* idea of accountability which identifies the agent with his actions and is articulated through the idea of *fate*; and a *moral* idea of accountability which separates the agent from his acts and is articulated through the notion of *guilt*.[2] Nietzsche argues that whereas the tragic notion of accountability illustrates the presence of a *good conscience*, the moral idea of accountability expresses the existence of a *bad conscience*. The precise character of the distinction between these conceptions of accountability can be simply put in terms of two different models of the self. On the one hand, the tragic model of the self supposes that the actor is not separable from his actions; he could not act otherwise because his actions are what he is. One is a piece of fate. On the other hand, the moral model of selfhood posits a distinction between the actor and his actions which locates actions as operations on an object (the world) authored by a subject (the self); consequently, this model claims that the actor could always have acted otherwise than he did. One is a 'free will'. The account which Nietzsche sketches focuses on suggesting how these forms of conscience emerge, although he will pay specific attention to the question of the origin of bad conscience since it is this type of conscience, he argues, which is entrenched within our modern liberal cultures.

Let's begin by asking what Nietzsche is getting at when he refers to the breeding of an animal with the capacity to make promises as the paradoxical task nature has set itself regarding man. What is paradoxical about this task? The following instance of Nietzsche's characterisation of the animal state provides a hint:

> Consider the cattle grazing as they pass you by: they leap about, eat, rest, digest, leap about again and so on from morn till night and from day to day, fettered to the moment and its pleasure or displeasure, and thus neither melancholy or bored. . . . Thus the animal lives *unhistorically*: for it is contained in the present. (GM II §1)

Animals are ahistorical beings; beings characterised by an active forgetting such that they live in a perpetual present.[3] Thus, the paradox of man is the production of a *historical* being; a being who lives in historical time (past, present, future). The task of producing a being with the capacity to make promises thus requires the development of a counterforce to the active force of forgetting – a memory:

> . . . a real *memory of the will*: so that between the original 'I will,' 'I shall do this' and the actual discharge of the will, its *act*, a world of strange new things, circumstances, even acts of will may be interposed without breaking this long chain of will. (GM II §1)

However, Nietzsche argues, this development itself involves a series of presuppositions: 'Man must first of all have become *calculable, regular, necessary*, even in his own image of himself, if he is to stand security for *his own future*, which is what one who promises does!' (GM II §1). Consequently, it is to Nietzsche's account of how we become calculable beings that I will now turn.

In an earlier work, Nietzsche had commented that the first proposition of civilisation is 'any custom is better than no custom' (D §16); now he explains why he takes this to be the case by suggesting that it is through customs, through the prehistoric labour of the 'morality of mores', that 'man was actually *made* calculable' (GM II §2). At the end of this pre-historic process lies 'the *sovereign individual*, like only to himself, liberated again from morality of custom, autonomous and supramoral (for "autonomous" and "moral" are mutually exclusive)' (GM II §2) and it is the production of the sovereign individual which redeems the severity, stupidity, tyranny and cruelty of prehistory. But how does the morality of custom teach us the law of obeying laws, teach us our responsibility for our actions, so that this law becomes 'the dominating instinct' which we term 'conscience'? Nietzsche's suggestion is that this is accomplished through punishment:

> 'If something is to stay in the memory it must be burned in: only that which never ceases to *hurt* stays in the memory' – this is a main clause of the oldest (unhappily also the most enduring) psychology on earth. (GM II §3)

Through this *mnemotechnics* – images and procedures such as stoning, breaking on the wheel, boiling in oil, flaying, quartering, etc. – 'one finally remembers five or six "I will not's," in regard to which one has given one's *promise* so as to participate in the advantages of society' (GM II §3). Thus, Nietzsche's claim is that it is customs which make man regular and calculable, while it is punishment for breach of customs which produces the memory of the will.

In order to contextualise this claim, Nietzsche notes that the emergence of punishment is tied not to a moral psychology of guilt predicated on the idea that the criminal could have acted otherwise (on the contrary, Nietzsche suggests that in pre-history punishment retards the development of the feeling of guilt),[4] but to a contractual psychology of equivalence in which the relationship between creditor and debtor is expressed through the idea that 'every injury has *its equivalent* and can actually be paid back, even if only through the *pain* of the culprit' (GM II §4). Punishment emerges in this form because it is contractual relations which articulate the activity of promising in which the debtor stands security for the future by agreeing that failure to repay will result in the substitution of something equivalent such as his body, his wife, his freedom, his life or even his salvation. On Nietzsche's account, this logic of equivalence is an unspiritualised expression of will to power in which recompense for injury is provided by a kind of pleasure:

> In 'punishing' the debtor, the creditor participates in a *right of the masters*: at last he, too, may experience for once the exalted sensation of being allowed to despise and mistreat someone as 'beneath him'. . . . The compensation, then, consists in a warrant for and title to cruelty. (GM II §5)

For Nietzsche, the particular significance of this contractual psychology of power is that it also characterises the relationship of the individual to the community. But how does this model of community as creditor and individual as debtor come about?

The argument Nietzsche presents is that this conception of community/ individual relations emerges through the tribal recognition of a debt on the part of the present generation to those preceding it:

> The conviction reigns that it is only through the sacrifices and accomplishments of the ancestors that the tribe *exists* – and that one has to *pay them back* with sacrifices and accomplishments: one recognizes a *debt* that constantly grows greater, since these forebears never cease, in their continued existence as powerful spirits, to accord the tribe new advantages and strength. (GM II §19)

Thus, Nietzsche argues that the conception of the community as creditor is predicated on the community as an expression of the power of the ancestor. Concomitantly, as the power of the community increases so too does the sense of the power of, and indebtedness to, the ancestor. Given this creditor/debtor model, Nietzsche suggests that the criminal is imagined as breaking his contract, that is, not merely failing to appreciate the credit extended to him (the advantages of society) but of attacking his creditor (the ancestor/society). Consequently, Nietzsche argues that, in its early stages, a community reacts to the lawbreaker by hurling him 'into the savage and outlaw state against which he has hitherto been protected' (GM II §9). By thrusting him into a state in which every form of hostility may be vented on him, the lawbreaker (and the rest of the community) are reminded what the benefits of community are really worth, while the feeling of power which attends being able to vent its anger on the outlaw acts as a recompense for the loss and attack suffered. However, Nietzsche goes on to argue that the severity of this reaction to the lawbreaker is inversely related to the strength of the community's consciousness of power; thus, as its feeling of power increases, so the harshness of its reaction decreases:

> As its power increases, a community ceases to take the individual's transgressions so seriously because they can no longer be considered as dangerous and destructive to the whole as they were formerly. (GM II §10)

In particular, Nietzsche suggests, there emerges 'the increasingly definite will to treat every crime as in some sense *dischargeable*, and thus at least to a certain extent to *isolate* the criminal and his deed from one another' (GM II §10).

Now although it might initially appear that there is a tension in Nietzsche's argument between the idea that the increasing consciousness of power of the community is simultaneously a sign of the increasing indebtedness of the individual to the community *and* the increasing capacity of the community to regard the crime as dischargeable, the important point to note is that an increase in the power of the community is equivalent to an increase in the power of the ancestor (who is transfigured in the end into a god) and thus in the capacity of the ancestor as creditor to treat the crime as dischargeable:

> The 'creditor' always becomes more humane to the extent that he has grown richer; finally, how much injury he can endure without suffering from it becomes the actual *measure* of his wealth. (GM II §10)

Indeed, extrapolating this relationship between the strength of the community (or god) and the severity of the penal code, Nietzsche postulates the existence of a community whose consciousness of power would be so great that it could let those who harmed it go unpunished; this possibility demarcating the self-overcoming of justice (the logic of equivalence) as *mercy*. Moreover, against those who read Nietzsche's idea of will to power as an expression of a politics of domination, it should be noted that, for Nietzsche, mercy is a form of will to power, but whereas the need for the compensation of cruelty as a form of will to power denotes the weakness of the individual or community concerned, the exercise of mercy is an expression of strength, that is to say, nobility.

Reflecting back over Nietzsche's argument thus far we can summarise by highlighting three points which are of significance. Firstly, the development of conscience as the law of obeying laws is tied to the morality of mores which renders man regular and to the punishment of transgressions which develops a memory of the will. Secondly, this memory of the will develops in the sphere of contractual relations between individuals and, more significantly, between the individual and the community (where this is an expression of indebtedness to preceding generations, particularly the founding generation). Thirdly, as the strength of the community (power of the ancestor) increases, so too does its capacity to regard crimes as dischargeable and to separate the criminal actor from the criminal act. In the context of our concern with liberal political theory, we can suggest that Nietzsche's concern in this opening section of his discussion is to show how the human capacity for autonomous reflection and agency is not given *a priori* but, rather, is the product of humanity's pre-historical labour on itself.

It's appropriate that our examination of the development of conscience concludes with the issue of the separability of criminal actor from the crime because it is in how this separation is treated that Nietzsche identifies the distinction between good conscience and bad conscience. For example, in his discussions of ancient Judaism Nietzsche regards good conscience as expressed through the idea of a god of justice and bad conscience as presented in the idea of a god of judgement. Thus he comments:

> Originally, above all in the period of the kingdom, Israel too stood in a *correct*, that is to say, natural relationship to all things. Their Yaweh was the expression of their consciousness of power, of their delight in themselves, their hopes of themselves: in him they anticipated victory and salvation, in him they trusted that nature would provide what the people needed – above all rain. Yaweh is the God of Israel and *consequently* the God of justice: the logic of every nation that is in power and has a good conscience about it. (AC §25)

The good conscience of the community and of the individuals within it finds its manifestation in a reverence for justice (as equivalence) and, even more, mercy. Yet this conception of Yaweh as a God of justice is *necessarily* displaced by a conception of him as a God of judgement (I will address the necessity of this displacement in the next section). Nietzsche represents the bad conscience of this latter conception thus:

> The new conception of him becomes an instrument in the hands of priestly agitators who henceforth interpret all good fortune as reward, all misfortune as punishment for disobedience of God, for 'sin'. (AC §25)

The significance of this example is, firstly, that it illustrates that Nietzsche regards good conscience as the initial state of human affairs which is displaced by bad conscience and, secondly, that it points to the articulation of good conscience and bad conscience through the two distinct models of the self sketched earlier: a tragic conception of the self as inseparable from its actions which is tied to concepts of character, fate and shame, and a moral conception of the self as distinct from its actions which is tied to concepts of soul, freedom and guilt.[5] We can clearly see this moral conception of bad conscience at work in the idea of 'guilt', which requires that one could have acted otherwise than one did; it is because one has free will that one is rewarded for choosing obedience and punished for choosing disobedience. While this Judaic example does not highlight the tragic conception particularly well, this can be rectified if we refer to the Greeks, of whom Nietzsche comments:

> For the longest time these Greeks used their gods precisely so as to ward off the 'bad conscience', so as to be able to rejoice in their freedom of soul. (GM II §23)

The dilemma confronted by the tragic model of the self is this: how, if the self is inseparable from its actions, can this model accommodate the isolation of the criminal from his crime? Nietzsche's suggestion is that when they were confronted by a Greek noble who committed ignoble, criminal actions, the Greeks separated the actor from the act by attributing his actions to possession or delusion by a god. This ad hoc device allows the Greeks to maintain the conceptual scheme (perspective) which sustains their good conscience:

> In this way the gods served in those days to justify man to a certain extent even in his wickedness, they served as the originators of evil – in those days they took upon themselves, not the punishment but, what is *nobler*, the guilt. (GM II §23)

The question raised by these considerations concerns how we came to think of ourselves in terms of free will. If, as Nietzsche suggests, the conception of self which emerges in the context of the morality of mores simply identifies the actor with his actions, how does this other model of the self arise? To pursue this topic, however, requires that we examine the origins of that other form of conscience, the bad conscience, which requires the idea of the free subject. However, before we move to this topic, we should note that Nietzsche's story about the development of conscience is also a story about the emergence of consciousness. Let us focus briefly on this issue.

This point can be simply put: insofar as one becomes a historical animal, an animal with the right to make promises, one must also develop certain minimal reflective capacities. Thus Nietzsche comments that to develop the capacity to promise requires

> man must first have learned to distinguish necessary events from chance ones, to think causally, to see and anticipate distant eventualities as if they belonged to the present, to decide with certainty what is the goal and what the means to it, and in general be able to calculate and compute. (GM II §1)

On Nietzsche's account, it is precisely through custom and punishment that we acquire these capacities.[6] However, it is the fundamental feature of consciousness that it introduces *meaning* into the world. Because one can now see life in a mirror, as it were, one no longer simply experiences living but asks what the meaning of life is. Indeed to experience oneself as a self (which is, after all, an integral aspect of experiencing one's self as powerful) requires that one make sense of one's experience of being in the world; consciousness compels us to assign meaning to the world. It is in this context that Nietzsche remarks:

> What really arouses indignation against suffering is not suffering as such but the senselessness of suffering: but neither for the Christian, who has interpreted a whole mysterious machinery of salvation into suffering, nor for the naive man of more ancient times, who understood all suffering in relation to the spectator of it or causer of it, was there any such thing as *senseless* suffering. (GM II §7)

The significance of this passage is that it suggests that another way of understanding good and bad conscience is to think of them as ways of accounting for suffering. The naive Greek makes sense of suffering in terms of fate – it is a destiny decreed by the gods for their enjoyment (where these gods are also 'pieces of fate'; they cannot act other than they are); while the more reflective man of bad conscience postulates a guilty agent as the cause of suffering, an agent who could have acted otherwise. We can sharpen our consideration of this topic by deploying Arthur Danto's distinction between extensional and intensional suffering:

> As I see Nietzsche's thesis, it is this: the main suffering human beings have throughout history been subject to is due to certain interpretive responses to the fact of extensional suffering. . . . For while extensional suffering is bad enough, often it is many times compounded by our interpretations of it, which are often far worse than the disorder itself. (1988: 21)

On this basis, Nietzsche's distinction between good and bad conscience is a distinction between a perspective which minimises intensional suffering through the idea of fate and one which maximises such suffering through the idea of free will. For example, if one breaks a leg, a recognition of this event as simply fate does not add intensional suffering to extensional suffering in any significant degree, while a recognition of this event as punishment for sin multiplies the suffering involved such that the extensional suffering (physical pain and inconvenience) is insignificant compared to the intensional suffering ('Lord, how have I failed you? I am a guilty, worthless sinner. Oh Lord, why do you even bother with me?') involved. Notably bad conscience involves far more self-reflection than good conscience, a point which supports my description of the man of bad conscience as more reflective. To grasp why I describe the man of bad conscience in this way, let us now turn to the origins of this other conscience, this bad conscience which invokes the idea of free will.

Like his account of the emergence of conscience, Nietzsche's account of the origins of bad conscience is speculative; his hypothesis is that bad conscience emerges when man is entrapped within the walls of society and of peace:

> The man who, from lack of external enemies and resistances and forcibly confined to the oppressive narrowness and punctiliousness of custom, impatiently lacerated, persecuted, gnawed at, assaulted, and maltreated himself; this animal that rubbed itself raw against the bars of its cage as one tried to 'tame' it; this deprived creature, racked with homesickness for the wild, who had to turn himself into an adventure, a torture chamber, an uncertain and dangerous wilderness – this fool, this yearning and desperate prisoner became the inventor of the 'bad conscience'. (GM II §16)

Reduced to the use of consciousness (his least developed organ) by this imprisonment within the institutions of society (punishment among them) which denies him the outward expression of his instincts, these same instincts turn inwards against man and it is this process of internalisation that leads to the development of the inner realm of the self and, concomitantly, to the idea of the self as subject. But who is the 'inventor' of bad conscience? This appears to be a straightforward question in that Nietzsche comments 'one can see who has the invention of "bad conscience" on his conscience –

the man of *ressentiment*!' (GM II §11). Yet this remark is perplexing because Nietzsche also suggests that the emergence of bad conscience is not simply a product of the most fundamental change man has undergone but also that this change was 'a break, a leap, a compulsion, an ineluctable disaster which precluded all struggle and even all *ressentiment*' (GM II §17). How, if at all, can we reconcile these positions?

Let's begin by considering this fundamental change. What Nietzsche is describing with the idea of the sudden enclosure of man within society and peace is the process of state formation, 'the welding of a hitherto unchecked and shapeless populace into a firm form' which takes place through the violent acts of a warrior tribe:

> . . . a conqueror and master race which, organized for war and with the ability to organize, unhesitatingly lays its claws upon a populace perhaps superior in numbers but still formless and nomad. (GM II §17, cf. BGE §257)

Developing this point, Nietzsche identifies the masters as producing the conditions of possibility of bad conscience but *not* themselves being its conditions of emergence:

> It is not in *them* [the conquerors] that the 'bad conscience' developed, that goes without saying – but it would not have developed *without them*, this ugly growth, it would be lacking if a tremendous quantity of freedom had not been expelled from the world . . . and made as it were *latent* under their hammer blows and artists' violence. This *instinct for freedom* forcibly made latent . . . that, and that alone, is what the *bad conscience* is in its beginnings. (GM II §17)

Reflecting on the violence wreaked upon a nomadic populace by these unconscious and involuntary artists of the state, then, it is necessary to note the obvious point that the state formed through this violence is characterised by (at least) two classes: nobles (the master race) and slaves (the subjugated populace). It is the victims of violence whom Nietzsche terms the men of *ressentiment*; for while the rapidity of the process of their subjugation may preclude *ressentiment*, the everyday experience of subjugation, the powerlessness of being a slave, which attends the completion of this process marks a fertile ground for the emergence of this vengeful sentiment.[7]

However, we should be clear that Nietzsche's claim is not that bad conscience is the product of *ressentiment*; on the contrary, it is simply that it is amongst those who are 'men of *ressentiment*' that it emerges because it is the powerless and subjugated who are the first to be enclosed in the walls of society and of peace. It is important to emphasise this point because Nietzsche's argument is the reverse of the claim that *ressentiment* produces bad conscience; his claim is that bad conscience is the condition of possibility of *ressentiment*. This becomes clear if we reflect on the idea of *ressentiment*, which is basically an expression of the claim that one is *wrongfully* subject to suffering, that one's suffering is undeserved (consider the Book of Job).[8] In other words, *ressentiment* is the site where the phrases 'why me?' and 'it's unfair' meet. Yet the reflective element of this sentiment makes no sense within a conceptual scheme structured around the idea of fate (good conscience). If it's simply my fate that I am what I am, the question of the justice or injustice of this state of being is not raised, indeed it is not a *possible* question within this paradigm. *Ressentiment* requires the idea that the fact that I am a slave is the product of some (guilty) agency which could have acted otherwise; one is resentful precisely because they did not do so.

However, for our immediate concerns, the significant point raised by Nietzsche's distinction between the conditions of possibility of bad conscience (state formation) and its conditions of emergence (the slave class of the formed state) is that it allows us to see that the apparent contradiction we noted within Nietzsche's remarks can be resolved if, and only if, he can provide an explanation of why it is that bad conscience emerges, at least initially, amongst the slave class and not the nobles.

Nietzsche's explanation of this point becomes immediately apparent if we recall his earlier formulation of the conditions of emergence of bad conscience as being 'finally enclosed within the walls of society and peace' (GM II §16). It is, after all, all too apparent that the slave class are so enclosed while, at least initially, the nobility are not. We can support this explanation with two references. Firstly, recall the comment cited in our discussion of creditor/debtor relations in which the right of the creditor to take payment in pain is characterised as participating in 'a *right of the masters*' (GM II §5). This remark suggests that the masters can exercise their instinct for freedom (will to power) within society insofar as they possess the power to inflict cruelty on the populace and, in particular, the slaves. Secondly, consider the following characterisation of the activity of the noble class outside society which Nietzsche offers in the first essay of *On the Genealogy of Morals*:

> Here is one thing we shall be the last to deny: he who knows these 'good men' only as enemies knows only *evil enemies*, and the same men who are held so sternly in check *inter pares* . . . – once they go outside, where the strange, the *stranger* is found, they are not much better than uncaged beasts of prey. There they savour a freedom from all social constraints, they compensate themselves in the wilderness for the tension engendered by protracted confinement within the peace of society. (GM I §11)

Both of these references confirm that the noble is free from bad conscience precisely insofar as he is not confined by society or by peace. However, as soon as the walls of society and peace come to enclose the noble, he too is subject to bad conscience.

But precisely how does the core of bad conscience, the idea of the self as free subject, develop from this enclosure and the attendant internalisation of the instincts? Thus far we have simply suggested that bad conscience is marked by the emergence of the idea of the self as subject which is produced by internalisation of the instincts – which Nietzsche groups collectively as the instinct for freedom and which he characterises as 'will to power' (GM II §18) – without analysing Nietzsche's argument as to how this idea emerges from man's sudden dependence on consciousness alone.

We can begin by returning to the relationship between the development of conscience and the emergence of consciousness with respect to the idea of will to power. It is notable that in this essay Nietzsche affirms his hypothesis that life is will to power (GM II §12) and, thus, that pre-historical humanity is characterised by the instinctual desire to strive 'for an optimum of favourable conditions under which it can expend all its strength and achieve its maximal feeling of power' (GM III §7, cf. BGE §13). However, insofar as one develops consciousness at the expense of instinct, so the feeling of power is increasingly mediated through meaning; the development of consciousness entails that the feeling of powerfulness requires that one experience one's self as meaningful. The significance of Nietzsche's account of bad conscience in this context as the juncture at which man is reduced to the use of consciousness *alone* is that it marks the transition from the rule of the instincts to the rule of consciousness.[9] The instinct for freedom/power turned fully back on itself becomes the conscious desire for the feeling of freedom/power, where this is entirely mediated through meaning.

However, while this point is significant, the crucial element of Nietzsche's argument is the incorporation of this recognition that bad conscience is tied to the development of our basic capacities for conscious reflection into his phenomenal account of willing (which he outlines in *Beyond Good and Evil*). In this account of willing as a conscious, reflective activity, Nietzsche distinguishes between three elements: a pathos of embodiment (our bodily experience of, and affective relation to, the world), a commanding thought (a goal) and the affect of command (a feeling of power).[10] Following this identification of the elements of willing, Nietzsche develops his argument to account for the idea of 'free will' as 'the phenomenal experience of efficacity that attends a certain threshold of affective investment' (Conway, 1992a: 25). He begins by claiming that the idea of 'freedom of will' is 'essentially the emotion of superiority over him who must obey: "I am free, 'he' must obey" – this consciousness adheres to every will' (BGE §19). This claim is developed in the following way:

> A man who *wills* – commands something in himself which obeys or which he believes obeys. But now observe the strangest thing of all about the will – about this so complex thing for which people have only *one* word: inasmuch as in the given circumstances we at the same time command *and* obey, and as the side which obeys know the sensations of constraint, compulsion, pressure, resistance, motion which usually begin immediately after the act of will; inasmuch as, on the other hand, we are in the habit of disregarding and deceiving ourselves over this duality by means of the synthetic concept 'I'; so a whole chain of erroneous conclusions and consequently of false evaluations of the will itself has become attached to the will as such – so that he who wills believes wholeheartedly that willing *suffices* for action. (BGE §19)

Thus, Nietzsche's argument is that the successful performance of any action which is consciously willed leads to the assumption of 'free will'. The combination of a pathos of embodiment with a conscious goal and an affect of command produces the idea that I am a free subject. He concludes:

> 'Freedom of the will' – is the expression for that complex condition of pleasure of the person who wills, who commands and at the same time identifies himself with

the executor of the command – who as such also enjoys the triumph over resistances involved but who thinks it was his will itself which overcame these resistances. (BGE §19)

It follows that Nietzsche's claim is that the idea of self as free subject is a consequence of the dependence of human beings on conscious reflection and willing alone. On this account, from the feeling that willing suffices for action, we are led inexorably to the idea of the self as free subject.[11] This idea is not, *contra* philosophical liberalism, an *a priori* truth but the product of humanity's enclosure within the walls of society and peace.

The clear implication of this argument is that bad conscience is simply the price we pay for the development of our basic capacities for conscious reflection which attends our reliance on consciousness alone. Thus, while the Jewish and Greek nobility of antiquity were able to act with good conscience because they retained an external outlet for their anti-social instincts, a consequence of this opportunity for instinctual expression is a relatively undeveloped capacity for reflective thought; whereas the bad conscience of the slave classes which is the consequence of the lack of any such outlet for instincts entails a greater capacity for conscious reflection. That Nietzsche recognises and acknowledges this implication is made clear in the first essay of *On the Genealogy of Morals* when he remarks:

> A race of such men of *ressentiment* is bound to become eventually *cleverer* than any noble race; it will honor cleverness to a far greater degree: namely, as a condition of existence of the first importance; while with noble men cleverness can easily acquire a subtle flavor of luxury and subtlety – for here it is far less essential than the perfect functioning of the regulating *unconscious* instincts. (GM I §10).

However, before we turn to the first essay, we should draw together the main points of our discussion of the development of conscience and, in particular, bad conscience.

According to the interpretation offered here, the first element of Nietzsche's reflections on conscience concerns an account of how man becomes a historical animal, an animal with the right to make promises, which focuses on the role of the morality of mores and the institution of punishment in producing man as a calculable, regular being capable of ordaining the future in advance (promising) and thus being held accountable for his actions. Indeed, there is a sense in which Nietzsche's argument suggests that historical time is constituted by the activity of promising as the paradigmatic exemplar of autonomous agency. Thus, *contra* philosophical liberalism's construction of the antinomy of reason and history,[12] Nietzsche locates the emergence of our capacity for autonomous rational reflection and agency as the emergence of human history; it is through autonomous agency that we constitute human time as historical time.[13]

The second element of Nietzsche's argument shifts to the bifurcation of conscience wherein Nietzsche differentiates good conscience (as articulated through a tragic conception of human accountability) from bad conscience (which is expressed through a moral conception of accountability). It is pointed out that these different notions of accountability involve different conceptions of the self. The remainder of Nietzsche's argument attempts to show how the idea of bad conscience articulated through the idea of free will is intrinsically interwoven with the development of our basic capacities for conscious reflection which attends man's enclosure within the walls of society and of peace. At this stage, the focus shifts to the forms of morality for which good and bad conscience act as the conditions of possibility.

'"Good and Bad", "Good and Evil"'

My claim with respect to this essay is that Nietzsche attempts to provide a historical account of the appearance/reality distinction and to reflect on both the practical interests embodied in this distinction and the liberal conception of autonomy which it articulates. To perform this task, Nietzsche examines two modalities of moral judgement by providing an ideal-typical account of their conditions of emergence and of their major characteristics. In particular Nietzsche seeks to delineate the features of the event which he terms 'the slave revolt in morals' since it is the demise of the form of moral reasoning engendered by this revolt which Nietzsche takes to be constitutive of the nihilist condition of our modernity. The significance of reflecting on this historical event is not simply that if we are to overcome the constraints of our modern condition (nihilism) it is necessary to understand how these constraints were constituted, but also that this recuperative activity discloses another form of moral reflection (a form which the slave revolt in morality attempts to displace and which has long been subject to the hegemony of slave morality) which Nietzsche seeks to recover in order to point beyond our human, all-too-human predicaments.[14]

What, then, are the conditions of emergence of these two forms of moral reflection which Nietzsche terms 'noble' and 'slave' morality? The claim made is that these modes of moral judgement emerge from the typical experiences of agency characteristic of the noble and slave classes in ancient society. On the one hand, there is the noble's experience of himself as able to command slaves. On the other hand, there is the slave's experience of himself as subject to the commands of the nobles. It is unsurprising, on Nietzsche's account, that these two kinds of sensuous experience of being in the world – the feeling of power which attends the noble and the feeling of powerlessness which characterises the slave – lead to radically different judgements as to the nature of the self, the world and their relationship. To explicate the relation between the distinct experiences of agency character-istic of these classes and the divergent forms of moral reasoning to which they give rise, Nietzsche focuses on their conditions of emergence.

Let us begin with noble morality, whose emergence Nietzsche character-ises as follows:

> The pathos of nobility and distance . . . the protracted and domineering fundamental total feeling on the part of a higher ruling order in relation to a lower order, to a 'below' – *that* is the origin of the antithesis 'good' and 'bad'. (GM I §2)

In other words, this good/bad form of moral reasoning emerges from the pathos of social distance in which the feeling of political superiority which stems from the power of command over slaves is translated into the feeling of superiority of soul (the pathos of inner distance) which Nietzsche ascribes to the noble (GM I §6). This perspective sustains the noble's experience of himself as an autonomous agent (an agent capable of commanding goals and obeying these commands) by identifying him as the source of the meaning and value of the world, an identification which is expressed by defining as 'good' the typical character traits of the nobility. Nietzsche notes, for example (GM I §5), that the Greek nobles referred to themselves as 'the truthful', where the root of the term deployed for this, *esthlos*, signifies good and brave, while the Latin term *bonus* (good) is traced back to *duonus* (war). In this context Frithjof Bergmann comments:

> [Noble] morality could not have been more direct and straightforward: Human beings were evaluated very naturally like all other things. There were desirable attributes: health, strength, physical or sexual attractiveness, but also talents and gifts of every sort: wit, imagination, as well as cunning, the capacity to sustain passion, and beyond this toughness and endurance, and much more. In the beginning the word 'good' simply stood for these traits; it was no more than a generic summary, or a spontaneous exclamation. For those who possessed these qualities the word 'good' signified the joy and pride and happiness of their possession; it reflected back to them the qualities in which they took delight. (1988: 29–30)

The concept 'bad' which develops alongside this conception of 'good' simply expresses the *lack* of these attributes. Nietzsche stresses this point, commenting that the concept of 'bad' as it operates in noble morality 'is only a subsequently-invented pale, contrasting image in relation to its positive basic concept' (GM I §10). Thus the good conscience of the nobility acts as a condition of possibility for, and finds expression in, a form of moral reflection which identifies what is valuable with the nobles and what lacks value with the slaves. In this context, Nietzsche comments:

> The essential thing in a good and healthy aristocracy is, however, that it does *not* feel itself to be a function (of the monarchy or of the commonwealth) but as their *meaning* and supreme justification – that it therefore accepts with a good conscience the sacrifice of innumerable men who *for its sake* have to be suppressed and reduced to imperfect men, to slaves and instruments. (BGE §258)

In other words, because the morality of nobles is predicated on the inseparability of actor and acts (good conscience), it identifies noble action with the noble class. This form of self-affirmation locates the existence of nobility as the *raison d'être* of society.

By contrast, the slave revolt in morals – the emergence of slave morality (which Nietzsche takes to be *anti-natural*)[15] – is a product of the slave's experience of himself as 'below', as subject to command, as powerless; a pathos of embodiment which expresses itself in the feeling of *ressentiment*. Within the perspective of nobility, the slave experiences himself as without value. But why does this experience of valuelessness and powerlessness express itself as *ressentiment*? This sentiment emerges because the slave accounts for his suffering, his experience of himself as lacking value, in terms of the idea of free will (bad conscience); the slave seeks a guilty agent for his experience of powerlessness and identifies this figure as the noble. In this context, it is clear that if the slave is to experience himself as an autonomous agent, an alternative paradigm to the noble perspective must be constructed; a paradigm which gives expression to the slave's *ressentiment*.

Nietzsche comments that

> [t]he slave revolt in morality begins when *ressentiment* itself becomes creative and gives birth to values: the *ressentiment* of natures that are denied the true reaction, that of deeds, and compensate themselves with an imaginary revenge. . . . slave morality from the outset says No to what is 'outside,' what is 'different,' what is 'not itself'; and *this* No is its creative act. (GM I §10)

In reflecting on this revolt, we should note that this creative No does not emerge *ex nihilo*. On the contrary, its possibility is already articulated in the idea of free will; thus, in *Twilight of the Idols*, Nietzsche argues that the distinction between being and becoming is a product of the distinction between will and willing which attends the idea that the will is something which produces effects (TI '"Reason" in Philosophy' §5). The creative aspect of the slave's No is that it projects the distinction between being and becoming into a distinction between the real world and the apparent world which is also a hierarchy in that the real (metaphysical) world is granted value through a negation of the value of the apparent (actual) world. Unable to exact revenge on the nobles in this world, the slave constructs an imaginary revenge by saying No to this world and positing another world, the 'real world', in which the hierarchy of values is entirely inverted:

> To be able to reject all that represents the *ascending* movement of life, well-constitutedness, power, beauty, self-affirmation on earth, the instinct for *ressentiment* here become genius had to invent *another* world from which that *life-affirmation* would appear evil, reprehensible as such. (AC §24)

Consequently, against the noble's stress on *heroic* values such as courage and wit (consider the *Iliad* and the *Odyssey*), the slave's inversion stresses obedience and humility. Thus, whereas the pathos of 'inner distance' which grounds the noble's self-affirmation is predicated on the pathos of *social* distance, the self-affirmation of the slave is grounded in a pathos of 'inner distance' predicated on the pathos of *metaphysical* distance (wherein, at this juncture, metaphysical distance involves simply the inversion of social order of rank). Thus, Nietzsche argues, *contra* philosophical liberalism, that the appearance/reality distinction is not an inescapable feature of the human condition but a specific historical construct which expresses a devaluation of this-worldly existence.

In the context of this metaphysical inversion of the social order of rank, it is unsurprising that a foundational belief of slave morality is the existence of the *soul* as the site on which the subject/object and appearance/reality distinctions are synthesised and the empirical self is devalued because it is this belief which articulates both the guilt of the noble and the autonomy of the slave:

> This type of man [the slave] *needs* to believe in a neutral independent 'subject,' prompted by an instinct for self-preservation in which every lie is sanctified. The subject (or, to use a more popular expression, the *soul*) has perhaps been believed in hitherto more firmly than anything else on earth because it makes possible to the majority of mortals, the weak and oppressed of every kind, the sublime self-deception that interprets weakness as freedom, and their being thus-and-thus as a *merit*. (GM I §13)

Reflecting on this belief, we should note that because slave morality constitutes obedience as its primary virtue, it requires a figure to whom obedience is owed and whose commands *must* be observed. In relation to ancient Israel, Nietzsche suggests that this figure is Yaweh as the God of judgement (as opposed to his earlier incarnation as the God of justice). In relation to the Greeks, Nietzsche claims that this figure is the Platonic ideal of Good which displaces the Olympic pantheon of gods; these two figures finding their synthesis in the figure of the Christian God.[16] But if one is subject to the commands of God, in what sense is one autonomous? A straightforward response to this question which is manifest in Kantian versions of liberalism is that one is autonomous *qua* transcendental self because these commands are identical to one's rational will and one is autonomous *qua* empirical self insofar as one obeys one's rational will.

At the same time, it is also important to note the fundamentally *reactive* character of this morality (and thus, by implication, this conception of autonomy): the slave needs the belief in the noble as evil in order to generate the belief in himself as good; he needs to devalue the other in order to secure the value of his own identity. In other words, whereas the noble's self-affirmation is predicated on a recognition and affirmation of his own qualities which constructs the identity of the slave as the unfortunate who lacks these qualities, the slave's self-affirmation is predicated on a recognition and affirmation of his own qualities which is constructed through a devaluation of the noble.

Taken together these points suggest that the conception of freedom articulated within this mode of moral reasoning is unlikely to be capable of valuing difference or affirming alterity. In positing a God's-eye view which rules out of moral reflection any recognition of the embedded and embodied character of human subjectivity in the name of a disinterested universalism, slave morality expresses itself as a logic of identity; a logic in which any recognition of the others of liberal reason (such as embodiment and embeddedness) is constructed as a threat to the security of reason *tout court* and in which the abstract anonymity of the transcendental self is presented as the condition of possibility of moral reflection.[17]

Of course, it might be objected that liberal reason is characterised precisely by its commitment to tolerance and this commitment is sustained by a conception of the self which is purely formal. But, on Nietzsche's account, this is to fail to recognise that liberal reason in its philosophical guise is tolerant only to the extent that its own presuppositions are accepted; the possibility of a God's-eye view is a non-negotiable truth (even if it is accepted that the correct formulation of, or means of attaining, this ideal has not yet been achieved). The tolerance of liberal reason does not extend to the contestation of its own conception and criteria of tolerance.

Again it might be objected that this intolerance with respect to criteria of tolerance is a feature of any account of, and argument for, tolerance which is meaningful (i.e., specifies some limit to what can be tolerated). However, the problem with liberalism is that precisely because it argues that a rational commitment to tolerance is *only* possible on the basis of the kind of argument it provides, it rules out of court (as *necessarily* irrational) any contestation of its criteria of tolerance. In terms of our discussion of concept/conception relations (in Chapter 1), liberalism seeks to specify the transcendent 'core' or 'consensus' of competing conceptions of tolerance and, thus, rules out *a priori* any conception of tolerance which does not overlap with this 'core consensus'.

Thus the basic character of Nietzsche's critique of the moral character of liberal reason becomes clear if we reiterate the point that slave morality is characterised by the conjunction of the subject/object and appearance/reality distinctions, whose synthesis entails the idea of the *univocity* of reason: just as the epistemological claims of liberal reason posit the univocity of truth, so too the moral claims of liberal reason posit the univocity of right. In the light of the preceding chapter in which the epistemological commitments of liberal reason were subject to critical censure, it is unsurprising that the moral commitments of this style of reasoning should similarly invoke Nietzsche's ire. In place of the *agonistic* struggle through which Nietzsche claims our epistemic and ethical judgements must prove their worth against other judgements, liberal reason posits *transcendental* judgements which rule other judgements out of court. However, Nietzsche's critique of slave morality is not limited to a critique of its presuppositions. On the contrary, the act of offering a historical (this-worldly) account of the emergence of values for which a *transcendent* (other-wordly) status is claimed performs a critique of this status which renders it open to question; to 'ground' his philosophical critique Nietzsche will seek to show how our contemporary condition of nihilism is a product of this form of reasoning. This conception of liberal reasoning as engendering nihilism requires, however, that Nietzsche can account for both the triumph of slave morality over noble morality (how does slave morality become hegemonic?) and the developments in this form of moral reasoning which construct the conditions of its own demise (how does slave morality overcome itself?). I will address the question of hegemony now, postponing the question of liberal reason's self-overcoming to our consideration of the essay on the meaning of ascetic ideals.

How does slave morality become hegemonic? An alternative way of putting this question which renders the answer obvious is to ask 'how do the nobles become subject to bad conscience?' After all, if noble morality is predicated on good conscience and slave morality is predicated on bad conscience, then it is the final enclosure of the *noble* within the walls of society and peace which ensures the triumph of noble morality. One can well imagine that the pressures entailing this enclosure must be overwhelming if the noble is to accept a perspective in which the nobility is characterised as guilty, the agency of evil. Indeed, we are constrained to ask under what conditions can this acceptance of the lowest position in the metaphysical order of rank be reconciled with the thesis of will to power? Only if it is a final expedient. To recognise oneself as willing evil is preferable to not willing at all, and this was the choice which confronted the nobility of ancient Israel and Greece! Thus Nietzsche comments that the attempt of the Jewish nobility to maintain the ideal of Yaweh as a God of justice could not be sustained since 'every hope remained unfulfilled' (AC §25). He remarks further:

> The Jews are the most remarkable nation in history because, faced with the question of being or not being, they preferred, with a perfectly uncanny conviction, being *at any price*: the price they had to pay was the radical *falsification* of all nature, all naturalness, all reality, the entire inner world as well as the outer. (AC §24)

While he states explicitly that the Greek disavowal of the gods in favour of rationality was 'their *last* expedient . . . one had only *one* choice: either to perish or – be *absurdly rational*' (TI 'The Problem of Socrates' §10). Thus the nobility accept enclosure within the walls of society and of peace because the alternative is non-existence.

It should be noted, however, that Nietzsche does not conclude that noble morality ceases to be a possibility once man is enclosed; on the contrary, he argues:

> The two *opposing* values 'good and bad,' 'good and evil' have been engaged in a fearful struggle on earth for thousands of years; and although the latter value has certainly been on top for a long time, there are still places where the struggle is as yet undecided. One might even say that it has risen ever higher and thus become more and more profound and spiritual: so that today there is perhaps no more decisive mark of a '*higher nature*,' a more spiritual nature, than that of being divided in this sense and a genuine battleground of these opposed values. (GM I §16)

In this passage, Nietzsche highlights both the possibility of more spiritual (i.e., reflective) forms of noble morality emerging under certain unspecified conditions and the identity of modernity as a site on which this confrontation is once more open to engagement. He emphasises the former point in citing the Renaissance as 'an uncanny and glittering reawakening of the classical ideal' (Nietzsche admires deeply Machiavelli's conception of *virtu*) before bemoaning its subsumption under 'that thoroughly plebian (German and English) *ressentiment* movement called the Reformation' (GM I §16). This point is reiterated with respect to the French Revolution:

> With the French Revolution, Judea once again triumphed over the classical ideal, and this time in a profound and decisive sense: the last political noblesse in

Europe, that of the *French* seventeenth and eighteenth century, collapsed beneath the popular instincts of *ressentiment*. . . . To be sure, in the midst of it there occurred the most tremendous, most unexpected thing: the ideal of antiquity stepped *incarnate* and in unheard-of splendour before the eyes and conscience of mankind – . . . Like a signpost to the *other* path, Napoleon appeared, the most isolated and late-born man there has ever been, and in him the problem of the *noble ideal as such* made flesh – one might well ponder *what* kind of problem it is: Napoleon, this synthesis of the *inhuman* and the *overhuman*. (GM I §16, translation adjusted).

I will conclude this section by reflecting on what is involved in this 'problem' because I suspect that such a discussion will help clarify the point that Nietzsche's commitment to a noble form of moral reasoning does not signify an anachronistic desire to return to the society of the ancient Greeks.[18]

In the second essay of *On the Genealogy of Morals*, Nietzsche comments that the significance of bad conscience lies in its rendering man '*pregnant with a future* . . . as if man were not a goal but only a way, an episode, a bridge, a great promise' (GM II §16). This image of man as a bridge is used frequently by Nietzsche; for example, in 'Zarathustra's Prologue' Nietzsche has his fictional *alter ego* pronounce thus:

Man is a rope, fastened between animal and Overman – a rope over an abyss.
A dangerous going-across, a dangerous wayfaring, a dangerous looking-back, a dangerous shuddering and staying-still.
What is great in man is that he is a bridge and not a goal; what can be loved in man is that he is a *going-across* and a *down-going*. (Z 'Zarathustra's Prologue' §4, translation adjusted)

Yet Nietzsche's characterisation of Napoleon as 'the ideal of antiquity' and his reference to Napoleon as 'late-born' suggests that the linearity of the metaphor of man as a bridge may be misleading in this instance, obscuring the *problem* of noble ethics which the figure of Napoleon represents. After all, if the relationship between the inhuman, human and overhuman is simply linear, it is difficult to see how a synthesis of the inhuman and overhuman might occur, and, if conceptualisable, such a synthesis would be simultaneously late-born (inhuman) and early-born (overhuman) – not simply late-born as Napoleon is characterised.[19] But if it is not simply linear, what is the character of the relationship between inhuman, human and overhuman?

To resolve this question – and to resolve it in such a way that it also resolves the apparently misleading character of Nietzsche's 'bridge' metaphor – consider the following schema:

1 the inhuman – the animal (the regulation of life by unconscious instinctive drives);
2 the human – the man of bad conscience and slave morality;
3 the overhuman – the man of good conscience and noble morality.

If we adopt this schema, it is clear both why Nietzsche refers to the synthesis of the inhuman and the overhuman as the *problem* of noble ethics and why he refers to man as a bridge. The former is simply a recognition of the fact (which we have already noted) that the good conscience and noble morality (the overhuman) are maintained in antiquity only because the noble has the opportunity to express his instinctive drives (the inhuman) outside of society. In other words, at this historical juncture it appears that the overhuman is non-contingently tied to the inhuman. Thus Nietzsche's characterisation of this synthesis as a *problem* reveals to his readers the central ethical concern of his genealogical reflection: *how is it possible to have the overhuman without the inhuman*? This reading is explicitly supported by an unpublished note from the period of November 1887 to March 1888 (i.e., immediately after finishing *On the Genealogy of Morals*):

> One recognizes the superiority of the Greek man and the Renaissance man – but one would like to have them without the causes and conditions which made them possible. (WP §882)

It is in this context that we can make sense of his metaphor of man as a bridge by suggesting that Nietzsche's claim is that the illness/pregnancy of bad conscience which results from 'a forcible sundering from his animal past' (GM II §16) and which constitutes the all-too-human figure of man raises the possibility of an overcoming of man in which the overhuman is not tied to the inhuman. On this account, the enclosure of man within the walls of society and of peace breaks the synthesis of the inhuman and superhuman; man is a bridge across the abyss constituted by this act of sundering not only in the sense of linking the inhuman and the overhuman but also in the sense of holding them apart. In other words, it is with the constitution of the human that a linear temporal relationship between the inhuman, the human and the overhuman becomes possible.

Consequently, we can conclude this section as Nietzsche concludes his essay on noble and slave morality by noting that his call to us to be beyond good and evil is not a call to be beyond good and bad. However, to explore Nietzsche's concern with the overcoming of man requires that we turn to the development and overcoming of liberal reason (as the expression of bad conscience and *ressentiment*) which Nietzsche considers in his essay on the meaning of ascetic ideals, not least since it is on the basis of the capacities which man develops under the aegis of asceticism that Nietzsche points to the possibility of the overhuman without the inhuman.

'What is the Meaning of Ascetic Ideals?'

My claim with respect to this essay is that Nietzsche provides a historical account of the emergence of the truth/*eros* distinction and its mobilisation in terms of an ethical injunction to overcome *eros* in the name of truth, to master the affects through the use of reason, while also illustrating the auto-destructive character of liberal reason. I will begin our reflection on this essay by suggesting two routes into Nietzsche's consideration of the meaning of ascetic ideals. The first route reflects on Nietzsche's idea of willing, while the second draws our attention to his critique of liberal reason with respect to the truth/*eros* distinction.

In considering Nietzsche's phenomenal account of willing, three aspects were noted: firstly, a pathos of embodiment (our sensuous experience of being in the world), secondly, a commanding thought (a goal) and, thirdly, an affect of command (the feeling of power). Let us deploy this schema of willing to reflect on the three essays of *On the Genealogy of Morals*. We can note to begin with that the second essay gives an account of how our instinct for freedom in turning back on itself becomes will to power and how this expresses itself as the idea of freedom of will which Nietzsche informs us 'is essentially the emotion of superiority over him who must obey' (BGE §19). Thus, the essay on bad conscience focuses its attention on the activity of willing *qua* the affect of command. By contrast, the essay on noble and slave morality gives an account of how different styles of moral reasoning emerge from different experiences of being in the world. Thus, this essay focuses its attention on willing *qua* pathos of embodiment or affectivity. Consequently, it should not surprise us if Nietzsche's essay on the meaning of ascetic ideals addresses itself to the topic of willing *qua* commanding thought, that is, to the question of the *telos* or goal of the activity of willing. We should also note that since the essay on bad conscience addresses the emergence of the subject/object distinction and the essay on morality attends to the emergence of the appearance/reality distinction, we might expect this final essay to focus on the emergence of the reason/ affectivity distinction. Nietzsche confirms the first of these routes into the discussion of the meaning of ascetic ideals in the opening section when he comments:

> *That* the ascetic ideal has meant so many things to man . . . is an expression of the basic fact of the human will, its *horror vacui*: *it needs a goal* – and it will rather will *nothingness* than *not* will. (GM III §1)

However, I will suggest that to explore the relation of this *horror vacui* with the ascetic ideal (why this goal?) requires that we take up the second route and attend to the emergence of the reason/affectivity (truth/*eros*) distinction and its deployment as the ethical imperative of vanquishing the affects through reason.

Let us start by recalling the context: the slave revolt in morals. I want to highlight two problems which are engendered by this event. The first problem concerns the slave's experience of existence as suffering. Of course, the slave revolt in morals gives meaning to this suffering by designating the nobility as the guilty agents responsible for it; the way in which this meaning is generated being through the projection of an imaginary inversion of the social order of rank as the 'real' world of being secured by the belief in the soul. However, precisely because this belief in the immortal soul equates death with freedom and existence with suffering, it removes any reason for living. Thus, an unintended consequence of the slave revolt in morals is that its very way of empowering the slave removes any rationale from persisting with earthly existence. The second problem concerns the explosive character of *ressentiment*. We can explain this problem by noting the slave revolt in morals is the expression of the collective experience of the slaves as a class-for-itself; the moment at which *ressentiment* becomes creative marks the shift from a class-in-itself to a class-for-itself – the revenge it imagines is collective. However, the belief in the soul entails that the slave distinguishes his self from any of its contingent social manifestations and, consequently, while the slave identifies the noble as guilty agent with respect to his suffering *as a slave*, he produces other guilty agents as necessary with respect to his other social identities: 'they [the slaves] make evildoers out of their friends, wives, children, and whoever else stands closest to them' (GM III §15). In seeking 'to *deaden pain by means of affects*' (Nietzsche identifies this desire being the cause of *ressentiment*), *ressentiment* threatens not only to undermine the solidarity of the slave class but to threaten sociality *per se*.

It is in this context that Nietzsche places the figure of the ascetic priest. Who is this figure? For Nietzsche, the ascetic priest 'appears in almost every age; he belongs to no one race; he prospers everywhere; he emerges from every class of society' (GM III §11). By contrast with the warrior-noble and the slave, the ascetic priest is one who adopts practices of self-denial in order to 'become master not over something in life but over life itself, its most profound, powerful, and basic conditions' (GM III §11). Eschewing the natural desires exhibited by the nobles for riches, fame and women (those things for which the slave envies the nobles), the ascetic priest practises poverty, humility and chastity in order to achieve supernatural desires, for example knowing the future and immortality; these examples indicate perhaps the wellspring out of which the ascetic spirit grows, the desire to avoid suffering from both the uncertainty of the future and the consciousness of our own mortality (both of these being basic conditions of life). Here, Nietzsche argues, 'rules a *ressentiment* without equal' (GM III §11). Moreover, the ascetic priest is such an anti-natural figure (taking the nobles as representatives of naturalness) that Nietzsche suggests:

> It must be a necessity of the first order that again and again promotes the growth and prosperity of the *life-inimical* species – it must indeed be in the *interest of life itself* that such a contradictory type does not die out. (GM III §10)

It is by placing the ascetic priest in the context of the problems raised for life by the slave revolt in morals that Nietzsche seeks to reveal the interest of life fulfilled by the ascetic priest.

We can now set out the *genius* of the ascetic priest. With respect to the problem of the lack of a goal, of a reason for living, Nietzsche notes that the ascetic priest provides a goal by idealising the ascetic life:

> The idea at issue here is the *valuation* the ascetic priest places on our life: he juxtaposes it . . . with a quite different mode of existence which it opposes and

excludes, *unless* it turn against itself, *deny itself*: in that case, the case of the ascetic life, life counts as a bridge to that other mode of existence. (GM III §11)

In other words, the ascetic priest provides a goal for life by making our experience of the next life (whether this takes the form of earthly reincarnation or some other-worldly existence) dependent on how we live this life. Thus, this *idealisation* of asceticism manifests itself as the absolute opposition of reason (mind/soul) and affectivity (body/flesh), and makes the pursuit of truth and the denial (transcendence and negation) of *eros* into the architectonic interest of humanity. However, this idealisation of the ascetic life also transforms the moral account of the meaning of suffering by inscribing *ressentiment* within the slave; the reactive logic of 'he is evil, therefore I am good' is projected onto the relation of the body to the soul (the body as prison of the soul). Within this perspective, the explanation of the suffering of the slave is articulated through the idea of sin, 'the greatest event so far in the history of the sick soul' (GM III §20). In the context, Nietzsche remarks:

'I suffer: someone must be to blame for it' – thus thinks every sick sheep. But his shepherd, the ascetic priest, tells him: 'Quite so, my sheep! someone must be to blame for it: but you yourself are this someone, you alone are to blame for it – *you alone are to blame for yourself*!' – This is brazen and false enough: but one thing at least is achieved by it, the direction of *ressentiment* is *altered*. (GM III §15)

By reinscribing the logic of *ressentiment* within the economy of the self, by making the ascetic ideal into the *telos* of the self's *rapport à soi*, the ascetic priest not only provides a goal for this-worldly existence but also defuses the threat which the build-up of *ressentiment* poses to society by allowing explosions under controlled conditions, that is, within the self: 'to detonate this explosive so that it does not blow up herd and herdsman is his essential art' (GM III §15).

Of course, the ascetic priest does not perform this resolution of the problems posed by the slave revolt in morals out of any spirit of civic duty or moral benevolence; on the contrary, the ascetic priest articulates a goal for life and the redirecting of *ressentiment* because this perspective maximises the feeling of power of the ascetic priest precisely by making the ascetic priest into the shepherd or herdsman. In other words, by transforming the ascetic life into the ideal life, the ascetic priest articulates, legitimates and establishes his authority over humanity. Consequently, Nietzsche argues that the ascetic priest serves the interest of life because '*the ascetic ideal springs from the protective instinct of a degenerating life* which tries by all means to sustain itself and to fight for its existence' (GM III §13). He continues:

The ascetic ideal is such an [life-preserving] expedient; this case is therefore the opposite of what those who reverence this idea believe: life wrestles in it and through it with death and *against* death; the ascetic ideal is an artifice for the *preservation* of life. (GM III §13)

Thus, it is Nietzsche's claim that the ascetic ideal is a paradox; it is a devaluation of life, a denial of life, which nevertheless acts to preserve it by providing a goal.

Let us conclude these opening reflections on the meaning of the ascetic ideal by reflecting on its relation to bad conscience. This reflection seems necessary because it appears that both bad conscience and the ascetic ideal have something to do with suffering and, specifically, with giving meaning to suffering. This point has led Daniel Conway to argue that we can think of the *horror vacui* of the will to which the ascetic ideal represents a response 'as a particular expression or by-product of the bad conscience' (1992a: 28). That this interpretation pushes us in the right direction can be seen by recalling our discussion of good and bad conscience as ways of explaining the fact of suffering. In that discussion, our focus was how the fact of suffering is given meaning and, in particular, how bad conscience explains extensional suffering through the idea of guilt. Now, at this juncture, we can distinguish two kinds of extensional suffering by distinguishing suffering which is independent of the fact of consciousness from suffering which is dependent on the fact of consciousness. Thus, for example, if I stub my toe, my extensional suffering is not dependent on the fact of consciousness (although my relation to this suffering, my intensional suffering, is so dependent); yet if I cannot answer the question of why I exist, of why my existence is meaningful, my extensional suffering is dependent on consciousness because such suffering is dependent on existence being mediated through meaning and this mediation is a consequence of the fact of consciousness. Consequently, we can distinguish between non-existential and existential forms of extensional suffering, and conclude that the *horror vacui* describes the fact of existential suffering, the fact that we live with the question of the meaning of life as an integral element of the human condition.

We should be clear that the *horror vacui* is a matter of our will to power, of the fact that the experience of ourselves as powerful or free requires goals in order to engage in willing, in order to experience the will as something which causes an effect. However, we should also note that the activity of willing takes place within the horizon of our consciousness of our mortality. The relation of the *horror vacui* to consciousness of mortality emerges when we reflect that, for humanity, the question 'what is the meaning of my existence?' takes the form of the question 'why be?', and that this latter question is only intelligible for a being for whom the possibility of not being is real.[20] Thus we may conclude with Conway that 'whereas the bad conscience represents the opportunity cost of relying on consciousness, the *horror vacui* is linked specifically to consciousness of one's mortality' (1992a: 28).

Following this discussion, we are in a position to specify the meaning of the ascetic ideal. It is a response to the *horror vacui*, the fact that 'man would rather will *nothingness* than *not* will' (GM III §28). The ascetic ideal is a way of closing the door 'to any kind of suicidal nihilism' by providing an architectonic goal for humanity, namely, truth (GM III §28). Thus, the ascetic ideal manifests itself as the will to truth. At the same time, this ascetic goal is nothingness, the transcendence and negation of our affective engagement with the world, the overcoming of earthly existence. We will see that Nietzsche argues that the ascetic ideal is not so much a solution to the problem of nihilism as a postponement, a deferral, of this dilemma; a deferral which has a high cost in human suffering but also opens up the possibility of ways of being through which this suffering can be redeemed.

It is in the context of this postponement, its price and possibilities, that Nietzsche raises the question of the relation of philosophy to the ascetic ideal (a question is demanded by Nietzsche's own claim to be engaged in the activity of philosophy). This discussion of the case of philosophers is prefaced by a discussion of artists in which Nietzsche highlights the issue of sensuality through the figure of Wagner, contrasting the attitude exhibited in his concern with the idea of Luther's wedding, in which chastity and sensuality are intertwined, with *Parsifal*, which manifests a hatred of sensuality (notably Nietzsche underlines his criticism of Wagner by suggesting that *Parsifal* is a much nobler achievement if taken as parody). However, Nietzsche soon dismisses the idea that artists can offer significant insight into the meaning of ascetic ideals because he claims that artists act variously as masks for, courtiers of and subjects of a philosophical (or theological) authority. Thus he notes that the later Wagner deploys Schopenhauer in order to legitimate his artistic practices. Consequently, Nietzsche turns to the question of the meaning of ascetic ideals for philosophers.

Again Nietzsche begins with a contrast; in this instance Kant's philosophical definition of the beautiful as that which gives us pleasure without interest is counterposed to the writer Stendhal's conception of the beautiful as *une promesse de bonheur* (a promise of happiness). As with the earlier contrast, Nietzsche is highlighting a position in which sensuality is an integral feature (Stendhal: the beautiful promises happiness because it arouses the will) with a counterposition in which sensuality is excluded (Kant's disinterested spectator). In this context, the later Wagner's deployment of Schopenhauer as his authority is revealing precisely because Schopenhauer radicalises the Kantian stance by defining the beautiful not simply as disinterested pleasure but as pleasurable because it releases us from interestedness, that is, the erotic will. Thus, a preliminary response to the meaning of ascetic ideals for philosophers is that it signals the desire to be free of *eros*:

> As long as there are philosophers on earth, . . . there unquestionably exists a peculiar philosophers' irritation at and rancor against sensuality: Schopenhauer is merely its most eloquent and, if one has ears for this, most ravishing and delightful expression. (GM III §7)

However, Nietzsche claims, a prejudice against sensuality does not exhaust the relation between philosophy and the ascetic ideal. Indeed, Nietzsche goes so far as to suggest that if a philosopher does not embrace the whole of the ascetic ideal (its three slogans – poverty, humility, chastity – are well known), his claim to the title 'philosopher' is held to be suspect.

Why is this the case on Nietzsche's account? Why is it that philosophers exhibit this prejudice in favour of the ascetic ideal? Consider the following passage:

> Every animal – therefore *la bête philosophe*, too – instinctively strives for an optimum of favorable conditions under which it can expend its strength and achieve its maximal feeling of power; every animal abhors, just as instinctively and with a subtlety of discernment that is 'higher than reason,' every kind of instrusion or hindrance that obstructs or could obstruct this path to the optimum. (GM III §7)

In this statement of the hypothesis of will to power, Nietzsche highlights the *teleological* aspect of our activity, that is, its directedness to the goal of establishing conditions under which we maximise our sense of ourselves as autonomous beings. In the case of philosophers, Nietzsche's suggestion is that the meaning of the ascetic ideal is that it provides the conditions under which the philosopher attains his optimum experience of himself as powerful. Thus Nietzsche comments: 'A philosopher may be recognized by the fact that he avoids three glittering and loud things: fame, princes and women' (GM II §8). However, significant as it is, this 'elective affinity' between philosophy and the ascetic ideal still does not exhaust their relation: 'A serious examination of history actually reveals that the bond between philosophy and the ascetic ideal is even much closer and stronger' (GM III §9).

Adopting a historical perspective, Nietzsche asserts that the emergence of philosophical activity is tied to 'the leading-strings of this ideal' (GM II §9). His argument is that philosophical contemplation emerges in the context of other forms of contemplative activity:

> Let us compress the facts into a few brief formulas: to begin with, the philosophic spirit always had to use as a mask and cocoon the *previously established* types of the contemplative man – priest, sorcerer, soothsayer, and in any case a religious type – in order to be able to *exist at all*: *the ascetic ideal* for a long time served the philosopher as a form in which to appear, as a precondition of existence – he had to *represent* it so as to be able to be a philosopher; he had to *believe* it in order to be able to represent it. . . . To put it vividly: the *ascetic priest* provided until the most modern times the repulsive and gloomy caterpillar form in which alone the philosopher could live and creep about. (GM III §10)

As the metaphor which concludes this passage reveals, Nietzsche is not claiming that philosophy is necessarily tied to the ascetic ideal; on the contrary, he suggests that this relation is 'a result of the emergency conditions under which philosophy arose', that is, the enclosure of man within the walls of society and of peace (GM III §10). However, he is claiming that insofar as philosophy is linked to the ascetic ideal, it posits objectivity, reason and truth as opposed to interestedness, affectivity and *eros*. Yet Nietzsche's metaphor also directs us to the possibility of another philosophy, a philosophy in which objectivity is 'the ability *to control* one's Pro and Con and to dispose of them, so that one knows how to employ a *variety* of perspectives and affective interpretations in the service of knowledge' (GM III §12). This other philosophy in which the affective structure of reason (will to power) and the erotic character of truth (the perspective theory of affects) are acknowledged is figured by this metaphor as philosophy reaching maturity; the transformation of caterpillar into butterfly. Yet how can such a philosophy – which is antagonistic not to asceticism but to its idealisation – come into existence? Or, to put this another way, what are the conditions of possibility of Nietzsche's philosophy? To address this question we need to return to the issue of how the development of liberal reason is articulated through the ascetic ideal as will to truth.

Nietzsche takes up the development of the perspective which I refer to as 'liberal reason' by posing the question of whether science opposes the ascetic ideal. After all, insofar as science is associated with the secularisation or disenchantment of the world and the ascetic ideal is tied historically to religion and metaphysics, it might be supposed that in freeing us from religion, science frees us from the ascetic ideal. With respect to this argument, Nietzsche comments:

> The truth is precisely the opposite of what is asserted here: science today has absolutely *no* belief in itself, let alone an ideal above it – and where it still inspires passion, love, ardor, and *suffering* at all, it is not the opposite of the ascetic ideal but rather *the latest and noblest form of it.* (GM III §23)

He re-emphasises and clarifies this claim in the following section when he writes:

> Strictly speaking, there is no such thing as science 'without any presuppositions'; this thought does not bear thinking through, it is paralogical: a philosophy, a 'faith' must always be there first of all, so that science can acquire from it a direction, a meaning, a limit, a method, a *right* to exist. (GM III §24)

Nietzsche's point is straightforward: science cannot tell us why scientific knowledge is worth knowing; the activity of science *presupposes* the value of truth. It is this 'overestimation of truth', this belief that 'truth is inestimable and cannot be criticized' (GM III §25), which reveals science as the latest form of the ascetic ideal.

Science is not merely the latest form of the ascetic ideal, however, it is also the *noblest* form of the ascetic ideal. We can account for this designation by noting that Nietzsche regards the commitment to intellectual probity, the incarnation of intellectual conscience, exhibited by scientific conscience as the most spiritual form of the ascetic ideal (cf. GS §2 and 335, AC §50, GM III §24) and that it is this commitment to truthfulness which acts as the agent of the self-overcoming of the ascetic ideal:

> All great things bring about their own destruction through an act of self-overcoming: thus the law of life will have it, the law of the necessity of 'self-overcoming' in the nature of life – the lawyer himself eventually receives the call: '*patere legeum, quam ipse tulisti* [submit to the law you yourself proposed].' In this way Christianity *as a dogma* was destroyed by its own morality; in the same way Christianity *as morality* must now perish, too: we stand on the threshold of *this* event. After Christian truthfulness has drawn one inference after another, it must end by drawing its *most striking inference*, its inference *against* itself; this will

happen, however, when it poses the question '*what is the meaning of all will to truth?*' (GM III §27)

In other words, it is our probity which undermines the religious, moral and scientific forms of the ascetic ideal and in doing so opens the possibility of rethinking truth, of a will to truth which serves *eros* rather than one which attempts to deny our affective engagement with the world. However, the process by which the will to truth undermines the ascetic ideal is also the process of revealing the meaning of the ascetic ideal as '*a will to nothingness*' and introducing that uncanniest of all guests, *nihilism*. Worn down by the battle of our will to truth against all other affective forces (including finally itself), we find ourselves deprived of the grounds on which we valued life. From the point at which the will to truth turns on Christianity as *religion* – the death of God – to the point at which it turns on itself and recognises itself as a problem, we can only be nihilists:

> . . . this is the great spectacle in a hundred acts reserved for the next two centuries in Europe – the most terrible, most questionable, and perhaps also the most hopeful of all spectacles. (GM III §27)

The most terrible because it involves the destruction of our most cherished beliefs and the most hopeful because it raises the possibility of articulating a counter-ideal which expresses a good conscience and a noble morality.

In summary, then, we can see that in focusing on the meaning of ascetic ideals Nietzsche is concerned with explicating the emergence of the reason/affectivity or truth/*eros* distinction and accounting for the transformation of this distinction into a dialectical structure in which the *telos* is a reason without affects (which is signified by the idea of a God's-eye view, the view from nowhere). At the same time, Nietzsche attempts to account for the conditions of possibility of his own erotic philosophy by showing how the will to truth cultivated by the ascetic ideal eventually turns on the ascetic ideal itself. This process of the self-overcoming, of the will to truth which marks our modernity is given the name 'nihilism' and it is Nietzsche's diagnosis of the terror and hope of this condition to which we turn in the following chapter.

Conclusion

In the preceding chapter, I argued that Nietzsche offers a philosophical critique of liberal reason, this form of rationality being characterised by two distinctions – subject/object, appearance/reality – which taken together generate two further distinctions, namely, reason/affectivity and reason/history. In this chapter, I've tried to show that the three essays which make up Nietzsche's *On the Genealogy of Morals* offer speculative accounts of the emergence and entrenchment of the two primary distinctions of liberal reason and their articulation through the moral deployment of the reason/affectivity distinction manifested by the ascetic ideal, while marking the moment of their demise as the moment at which Nietzsche's own erotic philosophy becomes possible. But what of the reason/history distinction? While it would undoubtedly flesh out Nietzsche's manifest dislike of dialectical philosophy if he were to point to the fact that the ascetic ideal can exhibit itself not simply as the desire to overcome affectivity but also as the desire to overcome or control history, his comments on the lack of historical sense exhibited by philosophers are all too numerous (cf. TI '"Reason" in Philosophy' §1, for example). Indeed, we may go further and cite a note from 1887 in which Nietzsche comments that one of the forms of eliding the significance of the death of God is to place oneself under the authority of '*history* with an immanent spirit and a goal within, so that one can entrust oneself to it' (WP §20). These points suggest that the reason/history distinction marks another side to the ascetic ideal in which the triumph of reason over the affects is simultaneously the triumph of reason over history (one might note in this context the recent emergence of liberal 'end of history' arguments). Perhaps for our concerns we need merely note that the essays which make up *On the Genealogy of Morals* perform a critique of the reason/history distinction and turn our attention to the conditions under which this critique becomes possible: nihilism.

Notes

1 I develop this claim against the position adopted in Deleuze's excellent and influential *Nietzsche and Philosophy* (1983).

2 Charles Turner has pointed out to me that Hegel makes this distinction, albeit with quite different purposes in mind, in the sub-section 'Purpose and Responsibility' §§115–18 in his *Philosophy of Right* (1952).

3 I'm by no means convinced of the truth of this statement. Consider ability of higher mammals to be taught (is conscious memory just fluid instinct produced by conditioning?).

4 See GM II §14.

5 For some pertinent and interesting observations on shame and guilt which are generally supportive of Nietzsche's argument, see Chapter 4 of Bernard Williams' *Shame and Necessity* (1993).

6 For a detailed account of this topic, see Owen (1994: Ch 3).

7 One does not tend to think 'why me?' until after the unintelligible attack is complete.

8 For a fascinating discussion of Job, see Connolly (1993).

9 A more precise way of putting this might be to suggest that with instinctive will to power an increase in power and an increase in feeling of power are identical while this is no longer the case once consciousness is introduced and the feeling of power becomes the sole criterion.

10 For an interesting attempt to develop this point re. will to power in general, see Warren (1988: Ch 4).

11 This argument is supported by other comments on the development of consciousness (GS §354) and on the relation of the idea that the will is something which causes an effect to the subject/object distinction in our grammar (TI '"Reason" in Philosophy' §5), particularly when these are read together.

12 Note Kant's 'historical antinomy' in this context (Yovel, 1980).

13 This position is given recent expression in Michel Foucault's essay 'Is it Useless to Revolt?' (1981).

14 Although not in the same form; rather, Nietzsche seeks to encourage noble forms of will to power through the rule of eternal recurrence and the *telos* of the Overman.

15 See, for example, AC §25 – but this is a natural piece of anti-nature. The paradoxical flavour of this statement is neatly resolved by Nehamas (1985).

16 For a fuller discussion of this topic, see Owen (1994).

17 One can see here why Adorno draws on Nietzsche in formulating his critique of the logic of identity.

18 For this view of Nietzsche, see Habermas (1987).

19 This was one of the many errors of Owen (1994) in discussion of the figure of the Overman with respect to Napoleon and Goethe.

20 It seems to me that a conscious, immortal being might ask 'what is the meaning of my existence?' but that this question would not be synonymous with or substitutable for the question 'why be?', but wouldn't this be to say that what this being means by 'meaning' is different from what we mean by 'meaning' – and isn't this just another way of saying that the grammar of the concept 'meaning' is inseparable from the grammar of the concept 'being'?

4

Modernity and the Destruction of the Ascetic Ideal

Nihilism, Decadence and the Necessity of a Counter-Ideal

> To stand outside [the] stream of history and reflect at some remove does not mean simply detaching oneself from history. It means reflecting not upon history as it is, but upon where it is headed. It does not mean to observe the reality of history and its idea objectively as historians or philosophers of history do, but to experiment with the future tendencies and issues of history by making the self one's laboratory. . . . This is the meaning of 'living nihilism through to its end' and the standpoint of 'one who is a philosopher and a hermit by instinct.' It is in this sense that Nietzsche claims to be doing nothing other than reflecting upon himself. (Nishitani, 1990: 30)

Nietzsche's genealogical reflections suggest that our modernity marks a juncture at which the hegemony of slave morality (i.e., bad conscience and *ressentiment* as they are expressed through the ascetic ideal) is progressively undermined by forces which were cultivated under its aegis, most notably the will to truth. For Nietzsche, in other words, we dwell within the death-throes of liberal reason (at least in its metaphysical form). He explores this process of the self-overcoming of slave morality, the auto-destruction of philosophical liberalism, through an account of modernity as *nihilism* – the will to nothingness – and as *decadence* – the experience of affective exhaustion. In this chapter I will be concerned to elucidate Nietzsche's account of modernity as nihilism and decadence before turning to his reasons for articulating a counter-ideal to the ascetic ideal.

Nihilism and Decadence

Let us open this discussion of the topic of nihilism with some remarks from the third essay of *On the Genealogy of Morals*:

> What is to be feared, what has a more calamitous effect than any other calamity, is that man should inspire not profound fear but profound *nausea*; also not fear but great *pity*. Suppose these two were one day to unite, they would inevitably beget one of the uncanniest monsters: the 'last will' of man, his will to nothingness, nihilism. (GM III §14)

Since it is precisely Nietzsche's claim that this will to nothingness is the most significant feature of the modern condition, to address the topic of nihilism requires that we account for the nausea and pity which beget this most uncanny monster. To provide such an account entails that we must *both* identify the forms in which the affective dispositions of nausea and pity disclose themselves *and* specify the process through which they engender the will to nothingness.

Although one should be wary in using the unpublished materials collected together in the volume entitled *The Will to Power*, a note from June 1887 provides an account of the *logic* of nihilism which is entirely consonant with Nietzsche's published reflections:

> But among the forces cultivated by morality was *truthfulness (Wahrhäftigkeit)*: this eventually turned against morality, discovered its teleology, its partial perspective – and now the recognition of this inveterate mendaciousness that one despairs of shedding becomes a stimulant. Now we discover in ourselves needs implanted by centuries of moral interpretation – needs that now appear to us as needs for untruth; on the other hand, the value for which we endure life seems to hinge on these needs. This antagonism – *not* to esteem what we know, and not to be *allowed* any longer to esteem the lies we should like to tell ourselves – results in a process of dissolution. (WP §5, cf. also GS §357 and GM III §27)

In this passage, the cognitive correlate of nausea is revealed as an inability to value our knowledge of the world because it doesn't satisfy the needs implanted in us by morality, while that of pity is disclosed as an inability to satisfy our need to value ourselves because our very truthfulness prevents us from satisfying our need for the untruths of morality. Taken together these affective dispositions and their cognitive correlates engender a process of dissolution which takes the affective form of decadence and the cognitive form of nihilism. But doesn't this passage elide the fact that our truthfulness satisfies our central 'moral' need under the aegis of the ascetic ideal, namely, the need for truth? If this were the case, it would be unclear why Nietzsche's claim that we are characterised by nihilism should be taken seriously. Yet Nietzsche is not unaware of this point, and it is, perhaps, precisely for this reason that he presents the *radical* character of contemporary nihilism as being disclosed at the moment at which our truthfulness addresses itself to the meaning and value of truth and recognises the fallacious character of metaphysical realist accounts of truth, thereby devaluing this highest (*oberst*) value by depriving it of its metaphysical ground. To clarify this point, we can sketch Nietzsche's account of the stages which occur in the development of nihilism.

Let us begin by distinguishing three stages within Nietzsche's account of the development of nihilism as he sets it out in the essay on the meaning of ascetic ideals and juxtaposing these three stages to the third, fourth and fifth/sixth positions in his account of how the 'real world' at last became a myth. The suggestion which will be elaborated by this juxtaposition is that the threefold movement of the will to truth against the metaphysics of God, morality and truth itself may be fruitfully read with the four stages in the transformation of our understanding of truth which concludes with Nietzsche's mature position as this is expressed in the perspective theory of affects. Let us begin by citing the relevant passage from *On the Genealogy of Morals*:

> . . . Christianity *as a dogma* was destroyed by its own morality; in the same way Christianity as *morality* must now perish too: we stand on the threshold of *this* event. After Christian truthfulness has drawn one inference after another, it must end by drawing its *most striking inference*, its inference *against* itself; this will happen, however, when it poses the question '*what is the meaning of all will to truth?*' (GM III §27)

But how did Christian morality overcome Christian dogma? Why must morality perish? And why must our truthfulness undermine our belief in the value of truth? To explicate Nietzsche's understanding of nihilism, we need to address these questions.

Morality contra *Dogma and the Spectre of Nihilism*

In *The Gay Science*, Nietzsche characterises Christian dogmatism in terms of the following ideas:

> Looking at nature as if it were proof of the goodness and governance of a god; interpreting history in honor of some divine reason, as a continual testimony of a moral world order and ultimately moral purposes; interpreting one's own experiences as pious people have long interpreted theirs, as if everything were providential, a hint, designed and ordained for the salvation of the soul – (GS §357)

Nietzsche's claim is that the first of these ideas is undermined by Kant, the second by Hegel and the third by Schopenhauer. Consequently we can begin by recalling his characterisation of Kant's position with respect to the appearance/reality distinction:

> The real world, unattainable, undemonstrable, cannot be promised, but even when merely thought of a consolation, a duty, an imperative. (TI 'How the "Real World" At Last Became a Myth' §3)

The importance of this position for Nietzsche's concerns emerges if we substitute 'God' for 'the real world' (recall Nietzsche's comments on slave morality) and lies in its transformation of the relation of God and humanity. On the one hand, Kant rules out the possibility of knowledge of God. On the other hand, Kant grounds morality in existence of God as a *matter of faith*. The first of these points has been neatly elaborated by Karl Loewith:

> Copernicus, Kepler, Galileo and Newton were all equally convinced that God had ordained the world mathematically and that they could come to know Him by reading from what, by analogy with the Bible, they termed the 'book' of nature. The biologist Swammerdamm's triumphant declaration, 'I bring you here proof of God's Providence in the anatomy of a louse', gives an indication of the confidence with which a belief in natural science as a pathway to God could be assumed in the period before Kant produced his critique of physico-teleological arguments for God's existence. (1989: 142)

Yet, at the same time as it rules out knowledge of God, Kant's critical system requires the idea of God in order to secure morality. Kant states this point in his famous claim to have found it necessary to deny knowledge in order to make room for faith, which finds its expression in his recognition that the possibility of the highest good (*summum bonum*) – the apex of his moral thinking – cannot be proved but must be assumed if morality is to be given firm foundations, and, thus, he comments:

> The effect which is commanded [by the idea of the highest good], together with the only conditions on which its possibility is conceivable by us, namely the existence of God and the immortality of the Soul, are matters of faith (*res fidei*). (1957: §91)

By acknowledging that we cannot have any knowledge of God because we cannot have knowledge of the 'real world' (the noumenal realm) and simultaneously, offering a 'proof' of the existence of God (and, therefore, of the *reality* of the noumenal realm) which basically consists in asserting that moral action is meaningless unless we assume the existence of God, Kant both undermines the idea of reading the 'book' of nature as a way of gaining knowledge of God and, unwittingly, raises the spectre of nihilism (i.e., the meaninglessness of moral action).

Nietzsche's suggestion is that the next stage in the critique of dogmatism comes with Hegel's commitment to the idea 'that species concepts *develop out of each other*' (GS §357). The important point for Nietzsche can be made plain by recalling that Kant resolved the debate between rationalists (e.g., Descartes) and empiricists (e.g., Hume) by arguing that our basic conceptual categories (e.g., causality) are the product of the 'synthesising' activity of the faculty of understanding, that is, of the transcendental structure of human consciousness. The significance of Hegel in this context is, firstly, that he recasts the question of our conceptual categories in terms of the *historical development* of human consciousness and, secondly, that this 'historical' turn continues Kant's transformation of the relationship between God and humanity by conceptualising this developmental process in terms of the collective, rational activity of humanity. Thus, on Nietzsche's account, Hegel rules out the Protestant idea that history is simply the passive working out of divine reason, a kind of clock mechanism that has been designed, wound up and let go by God and is simply working its way towards a predestined terminus.[2]

Despite the radical character of the transformations wrought by Kant and Hegel in terms of a critique of Christian dogmatism, Nietzsche recognises that, precisely to the extent these thinkers were non-dogmatic Christians, 'they *delayed* [the] triumph of atheism most dangerously for the longest time' (GS §357). On Nietzsche's interpretation, Kant's presupposition of the existence of God and Hegel's identification of God with *Geist* undermine dogmatism but, by doing so, sustain Christianity. Indeed, Feuerbach described Hegel's system as 'the last rational supporting pillar of theology' (cited in Nishitani, 1990: 13). It is Schopenhauer whom Nietzsche credits with taking the critique of dogmatism to its conclusion with the elaboration of a 'scientific atheism' which undermines the very idea of God and, concomitantly, the salvation of the soul. The point which Nietzsche emphasises in his account of Schopenhauer is the latter's stress, *contra* Hegel, on 'the *nullity* of all existence' (Nishitani, 1990: 14). Nishitani offers a clear characterisation of Schopenhauer's position:

> The will to life appears as desire in the individual things that are its phenomena, and this desire harbors profound dissatisfaction. As long as the will to life is operative, dissatisfaction arises ceaselessly from within. Therefore, life is essentially *suffering* (*Leiden*). . . . Herein rests true metaphysics and philosophy, as well as the basis for true morality. . . . I would simply note that for Schopenhauer blind will and emancipation from it are connected with *pity* (*Mitleiden*) for suffering, or with the highest *askesis* (*Askese*) – that is, with a morality of the complete negation of the will. . . . He therefore presents his metaphysics . . . as a true grounding for Christian morality. (1990: 14–15)

For Nietzsche, Schopenhauer sacrifices the idea of God in order to secure Christian morality and, consequently, confronts Kant's question concerning the meaningfulness of moral action and, indeed, of existence as such. Schopenhauer responds to this question by making the negation of the will into the meaning of existence and, thus, from Nietzsche's perspective, 'remaining stuck – in precisely those Christian-ascetic moral perspectives in which one had *renounced faith* along with the faith in God' (GS §357):

> Schopenhauer's metaphysics demonstrates that even now the scientific spirit is not yet sufficiently strong: so that, although all the dogmas of Christianity have long since been demolished, the whole medieval Christian conception of the world and of the nature of man could in Schopenhauer's teaching celebrate a resurrection. (HAH I §26)

However, even as the spectre of nihilism becomes fully developed with Schopenhauer's philosophy, the force of Nietzsche's critique is dependent on his claim concerning the second stage of nihilism – the advent of nihilism – in which the will to truth cultivated by Christian asceticism turns its critical eye on Christian morality.

Truthfulness contra *Morality and the Advent of Nihilism*

We can open up this topic by citing the fourth stage in Nietzsche's account of the history of the appearance/reality distinction:

> The real world – unattainable? Unattained, at any rate. And if unattained also *unknown*. Consequently also no consolation, no redemption, no duty: how could we have a duty towards something unknown?
> (The grey of dawn. First yawnings of reason. Cockcrow of positivism.) (TI 'How the "Real World" At Last Became a Myth' §4)

Nietzsche's parenthetic comments refer us to his early text *Daybreak* and the 'positivist' period of his writing in which he develops his critique of the significance of the real world and opposes morality in the name of science. These two elements are related: on the one hand, by locating the real world as utterly unknowable, Nietzsche places both morality and science firmly in the phenomenal realm; and, on the other hand, in so doing, he specifies their relation as one of opposition. The character of this twofold claim is clarified in *Human, All Too Human*, when Nietzsche comments:

> It is true, that there could be a metaphysical world; the absolute possibility of it can hardly be disputed. We behold all things through the human head and cannot cut off this head; while the question remains what of the world would still be there if one had cut it off. This is a purely scientific problem and one not very well calculated to bother people overmuch; but all that has hitherto made metaphysical assumptions *valuable, terrible, delightful* to them, all that has begotten these assumptions, is passion, error and self-deception. When one has disclosed these methods as the foundation of all extant religions and metaphysical systems, one has refuted them! Then that possibility remains over; but one can do absolutely nothing with it, not to speak of letting happiness, salvation and life depend on the gossamer of such a possibility. – For one could assert nothing at all of the metaphysical world except that it was a being-other, an inaccessible, incomprehensible being-other; it would be a thing with negative qualities. (HAH I §9)

There are two aspects to the claim developed in this passage. Firstly, as the following section makes clear, Nietzsche is suggesting both that religion and morality belong to 'the realm of ideas' (HAH I §10), because if we can have no knowledge of the metaphysical realm, this truth necessarily applies to the 'truths' of religion and morality; consequently, the presuppositions of morality offered by Kant and by Schopenhauer are unwarranted assertions (that such presuppositions are necessary conditions for the authority of morality does *nothing* to establish the truth of these presuppositions). Secondly, if this claim is correct, not only are religious and moral modes of reasoning (precisely insofar as they ground their claim to authority in a claim to knowledge of the 'transcendent truths' of the metaphysical realm) opposed to scientific reason (which is concerned simply with the phenomenal or empirical realm) but we should also be able – at least in principle – to give a historical (i.e., scientific) account of the emergence and development of religious and moral ideas. In other words, to support his argument, Nietzsche needs to show that scientific reason undermines theological/moral reason by demonstrating both that this latter form of reasoning is committed to forms of explanation which are incompatible with science and that science can provide us with an explanation of how these erroneous forms of explanation have arisen.

In *Daybreak*, Nietzsche suggests that '[i]n the same measure as the sense for causality increases, the extent of the domain of morality decreases' (D §10). This claim immediately reveals the character of Nietzsche's argument concerning the opposition of science and morality, namely, that moral explanations of the world involve *imaginary* causalities which we cease to need to the extent that scientific explanations of phenomena become available. On this understanding (which is present throughout Nietzsche's work from this stage onwards), morality is a product of humanity's need to account for its experiences of the world, and it is in *Twilight of the Idols* that Nietzsche gives this view its sharpest expression by providing both a psychological explanation of 'the cause-creating drive' and an identification of morality in terms of the error of 'imaginary causes'. Nietzsche's psychological account develops from his notion of will to power:

> To trace something unknown back to something known is alleviating, soothing, gratifying and gives moreover a feeling of power. Danger, disquiet, anxiety attend the unknown – the first instinct is to *eliminate* these distressing states. First principle: any explanation is better than none. . . . The cause-creating drive is thus conditioned and excited by a feeling of fear. The question 'why?' should furnish, if at all possible, not so much the cause for its own sake as a *certain kind of cause* – a soothing, liberating, alleviating cause. . . . Thus there is sought not only some kind of explanation as cause, but a *selected* and *preferred* kind of explanation, the kind by means of which the feeling of the strange, new, unexperienced is most speedily and most frequently abolished – the *most common* explanations. (TI 'The Four Great Errors' §5)

If Nietzsche's naturalistic account is plausible, it is not difficult to see both the power of religious/moral explanations and how this form of explanation should come to predominate precisely because, prior to the development of science, it provides an efficient way of subsuming the unknown under the familiar (i.e., God). However, to effect his critique, Nietzsche still needs to establish that such forms of explanation involve an imaginary causality; in other words, to establish his claim, which we can express in its precise form as follows:

> Morality and religion fall entirely under the *psychology of error*: in every single case cause is mistaken for effect; or the effect of what is *believed* true is mistaken for truth; or a state of consciousness is mistaken for the causation of this state. (TI 'The Four Great Errors' §7)

Nietzsche needs to provide a *philosophical* critique to supplement his *psychological* claims. To elucidate Nietzsche's position, we can take up the specific error of 'free will', which he addresses in the following section, focusing in particular on the state of consciousness which we term 'guilt'. Here Nietzsche's point – as a recollection of his account in *On the Genealogy of Morals* will confirm – is that consciousness of guilt is taken to be an *effect* of the fact that one is *guilty*, that is, we project back from our consciousness of guilt to the *cause* of this state of consciousness, namely, that one has freely chosen to act immorally (i.e., one could have acted otherwise). Thus, this moral explanation of consciousness of guilt is predicated on the *reality* of 'free will', the will as cause. Yet, in the last two chapters, we have seen that Nietzsche has provided both good reasons for rejecting this account and a historical explanation of its conditions of emergence. His point is simply this: the consciousness of guilt is not *explained* by the idea of 'free will', rather, the consciousness of guilt is a product of belief in the idea of 'free will', that is, 'the effect of what is *believed* true is mistaken for the truth' (TI 'The Four Great Errors' §6).

Earlier in this section, I claimed that to illustrate his critique of religious and moral explanations, Nietzsche needed to show both that such explanations were incompatible with scientific explanations and that the existence of religious/moral explanations could be explained by science (thus making metaphysical accounts unnecessary). We can now summarise Nietzsche's argument thus: firstly, the authority of religious/moral explanations is dependent on the claim to know inaccessible 'truths' (which Nietzsche latterly terms 'imaginary' truths, i.e., to have knowledge of the metaphysical realm); as such these unjustifiable forms of reasoning are opposed to science, whose authority is grounded in its claim to offer empirical truths. Secondly, we can give a naturalistic historical account of how we come to hold these religious/moral views in terms of their psychological efficacy and, concomitantly, their tendency to exclude other forms of explanation, while our capacity to generate a scientific account undermines the need for a metaphysical account of the other-worldly origins of morality. Although I have not explored the historical accounts Nietzsche offers – partly because the psychological explanation cited above indicates the character of this form of accounting and partly because the 'natural history of morals' which Nietzsche develops in *Daybreak* and *Human, All Too Human* finds mature expression in *On the Genealogy of Morals* which we have already addressed at length – we can see that the type of explanation Nietzsche adopts can explain why we should cease to regard the truth of morality as a warranted assertion precisely because our recognition of the inaccessibility of the real world combined with our capacity to explain morality in scientific terms entails that morality loses its 'proof of power'.

If we reflect back on this argument we can see that Nietzsche is offering an account of his 'positivist' works as part of the working through of the problematic of nihilism by characterising them in terms of the scientific assault on morality. We can conclude (and support) this interpretation of Nietzsche's account by reflecting on the following passage:

> *Historical refutation as the definitive refutation*: In former times, one sought to prove that there is no God – today one indicates how the belief that there is a God could *arise* and how this belief acquired its weight and importance: a counter-proof that there is no God thereby becomes superfluous. (D §95)

Recalling the relative interchangeability of the terms 'God' and the 'real world' in the context of Nietzsche's work, reflect for a moment on the term 'superfluous' in the passage cited above. Nietzsche's use of this term suggests that he thinks that the business of providing proofs and counter-proofs of the existence or non-existence of God (or the real world) is a fairly sterile activity in which we don't need to engage. Nietzsche's reason for adopting this disdainful position is twofold. On the one hand, with the development of science, we no longer need religious/moral explanations of worldly phenomena, and, more particularly, with the development of scientific accounts of the emergence and development of morality, we do not need to posit the other-worldly origin of moral values. On the other hand, since we can have no knowledge of God or the real world, we are utterly unwarranted in asserting claims about God or the real world *even* if the only way we can ground the meaning and value of moral action (and, indeed, of existence) is to make such claims. The point of Nietzsche's 'positivist' account is not to engender moral relativism and subjectivism (although this is one of its possible effects) so much as to indicate that the loss of authority of moral claims renders moral action meaningless: we can no longer ground the meaning and value of existence in terms of a moral explanation of the world insofar as such explanations are simply contingent historical products which appear to us as unwarranted assertions. At this juncture, therefore, the moral needs implanted in us by Christian asceticism appear to us as needs for untruth, yet the value and meaning of existence seems to depend on these lies we can no longer tell ourselves. In other words, the spectre of nihilism raised by Kant's contention that unless we presuppose certain metaphysical truths as matters of faith, moral action (and existence as such) becomes meaningless, enters into the world as the *reality* of nihilism. However, the advent of nihilism does not mark its completion.

Truthfulness contra *Truth and the Fulfilment of Nihilism*

The question raised by the overcoming of morality concerns the value of our will to truth and, relatedly, the value of truth if we can no longer give moral reasons for valuing the will to truth and truth. Of course, at this stage we can still sustain our central 'moral' commitment under the ascetic ideal, namely, our commitment to truthfulness. Indeed, while it is this commitment which drives the development of nihilism, precisely because it is the 'kernel' of the ascetic ideal, it can sustain our experience of ourselves as valuable. Recall that the ascetic ideal resolves the initial problem of nihilism by providing a *goal* for human agency in terms of which we can experience ourselves as valuable; this goal is the idealisation of an anti-erotic asceticism (which idealisation is made possible by the distinction between real and apparent worlds). Consequently, while the previous two stages may restrict the realm of the ascetic ideal, they do not undermine it as such. However, the third stage in the development of nihilism, which is characterised by Nietzsche's fifth and sixth positions on the appearance/reality distinction, signals the point at which the legitimacy of the ascetic ideal itself becomes subject to attack.

To elucidate this stage, I will follow our established pattern and begin with the fifth stage in Nietzsche's account of the demise of the 'real world' hypothesis:

> The 'real world' – an idea no longer of any use, not even a duty any longer – an idea grown useless, superfluous, *consequently* a refuted idea: let us abolish it. (TI 'How the "Real World" At Last Became a Myth' §5)

With this position, Nietzsche is drawing the conclusion which follows from the utter indifference to the existence or non-existence of the 'real world' (now placed in inverted commas) developed in his 'positivist' period, namely, since there are no grounds on which we are warranted in asserting the reality of the 'real world', and since this idea does no epistemic work, why hold it at all? Under the aegis of our will to truth, we are forced to recognise that we cannot legitimately sustain this belief. Indeed, Nietzsche thinks that he can now show that the very idea of a thing-in-itself involves an internal contradiction which Clark elucidates as follows:

> . . . we can have no conception, or only a contradictory one, of something that would be independent of all knowers and therefore of all conceptualization, because to conceive of something is to conceive of it as satisfying some description or other, which is to think of it as being conceptualizable in some way or other. (1990: 46–7, cf. GS §54)

This contradiction entails junking the idea of the 'real world' and hence the metaphysical realist account of truth. However, as Clark points out (1990: 103-9), Nietzsche does not immediately draw the conclusion from the critique of the 'real world' to the critique of metaphysical realism, and, consequently, in several sections of *The Gay Science* and *Beyond Good and Evil* Nietzsche characterises all our beliefs about the world, including our scientific beliefs, as illusions (GS §§107–11, BGE §§4, 24, 34). At this juncture, in other words, Nietzsche thinks of the 'apparent world' as appearance and, consequently, is still in thrall to the idea that truth might be independent of all possible knowers which his critique of the thing-in-itself undermines. This somewhat incoherent stance does not survive very long and Nietzsche realises the consequences of his critique of the thing-in-itself for metaphysical realism with reasonable rapidity. Yet this very point raises an interesting (if perhaps incidental) question, namely, insofar as he abandons this incoherent stance, why does Nietzsche include it in his history of the demise of the appearence/reality distinction? Of course, we could simply respond that he is being honest, and this seems a reasonable response, *but* perhaps we may also suggest another reason (which is related to this honesty in the context of Nishitani's comment that Nietzsche's thinking consists in reflection and experimentation on himself), namely, that by including this stage Nietzsche reveals to us how deeply entrenched the metaphysical realist idea of truth is in our culture. In this sense, Nietzsche's inclusion of this position in the working through of his account of truth reveals a moment of *radical* nihilism in which we take all 'truths' to be lies. In other words, at this stage we can no longer value our will to truth because we hold that there is no truth.

Be that as it may, this position is displaced by the sixth and final position in Nietzsche's account:

> We have abolished the real world: what world is left? The apparent world perhaps? . . . But no! *with the real world we have also abolished the apparent world*! (TI 'How the "Real World" At Last Became a Myth' §6)

With the recognition that his critique of the thing-in-itself entails the abandonment of the appearance/reality distinction constitutive of metaphysical realism, Nietzsche re-establishes the idea of truth which his previous position had abandoned, albeit that truth is now construed in terms of dependence on our cognitive interests and, thus, on our will to power (i.e., *eros*). However, while this working through of the implications of his rejection of the 'real world' marks an overcoming of the radical nihilism of the fifth stage, it does not so much resolve the problem of nihilism as sharpen it. Recall that there are two questions at stake here: 'what is the value of our will to truth?' *and* 'what is the value of truth?' By identifying truth as illusion, the fifth stage responds to the first question by claiming that the will to truth is valueless because truths are illusion, and, consequently, does not respond to the second question because it is meaningless within the framework of this stance. In other words, if we hold all truths to be illusions, then the question of the value of truth is elided since we can't have truth anyway; only when we move to the sixth stage and recognise the possibility of truth does the full force of *both* questions emerge since both are meaningful within the frame of this understanding. Thus, from the perspective of Nietzsche's final position, the question of the value of the will to truth is *dependent* on the question of the value of truth. But why should we value truth?

Nietzsche's claim is that the 'inestimable' value of truth is the central feature of the ascetic ideal. Recall Nietzsche's comment that 'there is no such thing as science "without any presuppositions" . . . a "faith" must always be there first of all, so that science can acquire from it a direction, a meaning, a limit, a method, a *right* to exist' (GM III §24). With this comment, Nietzsche is claiming that science is the latest form of the ascetic ideal because it involves the metaphysical *presupposition* of the value of truth (GS §344). Nietzsche's point is given acute expression in Max Weber's essay 'Science as a Vocation':

> . . . what is the meaning of science as a vocation, now that all these earlier illusions – 'the way to the true being', 'the true way to art', 'the way to true nature', 'the way to the true God', 'the way to true happiness' – have been dispelled? . . . [S]cience . . . presupposes that what is produced by scientific work should be *important* in the sense of 'being worth knowing'. And it is obvious that all our problems lie here, for this presupposition cannot be proved by scientific means. (1989: 18)

Weber goes on to give a series of examples to illustrate his – and Nietzsche's – case, of which I will consider one which seems particular appropriate in this context, namely, medicine. Expressed crudely, Weber's point is this: medicine may be able to tell us how to save a life but it cannot tell us why any life is worth saving without appealing to 'moral' claims about the value of existence which the practice of medicine presupposes. But if the ground of this presupposition of the value of existence (i.e., the ascetic ideal) is undermined, we are left with no reasons to value truth. The point is simply this: insofar as the sixth stage of Nietzsche's reflection of the appearance/ reality distinction involves the abolition of this distinction, it completes the nihilistic process of undermining the ascetic ideal. The implication of this abolition is that human agency lacks a goal, a commanding thought, in terms of which to mobilise its volitional resources; we are confronted with the *horror vacui*, and it is in this context that we would rather will nothingness than not will. As Daniel Conway elegantly expresses it:

> At this point our maximal experience of power derives from our affective engagement in our own annihilation. We will never to will again. (1992a: 36)[3]

In other words, with the destruction of the ascetic ideal, with the loss of our grounds for valuing truth and, concomitantly, our will to truth, we reach the completion of the process of nihilism; our highest values have been devalued, our existence has no value – the last will of mankind, the will to nothingness, is all we have left.

In this discussion thus far I have focused primarily on Nietzsche's account of nihilism, that is, the cognitive character of our contemporary condition. At this juncture, let us recall the question of decadence, that is, the affective correlate of our cognitive position which was specified at the beginning of this section in terms of the combination of *nausea* as the affective correlate of no longer esteeming truth and *pity* as the affective correlate of no longer being able to value existence. If we reflect on the development of decadence in terms of the development of nihilism which we've sketched, we can note that it is characterised by the increasing exhaustion of our volitional resources as these two affective dispositions gradually merge with each other in the context of the progressive weakening of the ascetic ideal as a way of defining the *telos* of human agency. The process reaches its (anti-)climax with the abolition of the appearance/ reality distinction which legitimates the ascetic ideal because it is at this juncture that not being able to value truth (nausea) and not being able to value existence (pity) become one and the same. Unable to answer the question 'why be?', we are overwhelmed by nausea/pity and can only overcome our state of volitional exhaustion by surrendering to the affective imperative which this combination constructs: suicide. Only self-annihilation will release us from the existential suffering expressed in the combination of nausea and pity.

In the context of these deeply depressing reflections, it is important to recall the quotation from the work of Nishitani which prefaces this chapter and suggests that Nietzsche's dangerous experiment on himself is concerned with revealing the direction in which history is heading. This claim is confirmed by Nietzsche's comment at the end of *On the Genealogy of Morals* that he is speaking from a point at which European culture is involved in the second stage of nihilism in which the will to truth is in the process of undermining morality but that the third stage 'is the great spectacle in a hundred acts reserved for the next two centuries' (GM III §27). It is Nietzsche's recognition that we are caught up in the logic of nihilism but not yet subject to its destructive conclusions which motivates his attempt to articulate a *counter-ideal*. The purpose of this quest is not to relieve us from the necessity of undergoing nihilism but – if I may be excused a cliché – to provide a light at the end of the tunnel, to conjoin terror and hope. To recognise the necessity of undergoing nihilism is an abysmal thought but it is, at least potentially, a bearable thought if we also recognise the possibilities for overcoming *ressentiment* and bad conscience implicit within this experience. The task of elucidating the counter-ideal which Nietzsche elaborates will be the task of the next chapter; however, at this stage it seems appropriate to explicate his reasons for articulating a counter-ideal.

On the Necessity of a Counter-Ideal

If my account of Nietzsche's understanding of nihilism and decadence is plausible, then it seems that the articulation of a counter-ideal to the ascetic ideal becomes an existential and ethical imperative for his work. Nietzsche's recognition that he is engaged in this activity is given gleeful expression in *Ecce Homo* when he comments: 'Above all, a *counter-ideal* was lacking – *until Zarathustra*' (EH 'Genealogy of Morals'). But why does Nietzsche regard the construction of a counter-ideal to the ascetic ideal as the only option? And why do I suggest that this activity is conceptualised by Nietzsche as both an existential *and* ethical imperative? Before we examine the possible counter-ideals which Nietzsche claims are immanent within modern culture in the next section, it may be as well to address these preliminary questions. I will begin this discussion by reference to the work of Alasdair MacIntyre and Charles Taylor before suggesting why I think that reflecting on these thinkers is fruitful for an understanding of Nietzsche's reasons for engaging in the activity of constructing and recommending an ideal.

In *After Virtue* (1981), Alasdair MacIntyre offers a closely argued and highly polemical critique of the Enlightenment and, thus, of liberal reason in order to recommend a return to Aristotelian ethics (shorn of its biological trappings). At the heart of MacIntyre's argument is a claim that modern culture is characterised by an *emotivist* notion of the self in which any moral attitude is presented as simply an expression of arbitary and subjective preferences. By divorcing the self from its social roles (and their ends) and locating the capacity for moral agency in this disembodied and disembedded self, MacIntyre claims, the Enlightenment ultimately undermines the possibility of generating a rational justification of morality because the Enlightenment philosophers 'share in the project of constructing valid arguments which will move from premises concerning human nature as they understand it to be to conclusions about the authority of moral rules and precepts' (1981: 52). The problem with this project, on MacIntyre's account, is that it fails to recognise that, if we are to have a rational justification of ethics, we require an account of the human *telos*. MacIntyre's reason for making this claim is straightforward, as Stephen Mulhall and Adam Swift make clear with the following example:

> We can move immediately from the knowledge that a knife is blunt and bent to the conclusion that it is a bad knife, and from the fact that it is sharp and evenly balanced to the judgement that it is a good knife, because we know that a knife is a tool for cutting things – we know, in other words, what the purpose or end (the telos) of such a thing is. (1992: 79)

The point of this example is that it elucidates MacIntyre's claim that a notion of *telos* is what enables us to move from 'is' to 'ought': 'this knife is blunt, it ought to be sharp (because its purpose *qua* knife is cutting).' On this account, the Enlightenment project of providing a rational justification of morality fails because in lacking a notion of *telos*, it lacks the element of ethical reflection necessary to move from statements of what 'is' to statements about what 'ought to be'. Consequently, MacIntyre argues that ethical reflection requires

> a threefold scheme in which human nature-as-it-happens-to-be (human nature in its untutored state) is initially discrepant and discordant with the precepts of ethics and needs to be transformed by the instruction of practical reason and experience into human-nature-as-it-could-be-if-it-realized-its-*telos*. (1981: 53)

MacIntyre goes on to argue that the narrative unity of a human life (the story of one's life) acquires its unity precisely through its quest to realise the *telos* of human nature and that the virtues are both the qualities which enable one to engage in this quest and part of its realisation.

This emphasis on the need for a *telos* (or hypergood) is taken up by Charles Taylor in a series of essays[4] and, most recently, in *Sources of the Self*, but whereas MacIntyre thinks that this need necessarily entails a complete commitment to an Aristotelian ethics, Taylor suggests that this need entails simply that any coherent system of ethical reflection requires a particular ontology (an account of what it is to be human), a set of ethical precepts and practices (a notion of practical reasoning), and a substantive conception of the good (a *telos*); he argues that liberal reason, despite its frequent claim to provide merely a *formal* conception of the good, is no exception in this regard. In developing his reflections, Taylor highlights three points which are relevant for our concerns. Firstly, he emphasises the fact that humans are self-interpreting animals, that is, 'beings whose nature and identity is not specifiable independently of their self-interpretations' (Mulhall and Swift, 1992: 107, cf. Taylor, 1985a: 45–76). In other words, part of what makes us what we are is our self-interpretations, and our becoming what we are can be expressed in terms of the narration of the self-interpretations which constitute the history of our selves. Secondly, Taylor argues that recognition of the self-interpreting character of human beings entails recognition of the individual as a member of a linguistic community since our self-interpretations are expressed within, and can only be expressed within, the conceptual resources available within the culture to which we belong. Thirdly, Taylor suggests that if we reflect on the self-interpretive character of human action, we recognise that the meaning of our actions is specifiable in terms of a description of the goals and the affects which our actions involve. Mulhall and Swift gloss this position as follows:

> Our actions are ordinarily characterised by the purpose sought and explained by reference to desires, thoughts, and emotions; but the language by which we describe those goals and feelings or emotions is also that used to describe the meaning of a situation for an agent. The vocabulary defining such meaning ('terrifying', 'attractive') is closely linked with that describing feeling ('fear', 'desire') and that describing goals ('safety', 'possession'). (1992: 107)

The inextricable entwinement of meaning, affect and goal points out to us that a description of the purposes and affects which characterise a piece of human agency provides an account of the meaning of that agency for the agent.

How do these observations on MacIntyre and Taylor enrich our understanding of Nietzsche's concern to construct an ideal? My first claim is that Nietzsche also argues that ethical reflection requires an ontological account, a set of ethical precepts and practices, and a *telos*. In making this claim, I want to suggest that MacIntyre and Taylor may be unintentionally misleading when they present ethics in terms of a threefold schema, since the second element, namely, practical reasoning – ethical precepts and practices – combines two elements, namely, ethical rules and ascetic practices (in a very broad sense); consequently, following Foucault,[5] I will argue that ethics involves four analytically distinct elements. The second claim which I want to make is that this reflection on the character of ethics leads Nietzsche both to reflect on the narrative character of selfhood and to a concern with the narrative unity of a human life. My third claim is that Nietzsche regards human beings as 'self-interpreting' animals and recognises that this claim entails both that individuals are members of a linguistic/cultural community and the entwinement of affect, purpose and meaning. However, I also want to suggest that Taylor's emphasis on self-*interpretation* is somewhat misleading with respect to Nietzsche's account because it conflates interpretation and understanding.[6] The distinction between interpretation and understanding can be brought out by noting that the activity of interpretation involves, for example, giving reasons for acting in a particular way ('I interpreted the rule in this way and not another way because . . .'), while the activity of understanding involves knowing how to follow a rule because one has mastered the relevant practice. As Tully comments:

> Far from being equivalent or essential to understanding, interpretation begins when our conventional self-understandings break down and we do not know how to go on. (1989: 195–6)

For this reason, it may be more appropriate to speak simply of human beings as animals characterised by particular self-understandings (and, under certain circumstances, self-interpretations) and to claim that the being of human beings is not separable from their self-understandings (and self-interpretations). I will explain why I think Nietzsche avoids Taylor's confusion shortly.

To elucidate the first claim, let us begin by reflecting on Nietzsche's account of the activity of the ascetic priest in resolving the initial threat of 'suicidal nihilism'. Firstly, Nietzsche presents the ascetic priest as committed to a particular ontology, namely, a conception of the person characterised by the idea of the transcendental subject. In other words, on Nietzsche's account, the ascetic priest deploys the ontology of *ressentiment* in which the rational self is conceptualised *both* as a disembodied and disembedded self, i.e., distinct from the empirical self (and its irrational bodily and cultural desires) *and* as a subject separable from its beliefs and actions, i.e., the rational self 'possesses' beliefs and 'performs' actions but is not constituted by these beliefs or actions. Nietzsche refers to this position as the thesis of '*soul atomism*' (BGE §12).

Secondly, Nietzsche argues that the ascetic priest solves the problem of nihilism by providing a *telos* for human existence in the form of an idealisation of the ascetic life as the good life which requires the quest to realise one's rational self by overcoming one's irrational bodily and cultural desires. But why does this 'solve' the problem of nihilism in its initial form? And why do we need an *architectonic* goal in terms of which to order and rank our other goals? Let us recall the distinction made between non-existential and existential forms of extensional suffering, that is, the distinction between existensional suffering which is independent of the fact of consciousness (e.g., stubbing my toe) and existensional suffering which is dependent on the fact of consciousness (e.g., worrying about the meaning of life). In the context of this distinction, Nietzsche's point is straightforward: insofar as we are self-interpreting animals who are conscious of our own mortality, we are confronted with the question of the meaning of our existence – the question 'why be?' – and the inability to answer this question results in an existential form of extensional suffering, the *horror vacui*. Consequently, we require an architectonic goal in order to provide a response to the question 'what is the meaning of my life?', where the primacy of this question lies in the fact that whereas the possibility of non-existential forms of extensional suffering is a contingent feature of being human, the possibility of the existential form of extensional suffering is an immanent feature of human existence. In this context, the ascetic priest provides a response to the question 'why be?' by providing a *telos* (the pursuit of the ascetic life) which renders existence meaningful as a way to the 'real world' and, thus, solves (or, more accurately, defers) the problem of nihilism.

Thirdly, Nietzsche claims that the ascetic priest provides a series of ethical precepts and ascetic practices by which to realise one's rational self. The primary rule provided by the ascetic priest, as we've already seen, is to be truthful and, thus, the primary ascetic practice is pursuit of the truth. Given the identification of truth and rationality, the primacy of this precept and practice is hardly surprising because it follows that the more truth we acquire, the more able we are to act rationally. Of course, the dictates of the ascetic priest are not limited to this rule and this practice but this feature does signify the central maxim of the ascetic ideal and is expressed in and through the construction of an Archimedean point, a God's-eye view, from which universal moral rules are legislated.

Thus we can see that Nietzsche recognises that an ontological account, a set of ethical precepts and ascetic practices, and a *telos* are integral features of ethical reflection – but why does this lead him to reflect on the narrative character of selfhood and the narrative unity of the self? To explicate the reasons for this move, which constitutes my second claim, we can begin by reflecting back on the first essay of *On the Genealogy of Morals*. In this essay, one of Nietzsche's implicit concerns is to point out that to experience oneself as valuable (autonomous) requires that one experience one's self as unified. In the case of the noble, the pathos of *social* distance is internalised as the power to command oneself, to impose an organisational unity on one's disparate drives and desires in the context of one's various social roles. Moreover, since the noble does not distinguish between himself and his beliefs or actions, his response to the question 'who are you?' would consist in simply referring to his place in society or recounting the narrative of his life. By contrast, in the case of the slave, the pathos of *social* distance is internalised as the lack of the power to command oneself, to impose order and rank on one's drives and desires. It is in the context of this experience of valuelessness (lack of autonomy) that *ressentiment* becomes creative and engages in an imaginary inversion of the social order of rank in constructing a pathos of *metaphysical* distance in which the slave's experience of the self as lacking unity is resolved by positing an *author* (the subject or soul) who lies behind and produces the disparate elements of the slave's life. In this context, the slave's response to the question 'who are you?' does not consist in telling the narrative of one's life but of naming the author of one's action. Thus, in this essay, Nietzsche constructs an implicit contrast between an understanding of the self in terms of the *narrative unity* of a life and an understanding of the self in terms of the *authorial unity* of a life. Since we know that Nietzsche rejects the subject/object and appearance/reality distinctions which underpin the authorial model of the self, it is not surprising that he adopts the idea of the narrative character of the self and accounts for the narrative unity of the self in terms of an architectonic goal. Of course, this is something in the way of a 'negative' proof of Nietzsche's position; to adopt a more 'positive' approach, we can turn to his comments on becoming what you are.

'*What does your conscience say?* – "You shall become the person you are"' (GS §270): how can we explicate this notion of becoming what you are? There are two related ways of grasping this aphorism and in a sense we can read it as playing with this ambiguity. On the one hand, this phrase may be read as proposing a narrative account of the self in which one is always already becoming what one is simply because the narrative which constitutes 'what one is' is always already ongoing. In this sense, we can read Nietzsche's aphorism as describing the *formal* character of selfhood disclosed to us by our *intellectual* conscience.[7] On the other hand, this aphorism may also be read as an injunction to realise one's potentiality (*telos*) and as a warning that one is responsible for becoming what one is (i.e., if I become a lazy slob, I am responsible for becoming what I am because in not, for example, pushing myself to work and be tidy, I reveal what I am). In this sense, Nietzsche's remark reveals to us the *teleological* character of selfhood disclosed to us by our *ethical* conscience. Thus, with a tight economy of language, Nietzsche exhibits his commitment both to a narrative account of the self and to an idea of the narrative unity of the self as provided by a commitment to a *telos*.

To conclude these preliminary reflections on why Nietzsche engages in the activity of constructing an ideal, we can reflect at some length on my third claim, namely, that Nietzsche recognises both that human beings are animals whose being is not separable from their self-understandings (and self-interpretations when self-understandings break down) and the consequences of this claim. To initiate this discussion, let us recall that Nietzsche characterises perspectives as 'grounded' in, and sustained by, particular ways of acting in the world. While he characterises the emergence of a perspective (for example, slave morality) as an interpretation of the world, Nietzsche's suggestion is that we only engage in interpretive activity when our self-understandings cease to enable our experience of ourselves as meaningful subjects and autonomous agents; the rest of the time we simply get on with going about our practices. Indeed, it is precisely because our self-understandings have broken down in modernity that Nietzsche engages in the interpretive activity of genealogy; unless our paradigmatic understanding of ourselves has ceased to hold good, we have no reason to engage in this activity. But does Nietzsche accept the consequences of this understanding of human beings? On the one hand, to establish that Nietzsche recognises that the individual must be a member of a linguistic community, we need merely note that Nietzsche accounts for the development of consciousness in terms of the development of language, which he ties to the development of community (GS §354). On the other hand, to ground the claim that Nietzsche recognises that affect and purpose are tied to meaning, we need simply refer to his account of willing, in which he specifies 'willing' as involving three elements. The first two elements are affectivity and purpose, that is, willing involves emotions and goals (BGE §19); consequently, Nietzsche would agree with Taylor that the meaning of an action for the actor involves a description of the affective and purposive elements of that activity.

However, Nietzsche also invokes a third element engaged in willing, namely, the feeling of power (or lack of power) which discloses itself in the successful (or unsuccessful) performance of an action. In other words, Nietzsche claims that an integral part of willing is agency's experience of itself as autonomous (powerful) agency, and he summarises the significance of this element when he comments:

> What is good? – All that heightens the feeling of power, the will to power, power itself in man.
>   What is bad? – All that proceeds from weakness.
>   What is happiness? – The feeling that power *increases* – that a resistance is overcome. (AC §2)

It is fairly easier to see what Nietzsche is attempting to draw out with this additional claim by giving an example. Suppose that I feel uncomfortable with my weight (for example, I am worried by my shortness of breath after mild exercise) and aim to go on a diet, but, after a few days, I can't resist tucking in to a large lunch of bacon, eggs, sausage and chips – and that is the end of my diet. In the context of this example of weakness of will, it seems reasonable to say that giving an account of the meaning of an action (dieting) *qua* self does not involve simply describing the affective dispositions (a sense of dis-ease and worry) and the *telos* (losing weight and, thus, better health) but also whether or not the actor is successful in achieving his or her goal (feeling of power). What is revealed in this discussion is, of course, Nietzsche's hypothesis of 'will to power' as an ontological account of the character of human agency and it is in the context of this account that Nietzsche argues that 'in the real world it is only a question of *strong* and *weak* wills' (BGE §21) as opposed to 'free' and 'unfree' wills. It is this emphasis on the feeling of power which leads Nietzsche to his account of autonomy as self-overcoming, that is, ethical labour on the self directed towards self-mastery, since it is in overcoming those aspects of ourselves which constrain our mastery of ourselves that we experience the feeling of power.

To conclude this section then, let us summarise the claims established. Firstly, it has been argued that, for Nietzsche, any ethical perspective must involve an ontological account of human agency, a set of ethical precepts and ascetic practices, and a *telos*. For Nietzsche, more specifically, the necessity of a *telos* is grounded in his account of willing and his hypothesis of will to power which specify this necessity in terms of the need of human beings to experience themselves as meaningful and autonomous. A *telos* provides an 'orientation' in existential-ethical space. The appropriateness of this space-analogue (which I borrow from Charles Taylor) for thinking about Nietzsche's reflections on the necessity of ideals can be drawn out by reflecting on the phrase 'a sense of direction' which we use both to refer to the capacity to orient oneself in space and to refer to the capacity to exhibit purpose with respect to the character of one's life. In this context, we can note in passing the following remark which Nietzsche offers in *Twilight of the Idols*: 'Formula for my happiness: a Yes, a No, a straight line, a *goal*.' (TI 'Maxims and Arrows' §44, also AC §1). Secondly, we have noted that this position leads Nietzsche to elaborate a narrative model of the self and to claim that the narrative unity of the self is achieved through the pursuit of an architectonic goal or *telos*. Thirdly, we have claimed that this account commits Nietzsche to an understanding of ethical activity in terms of 'self-overcoming', that is, the ongoing quest to realise one's *telos*.

Conclusion

In this chapter, we have examined Nietzsche's account of modernity as a condition characterised by the development of nihilism and decadence by attending to the three stages which Nietzsche assigns to the development of nihilism and juxtaposing these with his critical reflections on truth. The recognition that the *telos* of nihilism is the will to nothingness led us to examine Nietzsche's reasons for regarding the articulation of a counter-ideal as a necessary task for any contemporary ethical philosophy. At this juncture, having established why Nietzsche must provide a counter-ideal to the ascetic ideal, we can turn to the ideal which he elaborates and the character of the ethical schema of which it is the *telos*.

Notes

1 For a brilliant discussion of Kant's 'proof' of God's existence in the context of his philosophy, see Yovel (1980). I emphasise the point of the 'reality' of the noumenal realm against the 'dual aspect' interpretation of Kant offered by, for example, Allison (1983). For a critique of this type of interpretation, see Guyer (1987).

2 For a good account of Hegel and his relation to Christianity, see Houlgate (1991).

3 Conway regards this will to nothingness as the purest expression of the ascetic ideal; however, I would suggest that it marks the moment of the abolition of the ascetic ideal for the reasons stated.

4. These essays are collected in Taylor's *Philosophical Papers*. See in particular the essays 'Self-Interpreting Animals', 'The Concept of a Person', 'What is Wrong with Negative Liberty?' and 'The Diversity of Goods'.

5 These four elements correspond to Aristotle's four causes and to the four aspects highlighted by Foucault in his reflections on ethics, see *The Use of Pleasure* (1985).

6 See Tully (1989) for a brilliant discussion of this point.

7 Nietzsche has quite a lot to say about intellectual conscience, cf., for example, GS §§2 and 335.

5

Modernity, Ethics and Counter-Ideals
Amor Fati, Eternal Recurrence and the Overman

The problem I raise here is not what ought to succeed mankind in the sequence of species (– the human being is an *end* –); but what type of human being one ought to *breed*, ought to *will*, as more valuable, more worthy of life, more certain of the future. (AC §3)

At the same time as Nietzsche addresses modernity as nihilism and decadence, he also addresses modernity as the condition of possibility for a particular range of human types. Nietzsche presents his understanding of the possibilities for being human immanent within modern culture through the dramatic contrast of two ideal-typical figures which mark the limits of the range of possible types: the dystopian figure of the *Last Man* and the utopian figure of the *Overman*. As Laurence Lampert astutely comments: 'Last man and superman [i.e., Overman] represent the two extremes made possible by the malleability of man, "the as yet undetermined animal"' (1986: 24). This chapter will follow on from Nietzsche's account of modernity as *nihilism* and as *decadence* in which human beings are characterised by the affective dispositions of *nausea* and *pity* in order to show how Nietzsche seeks to articulate the overcoming of modernity by providing the conceptual resources (the doctrine of *eternal recurrence*) and communicating the affective dispositions (*heroism* and *irony*) necessary to such a task. In particular I will argue that through the contrasting figures of the *Last Man* (as the completion of modernity) and the *Overman* (as the overcoming of modernity) Nietzsche attempts to seduce his readers into adopting his perspective by providing a counter-ideal to the ascetic ideal in which the will to nothingness is displaced by the will to *amor fati*.

Amor Fati and the Overman

A consequence of Nietzsche's understanding of human beings as members of a linguistic community, a form of life, is that the construction of an ideal is necessarily disclosed in terms of the cultural resources of that community. In the context of his genealogical reflections on modern culture, Nietzsche argues that two distinct ideals – the Overman and the Last Man – can be formulated in modern culture which are consonant with both the collapse of the appearance/reality distinction and the capacities of modern individuals. In this section, I will focus on Nietzsche's recommendation of *amor fati* and the Overman as a counter-ideal and, in the next section, I will address the idea of eternal recurrence as the ethical rule appropriate to this *telos*. In the following two sections, I will seek to specify the characteristics which Nietzsche assigns to the Last Man, before going on to raise the question of the capacities of modern man to pursue these ideals.

Let us start, perhaps slightly obliquely, with a section from *The Gay Science* entitled 'Elevated Moods':

> It seems to me that most people simply do not believe in elevated moods, unless these last for moments only or at most a quarter of an hour – except for those few who know at first hand the longer duration of elevated feelings. But to be a human being with one elevated feeling – to be a single great mood incarnate – that has hitherto been a mere dream and a delightful possibility; as yet history does not offer us any certain examples. Nevertheless history might one day give birth to such people, too – once a great many favorable preconditions have been created and determined that even the dice throws of the luckiest chance could not bring together today. What has so far entered our souls only now and then as an exception that makes us shudder, might perhaps be the usual state for these future souls. (GS §288)

Despite the apparent pessimism expressed in this passage, my suggestion is that Nietzsche is concerned to facilitate the cultural conditions of possibility of such a future people and that he focuses on the affective disposition or mood which he calls *amor fati* and which is given incarnate form in the figure of the Overman.

We can begin by recalling that Nietzsche's account of the ascetic ideal – and his central objection to it – focuses on its devaluation of this-worldly existence; by contrast to the noble who affirms the sensuous relationship between self and world, the slave rejects this world in the name of a metaphysical world. Consequently, Nietzsche's product of reconstituting noble culture in the context of the deconstruction of metaphysics begins with the recognition that the ideal which he formulates must involve an affirmation of our sensuous this-worldly existence. It is at this juncture that Nietzsche's reflections on *amor fati* (love of fate) become significant:

> My formula for greatness in a human being is *amor fati*: that one wants nothing to be different, not forward, not backward, not in all eternity. Not merely bear what is necessary, still less conceal it – all idealism is mendaciousness in the face of what is necessary – but *love* it. (EH 'Why I Am So Clever' §10)

And, on a more personal note:

> I want to learn more and more to see as beautiful what is necessary in things; then I shall be one of those who make things beautiful. *Amor fati*: let that be my love henceforth! . . . And all in all and on the whole: some day I wish to be only a Yes-sayer. (GS §276)

But what is the experiential character of *amor fati* as an affective disposition? And what is the logical character of the concept of *amor fati*? What is the relationship between *amor fati*, eternal recurrence and the

Overman? To explicate Nietzsche's notion of *amor fati*, we need to address these questions, and this will be my task in the remainder of this section and the following section.

In specifying the experiential character of *amor fati*, Nietzsche seems to have in my mind that form of experience which we might term 'ecstatic epiphanies', moments of utter wonder and overflowing joy, moments of sublime rapture such as the moment when Nietzsche was struck by the revelation of the thought of eternal recurrence – 'six thousand feet beyond man and time' (EH 'Thus Spoke Zarathustra' §1): 'Immortal is the moment when I produced the recurrence. . . . For the sake of this moment I *endure* the recurrence' (cited in Thiele, 1990: 204). I think that it is relatively straightforward to depict the type of experience to which Nietzsche is referring by giving a few examples.

1   Lying in the grass on a summer's day, I am suddenly overwhelmed by a feeling of oneness with nature in which I 'see' myself as part of a shimmering, vibrant whole which makes my soul resonate, laugh and sing. In this moment, melancholy is stripped from my being and redeemed in wonder and joy.

2   Writing this book, I am suddenly grasped by a sense of utter clarity in which thought, being and word processor become continuous. I am simultaneously at one with this process and separate from it, watching myself as part of it. In this moment, all the blocks, frustrations and despair fall away like dead leaves and life breathes through me.

3   Playing tennis, I am caught in a sense of complete certainty that I can do no wrong and play without the need for conscious reflection on what I'm doing. The court, racket, balls and I are all one, flowing into and through each other, and I can somehow 'see' myself in this condition – knowing what to do without needing to reflect on it. All the days when the racket felt like an alien piece of wood are forgotten and redeemed in a moment of utter lightness of being.

While these elevated moods may be fairly commonplace in the sense that I suspect that everyone experiences such states at one time or another (often perhaps mistaking them for the presence of divinity), they are unfortunately also fleeting (at least in my experience – and I will return to this feature shortly), but I think that we can draw out certain features from these examples which help to illuminate what Nietzsche is gesturing towards.

Firstly, each of these examples points to the 'paradoxical' quality of this experiential state in which co-exist simultaneously a sense of the dissolution of subjectivity in an experience of 'oneness' and a sense of the presence of subjectivity in recognising and watching its own dissolution. We might express this paradox by saying that I experience the dissolution of subjectivity as an *actor* but that I experience the presence of subjectivity as a *spectator*. (As an aside, it is worth noting in this context that this distinction between unity and separation, dissolution and individuation, parallels Nietzsche's distinction between the *Dionysian* and the *Apollonian* in his first published book *The Birth of Tragedy*, in which he attributes 'Greek cheerfulness' to this type of experience as it is generated by Attic tragedy.) The second point we can develop from these examples can be specified by my reference to them as 'moments of wonder and joy', insofar as I would suggest that 'wonder' refers to our experience as *spectator* and 'joy' to our experience as *actor*. My suggestion is that our feeling of wonder is tied to a sense of *distance*, while our feeling of joy is tied to a sense of *passion* or erotic engagement. A third feature which can be drawn from these examples concerns the *redemptive* power of such moments of love of life, insofar as it seems to be a feature of these moments that we experience them as both a *liberation* from emotional states such as nausea and pity (to pick two random examples!) *and* as a *justification* of our past experience of these states. Thus, in a sense, we can suggest that the experience of *amor fati* implicitly involves the claim that one would suffer all the frustration, despair, etc., again as a condition of possibility of this rapturous moment.

These three features might seem pretty much to exhaust the elements of these examples cited, but I'd like to introduce a fourth feature which refers specifically to our second and third examples. The crucial difference between the first example and the other two is that while they all refer to human activities, the second and third examples refer to activities which are cultural practices involving specific skills.[1] To set out my claim, let us consider a comment by Nietzsche on *mastery*: 'One has attained mastery when one neither goes wrong *nor hesitates* in the performance' (D §537). If we recall the 'tennis' example cited above, it is notable that the features of the state described are captured by the sense that 'one can do no wrong' and has no need of 'conscious reflection' – 'knowing what to do without needing to think about it'. Indeed, it is a characteristic of such moods that as soon as something does go wrong or one is caught in hesitation, the mood is broken. This point suggests that the frequency and sustainability of such moments of *amor fati* is dependent on one's mastery of the activity in which one is engaged: to experience one's engagement in an activity as 'pure poetry' requires some degree of mastery of the activity (where our criteria of mastery are publicly constituted). Thus, for example, I suspect that – given his sublime genius – John McEnroe's experience of such moments is incomparably more regular and sustained than my rather infrequent and extremely fleeting experience of such moments *qua* the activity of tennis. We can confirm this relationship from the other direction by adducing a further example: having absolutely no mastery of dance entails that when I am engaged in this activity, I have to think about what I'm doing and, consequently, I am consumed with hesitation and a sense that what I'm doing is probably all wrong; whereas my partner surrenders herself to the music, I am utterly at sea and never experience (or expect to experience) moments of the type under discussion. The significance of this relationship between mastery and *amor fati* emerges if we consider that the tennis example, for instance, refers us to an affirmation of the relationship of self and world *qua* self as tennis player. The question which arises from this consideration is this: what would be required to affirm the relationship of self and world *qua* self as self, that is, to affirm one's self not simply with respect to one activity but with respect to the totality of one's activities? The obvious answer to this question, which is also the one that Nietzsche gives, is 'self-mastery', and we will illustrate this answer shortly.

At this stage, having sketched an understanding of *amor fati* as a mode of experience, we can turn to reflect on the conceptual character of *amor fati* within the context of Nietzsche's work. Let us begin by noting that *amor fati* represents love of life because Nietzsche posits the fateful character of existence. This identification is not the product of the philosophical claim that there is no freedom, only determination (not least because the freedom/determination antinomy is tied to the metaphysical realist position which Nietzsche rejects); rather it is an expression of the idea of becoming what one is (applied to both the individual and the cultural community). This point becomes clear if we note the relationship between the concepts 'fate' and 'character'.

Nietzsche's argument is that my actions express (and further constitute) my character (i.e., the narrative that is my self); thus, if I choose an action after long deliberation, both the chosen action and the process of deliberation are expressions of my character at this time, which is itself constituted by the previous actions and reflections which make up the narrative history of my self. (But perhaps this way of putting this point makes it sound as though 'becoming what one is' is a solitary activity; if given, this impression would be misleading because Nietzsche is in no way denying that my actions and reflections take place in the context of my relations with both my self and others, that is, within a dialogic context of intersubjective relations.) However, it might be objected to this expression of the notion of character that, in any given context, a number of different actions could express my character. This is a reasonable claim but it does not undermine Nietzsche's argument since he can simply respond that the fact that I do act in one way and not another, that I act on the basis of one evaluation and not another, illuminates the ranking of the different (perhaps contradictory) features of my character: 'A human being's evaluations betray something of the *structure* of his soul' (BGE §268).

Consider for a moment our response to someone we know who acts in an unexpected way, who acts 'out of character'; typically, in such cases, we seek reasons – 'She's not herself at the moment because . . .' – and if we can't find reasons (and/or the reasons offered by the person concerned don't seem adequate), we are likely to think that our assessment of their character is mistaken – 'She has more of a temper than I thought' (consider further the identical form of one's response to unexpected actions by oneself). These considerations seem to support Nietzsche's claims about character and, thus, his argument that one is fated to act as one does because how one acts is what one is. Human beings are pieces of fate. Thus, to love one's own fate is to love one's life, to affirm the relationship of self and world.

However, in the same way that we talk about the character of a person, we also talk about the character of a culture, of humanity and of the world.

Indeed, the piece of fate that I am is a part of the piece of fate that my culture is, which is part of the piece of fate that is humanity, which is, in turn, part of the fate of the world.[2] In other words, my narrative is part of the narrative of my culture, which is part of the narrative of humanity, which is part of the narrative of the world. Consequently, when Nietzsche talks about love of fate, we may suggest that he is not simply recommending love of one's own fate but love of the fate of one's culture, of humanity and of the world. A more precise way of putting this point would be to say that Nietzsche is arguing that the *total* love of one's fate requires the love of the *totality* of fate. This is not to say that one cannot love one's fate to different degrees, but simply to argue that the *highest* affirmation of the relationship of self and world involves the love of the fate of the world. Another way of putting this point is simply to say that *amor fati* represents our *maximal* possible feeling of power. To reflect on this claim, recall Nietzsche's characterisation of happiness as the feeling of the increase in power which attends the overcoming of resistances. In the context of this notion of happiness, love of the totality of fate reveals itself as the overcoming of all resistances to affirmation and, thus, as the maximal feeling of power.

Thus far, then, we have examined the experiential and conceptual aspects of Nietzsche's recommendation of *amor fati*, but what is the relationship between *amor fati* and the Overman? This relationship has already been gestured to by the passage on 'Elevated Moods' and is neatly expressed by Leslie Paul Thiele: '*Amor fati* is the disposition of the Overman' (1990: 200). Nietzsche gives lyrical expression to his vision of the Overman in the following passage, which is worth quoting at length:

> Anyone who manages to experience the history of humanity as a whole as *his own history* will feel in an enormously generalized way all the grief of an invalid who thinks of health, of an old man who thinks of the dreams of his youth, of a lover deprived of his beloved, of the martyr whose ideal is perishing, of the hero on the evening after a battle that has decided nothing but brought him wounds and the loss of his friend. But if one endured, if one *could* endure the immense sum of this grief of all kinds while yet being the hero who, as the second day of battle breaks, welcomes the dawn and his fortune, being a person whose horizon encompasses thousands of years past and future, being the heir of all the nobility of all past spirit – an heir with a sense of obligation, the most aristocratic of old nobles and at the same time the first of a new nobility – the like of which no age has yet seen or dreamed of; if one could burden one's soul with all of this – the oldest, the newest, losses, hopes, conquests, and the victories of humanity; if one could finally contain all this in one soul and crowd it into a single feeling – this would have to result in a happiness that humanity has not known so far: the laughter of a god full of power and love, full of tears and laughter, a happiness that, like the sun in the evening, continually bestows its inexhaustible riches, pouring them into the sea, feeling richest, as the sun does, only when even the poorest fisherman is still rowing with golden oars! This godlike feeling would then be called – humaneness. (GS §337)

In other words, the Overman is the being who can truthfully affirm the fate of the world and experiences in that affirmation of the maximal feeling of overflowing power. It is this affirmation that is the abysmal thought with which Zarathustra struggles for so long and finally comes to terms with at the end of part three of *Thus Spoke Zarathustra* in the section entitled 'The Seven Seals (or: the Song of Yes and Amen)' wherein Zarathustra's song, which marks his affirmation, echoes the disposition of the passage just cited in its refrain '*For I love you, O eternity!*'

However, given the relationship which I have claimed exists between *amor fati* and self-mastery, we can say more about the character of the Overman by suggesting that this figure represents a *perfectionist* ideal of self-mastery. This claim can be at least partially supported by Nietzsche's recommendation of self-mastery in the following passage, in which it is presented in terms of making oneself a work of art:

> *One thing is needful*: To 'give style' to one's character – a great and rare art! It is practiced by those who survey all the strengths and weaknesses of their nature and then fit them into an artistic plan until every one of them appears as art and reason and even weaknesses delight the eye. . . . In the end, when the work is finished, it becomes evident how the constraint of a single taste governed and formed everything large and small. Whether this taste was good or bad is less important than one might suppose, if only it was a single taste! (GS §290)

This passage suggests that becoming what one is can be likened to the process of creating a work of art in which the achievement of self-mastery is revealed as the constraint of style given content through a single taste. Our discussion of eternal recurrence will support and develop this relation to self-mastery, but before we move to this crucial discussion, we should note a possible line of objection to Nietzsche's recommendation of *amor fati*. Such an objection might proceed thus:

> In the context of twentieth-century history (let alone world history), isn't this idea of loving fate *obscene*? How can Nietzsche seriously recommend an ideal which seems to require the affirmation of, for example, the Holocaust? Moreover, in the context of the re-emergence of fascism and neo-Nazism in Europe (America, of course, has its own home-grown Christian varieties), isn't it utterly irresponsible (not to say abhorrent) to propagate the ideas of such a thinker?

These are serious questions and, while I think they are based on a misunderstanding of what Nietzsche means by 'affirmation' and 'love of fate', we should recognise the necessity of addressing these concerns. In order to take up this task, and to support earlier claims in this section, let us turn to Nietzsche's notion of eternal recurrence.

The Thought of Eternal Recurrence

There seems little doubt that Nietzsche regarded the thought of eternal recurrence as the linchpin of his mature thinking; however, there is considerable disagreement among Nietzsche scholars as to the form and function of this thought.[3] Typically such disagreements focus on the relationship between the ideas of will to power, eternal recurrence and the Overman which are often held to be incompatible in some way or other.[4] In this context, the need to situate the concept of eternal recurrence with respect to the concepts of will to power and the Overman becomes an important concern for any attempt to do justice to Nietzsche's thought; indeed, it was for this reason that I felt constrained to take up the question of the necessity of a counter-ideal by addressing the question of how Nietzsche thinks about the form of ethical reflection. It will be recalled that one of our conclusions was that, for Nietzsche, ethical reflection entails the provision of an ontological account of human beings, a set of ethical precepts and ascetic practices, and a *telos*. In this context, let me propose the following schema:

1 Ontological account: the thesis of will to power.
2 Ethical precept: the 'rule' of eternal recurrence.
3 Ascetic practices: self-overcoming – any form of artistic work on the style of one's character, the narrative unity of the self, consonant with the 'rule' of eternal recurrence; the practical cultivation of ethical virtues.
4 *Telos*: the Overman and *amor fati*.

In a sense, we have already explored arguments for the first and fourth dimensions of the schema but, in order to tie them into the second and third dimensions, I will spend this section arguing for the cogency of this way of thinking about the central concepts in Nietzsche's philosophy by focusing on the idea of eternal recurrence.

Let us begin by specifying the tasks involved in this project. Firstly, it is necessary to set out the formal character of eternal recurrence and its relationship to *amor fati*. Secondly, we need to develop the claim that eternal recurrence and *amor fati* are tied to self-mastery. This will involve clarifying the claim that *amor fati* represents our maximal experience of will to power. Thirdly, we must fulfil our commitment to explaining the sense of 'affirmation' revealed in this idea. We will leave the question of whether or not modern individuals have the capacity to pursue the ideal of the Overman through the thought of eternal recurrence until after our discussion of the Last Man.

What kind of thought is the thought of eternal recurrence? How does it relate to *amor fati*? Consider the following passage:

> *The greatest weight* – What, if some day or night, a demon were to steal after you into your loneliest loneliness and say to you: 'This life as you now live it and have lived it, you will have to live once more and innumerable times more; and there will be nothing new in it, but every pain and every joy and every thought and sigh and everything unutterably small or great in your life will have to return to you, all in the same succession and sequence – even this spider and this moonlight between the trees, and even this moment and I myself. The eternal hourglass of existence is turned upside down again and again, and you with it, speck of dust!'
>
> Would you not throw yourself down and gnash your teeth and curse the demon who spoke thus? Or have you once experienced a tremendous moment when you would have answered him: 'You are a god and never have I heard anything more divine.' If this thought gained possession of you, it would change you as you are or perhaps crush you. The question in each and everything, 'Do you desire this once more and innumerable times more?' would lie upon your actions as the

greatest weight. Or how well disposed would you have to become to yourself and to life *to crave nothing more fervently* than this ultimate confirmation and seal? (GS §341)

This passage is characterised by a lyrical simplicity of expression which conceals the complexity of its character. Let us begin by noting that this passage does not disclose a *cosmological* thesis but poses a *hypothetical* question: can you affirm (i.e., will) the eternal recurrence of your life? Nietzsche's reference to 'a tremendous moment' when one could make such an affirmation directs us to the moments of *amor fati* already discussed because we experience such moments as a *justification* or *redemption* of our being what we are (with all that this entails). In this context, we can grasp the relation of eternal recurrence to *amor fati* in this passage in a twofold sense. Firstly, the thought of eternal recurrence embodies the conceptual structure of *amor fati* in drawing our attention to the fact that to affirm the fleeting moments of the experience of *amor fati* entails not only affirming all the moments of one's life prior to this experience and as such constitutive of its possibility but also affirming the *necessity* (eternal recurrence) of one's being what one is. Secondly, the thought of eternal recurrence acts as a test of our *present* capacity to love fate, to embrace necessity of our being what we are, by posing the question 'Do you desire this once more and innumerable times more?' If we reflect on these two aspects of the thought of eternal recurrence, we can note that insofar as it reproduces the conceptual structure of the experience of *amor fati*, so too the experiential structure of the affirmation of eternal recurrence reveals itself as the experience of *amor fati*; it is this which makes the thought of eternal recurrence a test of one's capacity to love fate. In other words, our capacity to experience *amor fati* is tied to our capacity to affirm the thought of eternal recurrence; to affirm this thought truthfully is to experience *amor fati*.

Of course, to experience a moment in which one can affirm the thought of eternal recurrence is not to say that one can go on affirming this thought; such moments are all too fleeting. But insofar as we can both identify the affirmation of the thought of eternal recurrence with the experience of *amor fati* and recognise the *telos* of human existence in the ideal of a human being who is *amor fati* incarnate (the Overman), then the thought of eternal recurrence acts as an ethical imperative: 'act always according to that maxim which you can at the same time will as eternally recurring.' We can give this alternate expression by referring to the thought of eternal recurrence as the rule of an *eroticised asceticism*: 'erotic' because it does not abstract from the embodied and embedded character of human agency, and 'ascetic' because it places a purely formal constraint on the expression of our erotic nature, it channels the activity of willing towards the formal architectonic goal of the Overman. In this sense, the thought of eternal recurrence acts both as a test of our *present* capacity to love fate and as a ethical rule for our *future* actions – but what of our past actions? Does the thought of eternal recurrence have any significance here?

Consider the following passage from *Thus Spoke Zarathustra*, in which Zarathustra comments on the relationship between willing and the past:

> Will – that is what the liberator and bringer of joy is called: thus I have taught you, my friends! But now learn this as well: The will itself is still a prisoner.
>
> Willing liberates: but what it is that fastens in fetters even the liberator?
>
> 'It was': that is what the will's teeth-gnashing and most lonely affliction is called. Powerless against that which has been done, the will is the angry spectator of things past.
>
> The will cannot will backwards; that it cannot break time and time's desire – that is the will's most lonely affliction. (Z 'Of Redemption')

It is worth noting that the image of the will's 'teeth-gnashing' in Zarathustra's remarks recalls Nietzsche's phrase 'Would you not throw yourself down and *gnash your teeth* and curse the demon who spoke thus? (GS §341, my italics) from the presentation of eternal recurrence discussed above. Whatever we make of this similarity of expression, it seems clear that Zarathustra is drawing our attention to the fact that past actions and events have the character of *necessity*; however much we feel ashamed of our past actions and, thus, regret them, we cannot change either these actions or the fact that they are partially constitutive of what we are. Thus we may imagine that, confronted by the thought of eternal recurrence, one might be overwhelmed with nausea and pity – nausea because we regret these actions and pity because we recognise that we cannot change them. In such an all too imaginable situation, it seems likely one would feel crushed by the thought of eternal recurrence. But does the feeling of shame which attends our recognition of the ignoble character of certain of our actions have a *necessary* connection with the feeling of regret? In a remark from his 'positivist' period, Nietzsche comments:

> *Remorse* – Never give way to remorse, but immediately say to yourself: that would merely mean adding a second stupidity to the first. – If you have done harm, see how you can do good. (WS §323)

It is in this respect that I think that the thought of eternal recurrence is significant for past actions which one cannot in good conscience affirm, because in forcing us to confront the fact that our shameful past actions are constitutive of what we are, it reveals a way to redeem these actions by transforming them into motivational resources for overcoming our shame by *becoming* what we are through the pursuit of *amor fati*, that is, submission to the rule of eternal recurrence in its prospective role as ethical imperative. In other words, if the thought of eternal recurrence gains possession of us, we may experience this possession as feeling crushed (because we are ashamed of many of our past actions), yet precisely because this 'feeling crushed' is a feeling of a *decrease of power*, we are motivated to overcome this feeling and we recognise that we can overcome it by using it as an affective resource for performing noble actions in the future.

What is going on in this breaking of the connection between shame and regret? If we return to the example of my diet, which was deployed in our discussion of the necessity of a counter-ideal, we can see that the thought of eternal recurrence heightens my feeling of shame at failing to achieve my goal (my lack of self-mastery) by asking me to contemplate the eternal recurrence of this failure and the attendant feeling of shame. In the face of this abysmal prospect, I am motivated to overcome (and thus redeem) my failure by using my shame as a resource to embark on a new diet and to succeed in achieving my goal of weight-loss in the full recognition that my desire for sausage, bacon, egg and chips may overwhelm me once again. In this way, my feelings of *nausea* ('I regret failing. God, I'm feeble') and *pity* ('I wish I could change my past failure – what I am – but I know that I can't') are transformed into the dispositions of *heroism* which attends my embarkation on a new diet ('I am determined to succeed this time and redeem my past failure!') and *ironic cheerfulness* (or self-parody) which attends my recognition that, being what I am, I may fail again ('Once more unto the diet, dear friends . . .').

Having sketched the character of the thought of eternal recurrence and its relationship to *amor fati* by specifying it as the ethical rule of an eroticised ascetism, we can turn to the topics of self-mastery and will to power. Recalling Nietzsche's characterisation of self-mastery in terms of giving style to one's character, we can now see that the thought of eternal recurrence operates for Nietzsche as the law of stylistic constraint which constitutes self-mastery. Notably, it is in respect of this self-mastery that Nietzsche expresses his admiration for Goethe in a revealing passage:

> [Goethe] did not sever himself from life, he placed himself within it; nothing could discourage him and he took as much as possible upon himself, above himself, within himself. What he aspired to was *totality*; he strove against the separation of reason, sensuality, feeling, will . . .; he disciplined himself to a whole, he *created* himself. . . . A spirit thus *emancipated* stands in the midst of the universe with a joyful and trusting fatalism, in the *faith* that only what is separate and individual may be rejected, that in the totality everything is redeemed and affirmed – *he no longer denies*. (TI 'Expeditions of an Untimely Man' §49)

On the evidence of this passage, Nietzsche regards Goethe as the best exemplar of the Overman that Europe has produced. Here self-mastery reveals itself as the maximal feeling of power since it denotes the overcoming of all resistances in the affirmation of the totality of what is: 'Yes and Amen!'[5]

Yet we should also note another feature of the activity of giving style to one's character (achieving self-mastery), namely, that Nietzsche is not concerned with specifying what the content of one's character *ought* to be, that is, the *taste* which guides one's stylistic activity. In other words, the thought of eternal recurrence is not concerned with *what* is affirmed, only with submission to this law of affirmation. This point has been drawn out by Keith Ansell-Pearson through a comparison of Nietzsche's thought of eternal recurrence with Kant's categorical imperative:

> Like the categorical imperative, the thought of eternal recurrence has a universal character or form, but unlike the categorical imperative, it does not posit a universal content. However, it might be argued in response that the categorical

imperative too is a purely formal doctrine, for it has no determinate content. But the key point is that, although the categorical imperative is indeed formalistic, its willing does *presuppose* that the actions the autonomous will is to will are universal in content: always will in such a way that the maxims of your actions are capable of being universalized into universal natural laws. The eternal return, however, provides the form of universality in the act of returning, whereas what returns (the actual content) and is willed to be returned cannot be universal, since each life (each becoming) is unique. (Ansell-Pearson, 1991: 198)

The importance of this point is that it raises the question of whether or not it is appropriate to describe the thought of eternal recurrence as an *ethical* imperative since it is unclear if it has any ethical content. Another way of putting this point would be to ask if self-mastery can properly be regarded as an ethical (hyper)good. Couldn't I quite consistently act in ways which most people would find morally abhorrent while willing the eternal recurrence of these acts? Appealing to will to power will not help us here since this ontological thesis is quite consistent with obtaining a feeling of power by torturing others (recall the ancient noble); while appealing to *amor fati* or the figure of the Overman just restates the problem since I have argued that these notions are formulations of self-mastery and don't entail anything about the content of the self which is mastered. So in what sense, if any, does Nietzsche's notion of eternal recurrence involve an ethics?

Perhaps we can get some hints on this topic by noting the characteristics of the Kantian – God's-eye view – position which Nietzsche attacks, namely, impartiality and universalisability. With respect to impartiality, recall Nietzsche's comments on its epistemic correlate, namely, objectivity, which he argues should be 'understood not as "contemplation without interest" (which is a nonsensical absurdity), but as the ability *to control* one's Pro and Con' (GM III §12). On this analogy, impartiality is tied to self-mastery and means being able to consider 'a *variety* of perspectives and affective interpretations' in coming to an ethical judgement consonant with our being able to will its eternal recurrence. Thus, for example, if my mother and a great scientist are trapped in a burning lift and I can only get one of them out before they both die,[6] I can consider and weigh up a variety of perspectives against each other such as that of family loyalty and love versus utility to humanity. All that the law of eternal recurrence states is a rule which enables one to reflect on which evaluation one could will as eternally recurring, which evaluation one experiences under the aegis of this rule as *necessity*. Asked why I saved my mother or the great scientist, I respond 'Because I had to', and asked to expand on this statement, I respond 'Because that is what I am. I could not have lived with myself if I had not acted in this way.' We can note that this example reveals the reason for Nietzsche's attack on universality, namely, I cannot reasonably demand (as Kant's categorical imperative would have us do) that all persons should act in the way that I acted because other people may be committed to different evaluations (i.e., have different characters) which they experience as necessity under the aegis of eternal recurrence. This is Nietzsche's point when he comments:

A word against Kant as a *moralist*. A virtue has to be *our* invention, *our* most personal defence and necessity: in any other sense it is merely a danger. (AC §11)

Reflecting on this critique of Kant's notions of impartiality (as impersonal neutrality) and universality (as applying to the content of moral action), we can suggest that Nietzsche's thought of eternal recurrence does seem to involve at least one virtue which is tied to self-mastery, namely, *integrity*. Indeed, this point seems intuitively obvious if we recall that we use 'personal integrity' to refer to someone's life possessing a coherence and 'ethical integrity' to refer to someone's life exhibiting a coherence in terms of his or her substantive ethical commitments.[7]

To elucidate this point, let us turn once more to my recurring diet. What is the nature of the commitment I make when I decide to go on a diet? It seems reasonable to characterise this commitment as a *promise* which I make to myself, and if I say to other people 'I promise to stay on my diet', keeping this promise to others is predicated on keeping my promise to myself. Insofar as I stay on my diet, I keep my promise to myself, and we refer to this keeping of promises to oneself as 'personal integrity'; however, we also refer to my staying on my diet, my overcoming of my desire for fattening, as 'self-mastery'. We should note that this example helps draw out the point that a feature of integrity is that it involves self-mastery in the sense of overcoming resistances; this can be clarified by noting that if I did not have a desire for fattening food, we would not appropriately refer to my avoidance of such food as an example of integrity. In other words, to make a promise to oneself entails having a reason for making a promise, that is, placing a constraint on oneself, and if I have no desire for fattening food, I have no reason for placing myself under this constraint. This point makes clear the relationship between integrity and self-mastery, which we can state thus: integrity is the exhibition of self-mastery since one's capacity to keep one's promises to oneself is dependent on one's mastery of one's self at this time and is also the ethical work one does on oneself to develop one's capacity for self-mastery. With respect to 'ethical integrity', we can simply note that my substantive ethical commitments (whatever they may be) are, like my commitment to dieting, promises I make to myself, and as such the same conclusions follow. We should make clear that this position does entail an ethical rule immanent to the concept of integrity, namely, 'if you make promises, keep them', since to break a promise to another person is to break one's promise to oneself to keep promises (of course, this does not entail that one must make promises to others, but what would a life which included no commitments to others consist in?).

We should stress that this discussion does not entail that one's ethical (or other) commitments may not change in the course of one's life either in terms of how they are ranked or in terms of what they consist in; it does, however, entail that we can give reasons for these changes in terms of our reordered or new ethical commitments which sustain our commitment to integrity as the *ruling* virtue (or, to put it another way, maintain the narrative unity of one's life). Recalling our discussion of will to power and the displacement of one conceptual scheme by another, we can suggest that it is a *necessary* feature of our new substantive ethical scheme (the ordered totality of our substantive ethical commitments) that it not only provides an overcoming of the reasons which led us to abandon our previous scheme, but also offers an adequate account of the reasons for the failure of our previous substantive scheme. To avoid confusion, we should probably re-emphasise the point which began our discussion, namely, that a plurality of substantive schemes are compatible with the formal scheme which Nietzsche offers in terms of will to power, eternal recurrence and the Overman.

Three brief final – and possibly obvious – points on this question of the ethical character of eternal recurrence. Firstly, we can note that this formal ethical rule – or *law of integrity* as we may now call it – constructs an ethical framework structured around the concepts of *shame* (lack of integrity) and *honour* (integrity). Secondly, we can see that keeping a promise (i.e., submitting to the law of eternal recurrence) is both an instance of honour and, concomitantly, part of the constitution of an honourable life. It is in this context that Nietzsche refers to the affective disposition of *reverence* – the valuing of, and respect for, honour – as an integral feature of noble morality (see, for example, BGE §§260, 265, 287), which also draws into the affective dimension of this ethical framework, the opposite of reverence, namely, *disdain*. Thirdly, it is apparent that one exhibits one's nobility (self-mastery) *publicly* by acting in accordance with the commitments one espouses. In summary then, we can state that the law of eternal recurrence is an ethical rule and that the Overman is an ethical ideal but that this rule and ideal are formal in character. We can note in passing that this discussion indirectly clarifies why Nietzsche characterises self-mastery in terms of making the self into a work of art, because it is the defining feature of a work of art that it possesses internal coherence which we typically refer to as the integrity of the work.

At this juncture, let us turn to the objection posed to the idea of *amor fati* at the end of the preceding section, namely, that it is an abhorrent thought because it involves *affirming* events such as the Holocaust. Turning to this objection also draws our attention to the point that the thought of eternal recurrence does not entail simply becoming able to affirm one's own life but also becoming able to affirm the totality of fate (a feature somewhat elided in the discussion thus far). The point missed by this objection is that the act of affirmation does not occur outside of time but, on the contrary, is temporally situated and as such recognises the *necessary* character of past events, that is, our inability to will backwards – only the future is open to us. Consequently, Nietzsche's point is that rather than being consumed and, perhaps, paralysed by the remorse (nausea and pity) which attends our shame at humanity for committing such genocidal atrocities, we must *struggle* to redeem humanity by reflecting on such events in order to motivate us both to act with nobility ourselves and, concomitantly, to pursue the goal of a humanity characterised by nobility (in which such expressions of *ressentiment* are impossible). In other words, I think Nietzsche's commitment to the idea that *amor fati* requires the love of the totality of fate is tied to the argument that while as an individual I am accountable for my actions because these actions are constitutive of what I am, as a member of humanity I am accountable for the actions of humanity because these actions are also constitutive of what I am: the Holocaust is part of the conditions of possibility of my being what I am. This is a crushing thought and one might wonder what one can do to struggle to redeem humanity from its past and present barbarism or if one can do anything that makes a difference. Nietzsche's point is this: just as the performance of a noble action is partially constitutive of a noble life, so too the living of a noble life is partially constitutive of a noble humanity: in seeking to live noble lives ourselves (self-overcoming), we help to bring about the goal of a noble humanity, that is, we contribute to the self-overcoming of humanity. Thus, far from being ethically abhorrent, Nietzsche's teaching of eternal recurrence calls on us to take responsibility for ourselves and for humanity in developing an ethical culture characterised by honour and reverence.

The aim of this section has been to make plausible the ethical schema presented at its outset by reflecting on the thought of eternal recurrence and illustrating its connections to will to power, self-overcoming and the Overman as incarnate *amor fati*. The argument developed has suggested that we can grasp the rule of eternal recurrence as a law of integrity which tests our self-mastery (capacity to love fate) and enjoins us to cultivate an honourable life by seeking to overcome those aspects of ourselves which are ignoble, that is, involve dishonesty or self-deception (recall Nietzsche's noting of the fact that the ancient Greeks referred to themselves as 'the truthful'). This argument led to the conclusion that the law of eternal recurrence cultivates an ethical scheme characterised by the ethical virtues of honour and shame and, relatedly, as the valuing of honour and the devaluing of shame, the dispositions of reverence and disdain. We have also noted that the submission to the law of eternal recurrence is not a private, solipsistic activity but is a public activity in the sense of being subject to public criteria and exhibited through the consonance of actions and commitments, and as such is subject to public testing (I will return to the publicity of integrity in the next chapter). However, it must be stressed that we have said nothing about the capacity of modern individuals to submit to the law of eternal recurrence, to pursue the goal of the Overman; this topic is central to our concerns, but before we address it, let us turn to the other 'ideal' which Nietzsche specifies as immanent in modern culture: the Last Man.

'Happiness' and the Last Man

By contrast with the topics of *amor fati*, eternal recurrence and the Overman, Nietzsche says very little about the figure of the Last Man. However, since this figure emerges as a contrast to the figure of the Overman, we need to try to elucidate at least some of the characteristics of the Last Man. In opening this discussion, I want to make two claims which I think are necessary consequences of Nietzsche's deployment of the Last Man as a contrast to the Overman. Firstly, the Last Man must also be consonant with the collapse of the ascetic ideal and, concomitantly, beyond the legislative authority of the ascetic priest. Thus, for example, on this argument we cannot claim that Kantians are exemplars of the Last Man; while Nietzsche deeply objects to the Kantian position, he places it under the aegis of the ascetic ideal as an exemplification of an ascetic legislation. Secondly, insofar as Nietzsche is seeking to cultivate a feeling of reverence towards the figure of the Overman, he is also seeking to nourish a feeling of contempt towards the figure of the Last Man. Noting these claims, let us turn to the task of elucidating the characteristics of this figure.

The Last Man appears in *Thus Spoke Zarathustra* during 'Zarathustra's Prologue' and is explicitly presented by Zarathustra in terms of a contrast with the Overman. Zarathustra speaks thus:

> Behold! I shall show you the *Last Man*.
> 'What is love? What is creation? What is longing? What is a star?' thus asks the Last Man and blinks.
> The earth has become small, and upon it hops the Last Man, who makes everything small. His race is as inexterminable as the flea; the Last Man lives longest.
> 'We have discovered happiness,' say the Last Men and blink.
> They have left the places where living was hard: for one needs warmth. One still love's one's neighbour and rubs against him for one needs warmth.
> Sickness and mistrust count as sins with them: one should go about warily. He is a fool who still stumbles over stones or over men!
> A little poison now and then: that produces pleasant dreams. And a lot of poison at last, for a pleasant death.
> They still work, for work is entertainment. But they take care the entertainment does not exhaust them.
> Nobody grows rich or poor anymore: both are too much of a burden. Who still wants to rule? Who obey? Both are too much of a burden.
> No herdsman and one herd. Everyone wants the same thing, everyone is the same: whoever thinks otherwise goes voluntarily into the madhouse.
> 'Formerly all the world was mad,' say the most acute of them and blink.
> They are clever and know everything that has ever happened: so there is no end to their mockery. They still quarrel, but soon they make up – otherwise indigestion would result.
> They have their little pleasure for the day and their little pleasure for the night: but they respect health.
> 'We have discovered happiness,' say the Last Men and blink. (Z 'Zarathustra's Prologue' §5)

In this speech Zarathustra presents the Last Man as a being whose intellectual horizons are defined by the displacement of a concern for truth and a feeling of wonder at existence in favour of a concern for happiness characterised in terms of material comfort and spiritual complacency; the Last Man is troubled by suffering (unhappiness) and seeks to banish it through morality – by affirming the equal worth of all persons – and through technology – by overcoming scarcity – but only as long as this doesn't require too much effort (Lampert, 1986: 24–5). Characterised by a sense that the quest to achieve any ideal other than the preserving of a comfortable security in which to pursue one's preferences is mad, the Last Man engages in arguments as intellectual entertainment but doesn't take such arguments as being practically significant. He is too ironic and such constraints on superficiality might upset his indigestion. (Notably Zarathustra's attempt to deploy this contrast between the Overman and the Last Man at this stage is an utter failure; his audience embrace the 'ideal' of the Last Man.)

But why does Nietzsche despise the Last Man? In what sense is the Last Man an ideal-typical character embodying the features for which Nietzsche feels greatest contempt? Two answers present themselves. Firstly, Zara-thustra's speech outlines figures for whom integrity (which Nietzsche also refer to as 'intellectual conscience')[8] is sacrificed to comfort; the Last Men feel neither honour nor shame, their souls are too shallow for these ethical emotions:

> . . . at one in their faith in the morality of *mutual* pity, as if it were morality in itself and the pinnacle, the *attained* pinnacle of man, the sole hope of the future, the consolation of the present and the great redemption from all the guilt of the past – at one, one and all, in their faith in the community as the *saviour*, that is to say in the herd, in 'themselves'. (BGE §202).

Secondly, and relatedly, Nietzsche argues that the Last Man's desire to be free of suffering erodes the possibility of nobility:

> You want if possible – and there is no madder 'if possible' – *to abolish suffering*. . . . Wellbeing as you understand it – that is no goal, that seems to us an *end*! A state which renders man ludicrous and contemptible – which makes it *desirable* that he should perish! The discipline of suffering, of *great* suffering – do you not know that it is *this* discipline alone which has created every elevation of mankind hitherto? (BGE §225)

This second objection to the Last Man is related to the first objection since integrity requires suffering in the sense that it requires overcoming desires which one would like to indulge (think back to my diet and resistance to the temptation of fattening food). Together these reasons reveal the worry which Nietzsche confronts with respect to the Last Man, namely, that the erosion of intellectual conscience and the capacity to place oneself under constraint in the name of freedom and freedom from suffering undermines not merely the present nobility of humanity and thus the redemption of the past but also the possibility of the future nobility of humanity; the culture of the Last Man abrogates its responsibility both to redeeming humanity's past and to enabling the elevation of humanity's future.

We should note, however, that the Last Man does solve the problem of nihilism – the will to nothingness – posed by the collapse of the ascetic ideal, although it achieves this resolution in a curious way. Consider, to begin, that the Last Man as a post-ascetic ideal involves accepting the view of the self as a web of desires situated both culturally and historically, which also informs the idea of the Overman. But whereas the figure of the Overman is entwined with the rule of eternal recurrence as a law of integrity, the figure of the Last Man is interwoven with another rule: don't be cruel to yourself or others, don't inflict suffering on yourself or others, *or* – to put it another way – don't subject yourself or others to constraints, be 'free' and let others be 'free'. *This is an ethical position*: 'Be nice!'

It is important to note this point, namely, that the Last Man is a counter-ideal to the ascetic ideal, not least because, if it is expressed in this way, this ideal has a certain attraction which consists in its commitment to maximising pleasure and minimising pain within a framework of equal rights: 'Do what you want to do, express your emotions, your subjective preferences – just don't harm others!' The central claim of this position is that the collapse of the foundationalist project entails that all conceptions of the good are simply subjective preferences, and that since we lack grounds on which to decide between them, the only objective good we can specify in terms of the ethical interests of our public political culture is that anyone be able to pursue their preferences to the extent that this is compatible with everyone else being able to pursue their preferences. Or, to give this alternate expression, since persons are simply the conception(s) of the good which they pursue (their value-commitments) and we have no grounds on which to rank conceptions of the good, it follows that all persons are of equal worth and we recognise this fact in granting everyone equal rights.

As these comments may suggest, for Nietzsche, a culture characterised by Last Men is the fulfilment of the vision of 'the *autonomous* herd' (BGE §202), which he associates with liberalism, and I will be concerned to draw out the political aspects of the cultivation of the Last Man in the next chapter by arguing that the figure of the Last Man is given precise expression in contemporary political theory as the *postmodern bourgeois liberal* advocated by Richard Rorty. For the moment, however, having sketched the dystopian ideal which Nietzsche identifies as immanent in modern culture, we can turn to his arguments concerning the possibility of the Overman and the Last Man, that is, the capacity of modern individuals to pursue these ideals.

Culture, Capacities and Counter-Ideals

We have seen that the two ideals which Nietzsche presents involve very different features; whereas the Overman represents a utopian ideal of integrity, the Last Man is a manifestation of the dystopian (anti-)ideal of comfortable freedom – freedom to pursue desires and freedom from suffering. To explore the question of the capacities of modern individuals to attain these ideals, we can begin by noting that the context in which the quotations from *Beyond Good and Evil* cited in the last section are drawn is a critique of modern liberal democracy. This context suggests that Nietzsche regards the Last Man as the product of a liberal culture shorn of its theological and philosophical foundations. I will explore this aspect of Nietzsche's thought in the next chapter, but I mention it at this stage because it points us to the claim that Nietzsche regards the Last Man as simply involving the capacity of the Christian and the metaphysical liberal for engaging in rational calculation about one's desires (but without the spiritual discipline) which is developed under the aegis of anti-erotic asceticism,[9] and, since the Last Man does not seem to entail much more than this calculative capacity, I will focus my attention on the question of whether or not modern individuals possess the requisite capacities to submit to the rule of eternal recurrence and pursue the perfectionist ideal of integrity towards which it is directed.

Are modern individuals capable of integrity? We can address the question by dividing it into two distinct queries: firstly, what capacities are required for the pursuit of integrity and, secondly, do we find these capacities in modern individuals on the genealogical account of the constitution of modernity offered by Nietzsche? To take up the first of these questions, we can note that integrity seems to presuppose two capacities: *truthfulness*, which is required if we are to stand in a meaningful relation to the question of eternal recurrence (to make asking this question meaningful entails that we are capable of giving an honest response to it), and *the will to truth*, which is required if we are to have an interest in posing the question of eternal recurrence (if we do not value truth and specifically the truth about ourselves, we have no reason to ask this question of ourselves). These answers are revealing with respect to our second query, namely, whether or not modern man possesses these capacities, because a moment of reflection on the analysis of nihilism which began this chapter indicates that while Nietzsche certainly believes that modern individuals have the capacity for truthfulness which was bred under the aegis of Christian asceticism and was responsible finally for its self-destruction, he regards the will to truth as having been undermined by our truthfulness – this is the *telos* of the logic of nihilism. To offer further support for the idea that the capacity for truthfulness is immanent within modern culture, we can simply note a remark from the section 'Our Virtues' in *Beyond Good and Evil*:

> Honesty – granted that this is our virtue, from which we cannot get free, we free spirits – well, let us labor at it with all love and malice and not weary of 'perfecting' ourselves in *our* virtue, the only one we have: may its brightness one day overspread this ageing culture and its dull, gloomy seriousness like a gilded azure mocking evening glow! (BGE §227)

However, the fact that we are capable of truthfulness does not entail that we value truth; rather we require a reason to value truth in order to deploy and develop our capacity for truthfulness. This reason is given in Nietzsche's tying of integrity (i.e., self-mastery) in the form of the ideal of the Overman to *amor fati* as the maximum possible experience of the feeling of power (recall my three examples of fleeting moments of *amor fati*). This is revealed clearly in a comment already cited when Nietzsche remarks: 'Immortal is the moment when I produced the recurrence. . . . For the sake of this moment I *endure* the recurrence' (cited in Thiele, 1990: 204). The rapturous experience of such moments of wonder and joy is the fish-hook on which Nietzsche hopes to catch modern individuals by presenting the ideal of the Overman as incarnate *amor fati* and, thus, presenting integrity as the condition of experiencing such moments with respect to oneself. Within this framework, the will to truth is the will to *amor fati*.

But why do we value the experience – however fleeting – of *amor fati*? It may seem intuitively obvious that we do value such moments, but it is not so immediately apparent that we will necessarily continue to do so. Thus, for example, it is apparent that Nietzsche's portrayal of the Last Man presents a figure for whom the experience of such moments is not worth the cost in terms of self-discipline. My suggestion is that Nietzsche is seeking to mobilise the fact that we do value such moments to tackle the problem posed by the question of the *pathos of distance*. In order to state this problem, let us begin by reflecting on Nietzsche's concern with the pathos of distance. It will be recalled that it has been argued that a condition of experiencing oneself as autonomous (the feeling of power) is to experience oneself as a unified subject (and not just as an unorganised collection of social roles), and this is clearly central to Nietzsche's concern with integrity, but it was also argued that a condition of possibility of unified subjectivity is the pathos of distance, since it is this pathos which is internalised as 'inner distance' (the feeling of power over oneself). This is Nietzsche's point when he comments:

> Without the *pathos of distance* . . . that other, more mysterious pathos could not have developed either, that longing for an ever-increasing widening of distance within the soul itself, the formation of ever higher, rarer, more remote, tenser, more comprehensive states, in short, precisely the elevation of the type 'man', the continual 'self-overcoming of man', to take a moral formula in a super-moral sense. (BGE §257)

What, then, is the problem which Nietzsche confronts? We can note two types of pathos of distance recounted in Nietzsche's genealogy of modernity. On the one hand, the 'inner distance' of the ancient nobles is predicated on the pathos of *social* distance: 'a concept denoting political superiority always resolves itself into a concept denoting superiority of soul' (GM I §6). On the other hand, the 'inner distance' of the slave is predicated on a pathos of *metaphysical* distance, which appears, firstly, as a simple inversion of the social order of rank and, secondly, in the context of the ascetic priest, as the distinction between soul/mind/reason (grace) and flesh/body/affects (corruption). The problem raised by reflecting on these two types of pathos of distance is that *neither* is available to modern man! On the one hand, modern culture is characterised by a commitment to formal equality entrenched within the political institutions of democracy; besides which Nietzsche's comment that while he recognises the superiority of the ancient Greek to modern man, he wants nobility without the causes and conditions of Greek nobility (WP §882), although an unpublished note does suggest that he is not interested in advocating some anachronistic return to antiquity. On the other hand, given the collapse of the ascetic ideal wrought by our truthfulness, we cannot appeal to the imaginary constructions of metaphysics. To clarify how Nietzsche avoids being trapped by this problem, we can note the twist introduced by the ascetic priest, in which metaphysical distance is divorced from any relation to social distance; this strategy suggests that, under the aegis of asceticism, the pathos of distance is constructed *reflexively* in terms of distinct aspects of the self (in this case, soul versus body) which serve to mark the extremes of 'height' (soul) and 'depth' (body) requisite for the constitution of 'inner distance'. My suggestion is that Nietzsche's distinction between the utopian ideal of the Overman and the dystopian ideal of the Last Man is a post-metaphysical version of the same twist, in which the capacity for the reflexive constitution of 'inner distance' draws on the fact that, on Nietzsche's account, the Overman and the Last Man are the limit-ideals immanent within modern culture and the products of this culture, namely, modern individuals. *But* this strategy can only work if we value the experience of *amor fati*; if this ceases to be the case, the distance between the elevated heights of the Overman and the subterranean depths of the Last Man collapses.

On the account offered in this section, Nietzsche's claim that both the Overman and the Last Man are immanent possibilities within modern culture is consonant with his genealogy of modernity; indeed, one of the advantages of this account is that it explains why Nietzsche felt it to be necessary to sketch a dystopian ideal as well as a utopian ideal. But this account does raise a further question which can be addressed by way of a comment from Max Weber in one of his more Nietzschean moments:

> Without exception every order of social relations (however constituted) is, if one wishes to evaluate it, ultimately to be examined in terms of the human type (*menschlichen Typus*) to which it, by way of external or internal (motivational) selection, provides the optimal chances of becoming the dominant type. (cited in Hennis, 1983: 169)

The topic raised by this Nietzschean remark[10] is expressed by Nietzsche in terms of the relation between politics (external selection) and culture (internal selection). Of course, external and internal processes of selection are not independent of each other but reciprocally bound, and this is precisely Nietzsche's concern, namely, that the political institutions and processes of modern culture frame and constrain our forms of agency in ways which mitigate against the production and reproduction of the Overman as a cultural ideal and in favour of the cultivation of the Last Man. Elucidating how Nietzsche seeks to come to terms with this *political* question will be one of the tasks of the next chapter and, more specifically, of the critique of postmodern bourgeois liberalism. At this juncture, however, we need to take up a question which has been suspended throughout this chapter, namely, how is Nietzsche's claim to authority grounded? In other words, we need to ask on what ground Nietzsche claims the authority to recommend a cultural ideal at all.

Exemplarity and the Claim to Authority

Is Nietzsche an ascetic priest? While he offers an erotic asceticism, isn't Nietzsche simply taking up the role of the ascetic priest in specifying a cultural or, indeed, universal goal for humanity? As early as *Daybreak* Nietzsche is concerned to articulate the difference between himself and the type of ascetic priest characteristic of Christianity:

> Only if mankind possessed a universally recognised *goal* would it be possible to propose 'thus and thus is the *right* course of action': for the present there exists no such goal. It is thus irrational and trivial to impose the demands of morality upon mankind. – to *recommend* a goal to mankind is something quite different: the goal is then thought of as something which *lies in our own discretion*; supposing the recommendation appealed to mankind, it could in pursuit of it also *impose* upon itself a moral law, likewise at its own discretion. But up to now the moral law has been supposed to stand *above* our likes and dislikes; one did not want actually to *impose* this law upon oneself, one wanted to *take* it from somewhere or *discover* it somewhere or *have it commanded to one* from somewhere. (D §108)

This passage draws our attention to two points. Firstly, Nietzsche is concerned that we take responsibility for imposing our own law on ourselves, a point repeated in Zarathustra's injunction that the individual 'must become judge and avenger and victim of his own law' (Z 'Of Self-Overcoming'). Secondly, and more significantly for our current concerns, Nietzsche distinguishes between *recommending* a cultural ideal to us, that is, making a *claim* on us (in the way, for example, a work of art does), and *commanding* a universal ideal. This point suggests that Nietzsche's objection to the ascetic priest, quite apart from *what* he recommends (although related to it), is his activity as a *legislator*.

Of course, Nietzsche would object to this legislative activity on the part of the ascetic priest because the legislation of a goal for humanity presupposes a transcendental ground of authority – a God's-eye view – which is only possible on the presupposition of a metaphysical conception of truth (and is, thus, related to the devaluation of *eros*). In this respect, Nietzsche's cheerful acknowledgement that he can only recommend a cultural or universal ideal is a consequence of his post-metaphysical erotic theory of truth. But does this position entail that any recommendation of a cultural ideal has a claim to authority? What is at stake in this discussion may become clearer if we admit that any recommendation of a cultural ideal may claim authority (i.e., none can be ruled out *a priori*) but our concern is with the conditions under which such a claim to authority is recognised by the public community. There are, I think, two relevant considerations. Firstly, any recommendation of a cultural ideal must involve an acknowledgement of our ethical interests (in the same way that any theory claiming truth must acknowledge our cognitive interests). Although we may (and do) disagree about what these interests are and how to rank them, such disagreements are bounded by our form of life. Of course, this is a fairly weak constraint since it simply says that if a recommendation of an ethical ideal is to claim authority, it must be intelligible to us as an ethical ideal (i.e., address some ethical interest or set of interests). The second constraint provides a stronger criterion and we can draw this rule out by reference to a distinction which Max Weber makes between legislative prophets, who ground their claim to authority in a transcendental argument which legitimates their right to command a goal, and exemplary prophets, who ground their claim to authority in the exemplification of their ideal which legitimates their right to recommend a goal. If we transpose this distinction onto philosophical arguments, we get a distinction between legislative and exemplary forms of argument: in examining whether or not to grant the claim to authority of an argument, our question is whether or not this argument establishes *either* transcendental criteria of rational argumentation which guarantee its right to command *or* exemplifies in the structure of its reflection the cultural ideal which it seeks to recommend. Since we have already ruled out the possibility of specifying transcendental criteria of rationality (although this project has been interestingly – if, I think, still mistakenly – renewed in the recent work of Jürgen Habermas), we are left with the criteria of exemplification. 'But', it might be objected, 'why do we need any such criterion?' A straightforward response to this objection becomes clear once we recognise the logically isomorphic character of the claim to authority of the prophet and the claim to authority of argument: if I recommend a cultural ideal to you, and I, as a member of the same culture, do not exhibit my commitment to this ideal in my life, then I am engaged in a performative contradiction which utterly undermines not the ideal I recommend but the process of recommendation. In other words, you can only take me (assuming we are members of the same culture) to be recommending a cultural ideal if I show my commitment to this ideal, otherwise you have no reason to think that what I am doing is 'recommending' an ideal. The implication of this argument is that if Nietzsche's argument is to legitimate its right to recommend an ideal (if we are to recognise its claim to authority as a valid claim and this says *nothing* about the degree of authority it will be granted, only that it has established the right to be considered), it must exhibit in the performance of its argument the ideal which it seeks to recommend. But does it?

To address this question in detail would require a book in itself and consequently I shall confine myself to the attempt to make plausible the claim that Nietzsche's argument is an exemplification of its commitment to the ideal of the Overman and *amor fati*. To perform this task, I will focus very briefly on three topics: firstly, the exemplification of the cognitive commitment to truthfulness (and, thereby, the value of truth) in Nietzsche's strategies of argument; secondly, the exemplification of the affective commitment to heroism and irony in Nietzsche's stylistic strategies; and finally Nietzsche's reflection on this topic in *Thus Spoke Zarathustra*.

To establish the plausibility of Nietzsche's performance of a commitment to truthfulness, two points will suffice. Firstly, the relentless attack on idols which characterises his work is undertaken in terms of a valuing of truthfulness. To take but one example, consider the following passage:

> Even with the most modest claim to integrity, one *must* know today that a theologian, a priest, a pope does not merely err in every sentence he speaks, he *lies* – that he is no longer free to lie 'innocently', out of 'ignorance'. The priest knows as well as anyone else that there is no longer any 'God', any 'sinner', any 'redeemer' – that 'free will', 'moral world-order' are lies – intellectual seriousness, the profound self-overcoming of the intellect, no longer *permits* anyone *not* to know about these things. (AC §38)

The tone of moral indignation which characterises this passage may be less ironic than is typical of Nietzsche's voice, but it does seem typical of the commitment to intellectual probity which characterises his writing. The second point, which buttresses this claim, concerns Nietzsche's relationship to his own work, and here I simply want to refer back to our discussion of the section 'How the "Real World" At Last Became a Myth', in which it was noted that Nietzsche's critique of metaphysical accounts of truth develops through three stages which are characterised by an ongoing ethos of auto-critique. This self-critical relation to his work is given clearest expression in the 'Attempt at a Self-Criticism' attached to his first book, *The Birth of Tragedy*, in 1886.

If we turn to the question of whether Nietzsche's stylistic performance exhibits the dispositions of heroism and irony, the plausibility of our case may be less immediately obvious. However, we can note in this context that Alexander Nehamas has pointed out that the most pervasive figure deployed in Nietzsche's writing is that most unscholarly of tropes, '*hyperbole*', going so far as to claim that 'Nietzsche's writing is irreducibly hyperbolic' (1985: 22).[11] Why is this significant? I think that two considerations are relevant. Firstly, on his own account, Nietzsche is writing for an audience characterised by decadence, by the experience of affective exhaustion. As such, a stylistic strategy predicated on provocation, on a trope of exaggeration, might seem a prerequisite for generating affective engagement with his readers. In this sense, we can read Nietzsche's hyperbolic expressions of disdain for modern individuals and, in particular, Germans as attempts to engender an erotic agonism in the souls of his readers which parallels the cognitive agonism constructed by the contrast of the Overman and the Last Man. Recalling our discussion of the pathos of style, we can note that this topic is particularly significant in terms of the reading practices of his audience. By insulting, cajoling and provoking his readers to pay attention to his stylistic performance – the texture, tempo and tone of his language – Nietzsche can be seen to be attempting to constitute the conditions of affective communication whereby an affective investment in overcoming decadence is 'transferred' to his audience. The second consideration which we can bring to bear on this topic concerns the *ambivalence* of hyperbole as a rhetorical figure which oscillates between the heroic and the ironic (or self-parodic). Commenting on this trope both generally and in relation to Nietzsche's texts, Magnus, Stewart and Mileur note:

> Hyperbole is . . . inflated language, and since what goes up must come down, it follows from this deflated language as well. But hyperbole is not just the language of heights aspired to and depths fallen to, it is also the language of detours, of errancy, extravagance, and even errantry. . . . Exaggeration, extravagance, errantry, quest – synonymous with want of due proportion as error – hyperbole is also the excess that leads to quality, sublimity, greatness. (1993: 139)

Attending to the ambivalence of hyperbole as simultaneously inflated and deflated language (a kind of figural equivalent of the aspect change exhibited by pictures like Wittgenstein's duck/rabbit drawing), we can draw attention to Nietzsche's hyperbolic 'autobiography' *Ecce Homo*, which has been read by Nehamas (1985), amongst others, as an exemplification of the heroic self-overcoming of nihilism and decadence in which the dramatic structure of the text reveals Nietzsche's achievement of the task of giving style to his character. However, as Daniel Conway (1993) has argued, alongside the heroic Nietzsche, *Ecce Homo* also reveals an ironic or self-parodic Nietzsche who recognises that he may be engaged in self-deception and is concerned to deconstruct the monumental idol which the heroic register constructs. The double character of this hyperbolic text is revealed, for example, in the opening three chapter titles – 'Why I Am So Wise,' 'Why I Am So Clever,' and 'Why I Write Such Good Books' – which can be read as both an inflationary monumental construction of heroic authority and a deflationary critical and ironic undermining of such authority. Throughout *Ecce Homo*, I suggest, the figure of Nietzsche as heroic prophet is doubled by that of Nietzsche as ironic critic of idolatry through a deployment of the ambivalence of hyperbole which sets up a complementary relation between the heroic and the ironic as mutually limiting (Conway, 1993). Thus, against the dispositions of nausea and pity which characterise decadence, Nietzsche's play on the ambivalence of hyperbole may be read as attempting to communicate the dispositions of heroism and irony appropriate to the overcoming of decadence and, consequently, provoking an affective contest within the soul of the reader.

The final observations which will be brought to bear on this question of exemplarity concern Nietzsche's own reflections on the topic of teaching the Overman and the doctrine of eternal recurrence as these reflections are exhibited in *Thus Spoke Zarathustra*. Here I simply want to draw attention to some features of Zarathustra's journey and to make a claim on the basis of these observations. In the opening two parts of the book, Zarathustra comes down from his mountain to announce the death of God and to preach the vision of the Overman initially to the public and latterly to a small group of disciples. His attempt to present his clearly Nietzschean teaching to the public is a pathetic failure and he is mocked as a fool, while his teaching to his disciples is hardly less of a failure because they fail to understand him. This latter failure is contemporaneous with Zarathustra's recognition that he has not himself realised the implications of his teaching and he leaves his disciples in the realisation that he needs to be able to affirm this teaching himself before being able to teach it. In part three, Zarathustra struggles with the abysmal thought of eternal recurrence before finally overcoming his nausea at humanity and affirming this thought. Part four brings a series of bizarre visitors to Zarathustra, with whom he contests (in overcoming his pity for mankind), before ending on a note of climactic affirmation and preparedness to return to the world to resume his teaching.

Reflecting on this woefully schematic summary, we can note that in both parts one and two Zarathustra acts as an ascetic priest in attempting to legislate an ideal (the Overman). However, in announcing the death of God, Zarathustra undermines his claim to public authority, and this point is marked by the public's laughter at his preaching. His attempt to legislate for his disciples is similarly undercut by his failure to manifest the ideal which he preaches, and this point is marked by the failure of understanding which greets his pronouncements. In this context, parts three and four may be read as Zarathustra's coming to exemplify the ideal which characterises his teaching by overcoming both his nausea and his pity towards humanity (and himself). Thus, when Zarathustra commences once more to return amongst humanity and resume his teaching at the end of the book, he has found a way to recommend his ideal by exemplifying it. The suggestion which I want to attach to this claim is that Zarathustra can teach the Overman by doing precisely what Nietzsche has done in writing *Thus Spoke Zarathustra*, that is, offering an exemplary account of becoming what one is which manifests the ideal it recommends. In other words, I want to assert that, in his writings, Nietzsche is committed to the project of exemplarity which I have ascribed to him.

In summary, the purpose of this section has been to suggest that Nietzsche does not engage in ascetic acts of legislation, since he recognises both that he has no grounds on which to do so and that such an act undermines the ethics which he recommends. I have argued (or, perhaps, asserted) that a concern with exemplification can be found in Nietzsche's reflections on teaching his ethics as these are performed in *Thus Spoke Zarathustra*, and that by attending to his commitment to truthfulness and to communicating the dispositions of heroism and irony through his stylistic strategies, we can conclude that it is plausible to claim that Nietzsche's writing does exemplify the ideal it recommends.

Conclusion

The concern of this chapter has been to set out the counter-ideal to the ascetic ideal which Nietzsche elaborates and to try to draw out the ethical implications of this ideal. It has been argued that Nietzsche's ethical position can be best expressed in terms of the schema: will to power as ontological thesis, eternal recurrence as ethical rule, self-overcoming as ethical ascetics, and *amor fati* and the Overman as *telos*. I have claimed that the contrast between the Overman and the Last Man is an attempt to construct the pathos of distance requisite to this ethics and that the capacities required to pursue this ethics are immanent in modern culture. Finally I have argued that Nietzsche's claim to the authority to recommend the ideal of the Overman is grounded in the exemplification of the ethical commitments of this figure in his writing. At this stage, then, let us turn to the question of how this ethical counter-ideal is connected to Nietzsche's agonistic politics.

Notes

1 Of course we might make this claim of lying in the grass as well, but only, I think, as part of some practice such as relaxing or meditation which involves particular skills.

2 I am not going to develop this point here, but Nietzsche's argument expands to include the love of the fate of the world and, ultimately, the universe. This might have some interesting implications for human/non-human relations but this would require an argument which I do not have the space to develop.

3 Does the idea of eternal recurrence represent a cosmological thesis or a hypothetical thesis? Is it a statement of fact or an ethical imperative? Is it selective or non-selective?

4 For example, Erich Heller (1988: 12) argues that the Overman and eternal recurrence are contradictory, while Lawrence Lampert (1986) argues that Nietzsche drops the idea of the Overman in favour of the idea of eternal recurrence. While with respect to will to power and eternal recurrence Tracy Strong comments: 'The will to power and eternal return represent the greatest stumbling blocks in any interpretation of Nietzsche. Separately, they are obscure enough; but their relationship to each other leaves most commentators in the embarrassed position of having to make a choice' (1988: 218).

5 For a brilliant discussion of this 'Yes and Amen!', see Howard Caygill's essay 'Affirmation and Eternal Return in the Free-Spirit Trilogy' (1991).

6 I borrow this example from Anne MacLean's excellent attack on utilitarianism, *The Elimination of Morality* (1993).

7 For a fascinating discussion of integrity which clarified a number of issues for me, see Lynne McFall's article 'Integrity' (1987).

8 Nietzsche's advocation of integrity as tied to his concern with intellectual conscience is most clearly exhibited in GS §335.

9 In this context, the Last Man is rather like Hobbes' conception of human beings.

10 Weber's relation to Nietzsche has recently received much attention. I make my own view clear in 'Autonomy and "Inner Distance": A Trace of Nietzsche in Weber' (Owen, 1991).

11 Nehamas goes on from this claim to develop an extremely insightful discussion contrasting Nietzsche's use of hyperbole with Socrates' use of irony (1985: 22–41). For an insightful alternative reading of Nietzsche's style in terms of concinnity, which I do not think is incompatible with that stressed here, see Chapter 1 of Babette Babich's *Nietzsche's Philosophy of Science* (1994).

Agonism, Liberalism and the Cultivation of *Virtu*

Ethics, Politics and the Critique of Political Liberalism

Dying for the 'truth'. – We should not let ourselves be burnt for our opinions: we are not that sure of them. But perhaps for this: that we may have and change our opinions. (WS §333)

In the preceding chapters, we have focused on Nietzsche's critique of the philosophical commitments of liberal reason and his recommendation of an alternative ethical schema structured around the ontological thesis of will to power, the law of eternal recurrence, an ascetics of self-overcoming, and the *telos* of the Overman. However, Nietzsche is not alone in recognising that the implications of anti-foundationalism for a public philosophy include the abandonment of foundational arguments for liberalism; this position is also articulated by John Rawls' idea of *political liberalism* and Richard Rorty's notion of a *postmodern bourgeois liberalism*. Consequently, although Nietzsche's arguments may be effective against foundational justifications of liberalism deployed by philosophical liberals such as Kant and the early Rawls, it is not immediately apparent that these arguments would tell against the anti-foundational recommendations of liberalism adopted by Rorty and the later Rawls. These thinkers could, at least potentially, embrace Nietzsche's genealogical critique of the ascetic ideal without concluding that this critique has significant implications for the value of liberalism or implies that we need embrace Nietzsche's ethical position, indeed Rorty seems to adopt this very position. However, Nietzsche's critique of liberalism is not limited to an attack on the foundations of philosophical liberalism; on the contrary, Nietzsche is also concerned that a liberal polity undermines our capacity to sustain a commitment to human nobility. In this respect I will argue that Nietzsche articulates a critique of liberalism from the standpoint of a civic humanist position consonant with his admiration for Machiavelli.

To begin this chapter, I will briefly return to Nietzsche's critique of philosophical liberalism in order to show that this position is committed to the metaphysical conception of the self as antecedently individuated subject against which Nietzsche's criticisms of the presuppositions of foundational versions of liberal philosophy are directed. This sketch will also draw attention to Nietzsche's critique of philosophical liberalism as lacking an adequate conception of both culture and politics. Following this discussion, the rest of the chapter will be devoted to Nietzsche's critique of both political defences of liberalism and liberal politics. I will suggest that Nietzsche's worry about liberalism is predicated on a twofold claim: firstly, that our capacity to cultivate nobility is tied to our public culture and, more specifically, to the *agonistic* character of our public culture; and, secondly, that the liberalism articulated by Rorty and by Rawls[1] undermines the agonistic character of public culture both through the form of the public/private distinction which it institutes and, relatedly, through its commitment to an anti-perfectionist defence of state neutrality *qua* conceptions of the good. To make good this characterisation of Nietzsche as a political theorist and to elucidate the critique of liberalism embedded in it, I will begin this discussion by reflecting on the relationship between perspectivism, agonism and *virtu* in the context of Nietzsche's early essay 'Homer on Competition'. This reflection will lead to a confrontation between Nietzsche and Rorty on the significance of philosophy for political theory and, more particularly, the relationship between perspectivism and agonism. Following this confrontation, I will explore the contest between political agonism and political liberalism, that is, the reasons which can be offered for each of these contrasting political theories and the distinct conceptions of political community which they recommend. Finally I will compare the character of agonistic politics with that of liberal politics in order to address the question of the distinct human types which they cultivate. In this final section, I will suggest that, on Nietzsche's account, Rorty's postmodern bourgeois liberal and Rawls' political liberal act as representatives of the Last Man.

Philosophical Liberalism and the Ascetic Ideal

Thus far in our discussion of Nietzsche, I have tried to show how he attempts to undermine the founding dualisms involved in the philosophical justification of liberalism and, consequently, the account of the self as antecedentally individuated subject to which these presuppositions give rise. In this discussion, Nietzsche's critical project has been seen to involve both a philosophical critique of the coherence of these distinctions with respect to reason, subjectivity and truth, and a genealogical critique which ties them to the emergence of nihilism. This section will attempt to specify the pertinence of this critique with respect to liberal political theory in its foundational form by illustrating that philosophical liberalism is committed to a conception of the subjectivity as disembedded and disembodied, that is, as an unencumbered and antecedentally individuated self. However, although Kant is Nietzsche's main target, I will focus on the significance of Nietzsche's critique with respect to Rawls' *A Theory of Justice* (1971)[1], and there are two reasons for this: firstly, since the main aim of my argument is to illustrate Nietzsche's relevance to contemporary political theory, it seems appropriate to focus on what is probably the major text in terms of philosophical defences of liberalism to emerge in recent years (we can also point to the broadly Kantian character of Rawls' argument); and, secondly, since I will also be addressing Nietzsche's critique of political justifications of liberalism such as that offered by Rawls in his work after *A Theory of Justice* in the remainder of the chapter, a focus on Rawls' general position is probably more pertinent to the development of my argument. The main purpose of this section is to establish that Rawls is committed to the metaphysical conception of the person which Nietzsche's criticisms of liberal philosophy have attacked. Let us begin by setting out, albeit schematically, the relevant features of Rawls' account.

In *A Theory of Justice* Rawls' aim is to provide an account of justice which is appropriate to the liberal claim that individuals must be regarded as free and equal persons; Rawls pursues this goal through the ideas of the *original position* (1971: §4) and the *veil of ignorance* (1971: §24). The idea of the original position is an instance of the liberal tradition's conceptualisation of society as a contract between private individuals which can be found in thinkers as diverse as Hobbes, Locke, Rousseau and Kant. For Rawls, this is a hypothetical device which is set up to ask what principles of justice would be appropriate to a contract between mutually disinterested rational individuals. To specify these principles, Rawls introduces the device of a veil of ignorance behind which individuals know *neither* their position in society and their various talents or attributes *nor* the conceptions of the good (the beliefs about how best to live their lives) which they hold. Simplifying slightly, we can see that Rawls' reasons for introducing these constraints are fairly straightforward. On the one hand, the idea that one should not know one's position or attributes represents the commitment to equality in that it treats matters of position or ability as irrelevant to the concerns of justice. Thus, by including this restraint, Rawls seeks to rule out considerations which might import extraneous and distorting interests into the principles of justice derived from the original position. On the other hand, the idea that one should not know one's conception of the good represents the commitment to freedom in that it suggests that what is important with respect to justice is the right to choose our conceptions of good. By including this limitation, Rawls seeks to rule out consideration of conceptions of the good in order to entrench the priority of autonomy in the principles of justice at which rational (and therefore autonomous) persons would arrive.

Rawls' argument is that rational deliberation within these constraints would lead to two fundamental principles of justice:

> First: each person is to have an equal right to the most extensive total system of equal basic liberties compatible with a similar system of liberty for all.
>
> Second: social and economic inequalities are to be arranged so that they are both (a) to the greatest benefit of the least advantaged . . ., and (b) attached to offices and positions open to all under conditions of fair equality of opportunity. (1971: §47)

To this specification of the principles of justice, Rawls adds two rules of priority: firstly, that the first principle is lexically prior to the second and, secondly, that part (b) of the second principle has priority to part (a). But how does Rawls arrive at these conclusions from the original position? On the one hand, the first principle seeks to embody the idea that we would rationally agree on both the concern that justice protect our power to choose our conceptions of the good and on the priority of this role for justice (which is illustrated by both rules of priority). On the other hand, part (a) of the second principle, which is referred to as the 'difference principle', seeks to embody our concern with equality since our lack of knowledge concerning our position or attributes makes it rational for us to adopt a 'maximin' principle by virtue of which the least advantaged position is as good as possible and the only inequalities allowed are those which act to the advantage of the least advantaged position. In presenting the claim that Rawls is committed to a metaphysical conception of selfhood, I will not address questions concerning his derivation of these principles of justice,[2] but will focus on the claims embedded in the ideas of the original position and the veil of ignorance in the context of his remarks throughout the book.

Let us begin with the conception of the person manifest in Rawls' account of justice. In our sketch of the original position, it was noted that Rawls focuses on the idea of the subject as an autonomous chooser of ends as the morally relevant feature of human beings for considerations of justice. However, Rawls is not simply locating our capacity to choose ends and the virtue of justice as one capacity and virtue amongst others; rather he presents justice as the fundamental virtue and our capacity to choose ends as the essential feature of subjectivity:

> What we cannot do is express our nature by following a plan that views the sense of justice as but one desire to be weighed against others. For this sentiment reveals what the person is, and to compromise it is not to achieve for the self free rein, but to give way to the contingencies and accidents of the world. (1971: §86)

In a close textual reading of *A Theory of Justice*, Michel Sandel (1982) has argued that passages of this sort reveal that Rawls' assignation of moral priority to the autonomous choosing of ends over the ends chosen is committed to a metaphysical view of the self as antecedentally individuated in the sense of being fixed prior to, and distinct from, its chosen ends.[3] On this metaphysical view, the ends which I choose are not constitutive of my essential identity; rather I attach them to myself through an act of will, that is, I choose to 'clothe' myself in these beliefs but, however deeply I am attached to them, they are not essentially part of who I am. Reflecting on Sandel's reading of the passage cited above, Mulhall and Swift have summarised his argument thus:

> . . . a subject for whom justice is the first virtue is not just an autonomous chooser of ends but an antecedentally individuated subject: a self for whom justice has absolute priority over all other values is a self whose boundaries are fixed absolutely prior to its choice of ends. (1992: 47)

If Sandel's claim is correct, Rawls shares the ascetic priest's attachment to the thesis of *soul atomism* which Nietzsche regards as philosophically flawed and culturally disastrous in its abstraction from the embedded and embodied character of human subjectivity. But is Rawls committed to this metaphysical view? To adduce further evidence on this charge, we can turn to the related theme of asocial individualism.

Commenting on Rawls' construction of the original position in terms of the veil of ignorance which characterises it, Onora O'Neill has argued that it involves a misleading idealisation of human agents:

> The veil of ignorance described in *A Theory of Justice* was tailored to hide the interlocking structure of desires and attitudes that is typical of human agents. Once the social relations between agents were masked it could seem plausible to assign to each desires for a uniform shortlist of primary goods, and to build a determinate ideal of mutual independence into a conception of justice. This ideal is not met by any human agents. . . . The construction assumes a mutual independence of persons and their desires that is false of all human beings. (1989: 209)

Why does Rawls engage in this act of idealisation in which human agents are presented as asocial individuals? For Sandel, this idealisation reveals Rawls' commitment to a metaphysical view of the self. He argues that Rawls' commitment to asocial individualism is exhibited by the contractual character of the original position in which it assumed that the individual (including his or her understanding of himself/herself as an individual) is prior to society and that society is to be understood essentially as a civil association between individuals for the purpose of mutual advantage. However, to justify the connection of these features of Rawls' argument to the thesis of *soul atomism* requires reasons for thinking that Rawls is not simply claiming either that an understanding of the self as characterised by rational self-interest is simply appropriate to citizenship (the political sphere) in modern constitutional democracies or that our current cultural understanding of the individual is that of a rational self who exhibits specific interests and that the original position models this cultural self-understanding, but that we are – in reality, as it were – rational individuals who possess interests which may or may not coincide with the interests of others. In taking up this task, Sandel points, firstly, to Rawls' prioritisation of the fact of the distinctness of persons over the fact that the interests which we hold often overlap, and, secondly, to Rawls' stress on the mutual disinterest of persons in the original position. On Sandel's argument, Rawls' prioritisation of the distinctness of persons over the frequent commonality of interests illustrates his commitment to the idea that we are separate individuals first and members of society second because it entails that we are persons prior to our relations with others and, concomitantly, that our relations with others are not constitutive of our identities. In other words, the fact that we share interests with others is a contingent feature of subjectivity, while the fact that we are distinct is an essential feature of subjectivity. This view of Rawls' account is reinforced by his stress on the mutual disinterestedness of parties in the original position, since this feature suggests that we are not tied to each other by moral commitments in pursuing our interests, that is, interests are primarily attached to individuals and not to communities, where the form of this attachment is revealed in the claim that our interests are not *in* but *of* the self (Rawls, 1971: §22). As such, this asocial individual must also be an antecedently individuated subject.

If this claim about the metaphysical character of Rawls' conception of the person is accurate, it should be confirmed by the status which Rawls claims for his theory of justice. If Rawls is claiming that his account has universal (i.e., ahistorical and trans-cultural) application, this would appear to confirm his commitment to the metaphysics which Sandel ascribes to him, *but* if Rawls is not claiming a universal status for his account of justice, we may be mistaken in reading *A Theory of Justice* as committed to the metaphysics of the ascetic ideal and as another act of priestly legislation. Rawls makes his position clear in the final section of the book, when he comments on the status of the original position:

> Thus to see our place in society from the perspective of this [original] position is to see it *sub specie aeternitatis*: it is to regard the human situation not only from all social but also all temporal points of view. The perspective of eternity is not a perspective from a certain place beyond the world, nor from the point of view of a transcendent being; rather it is a form of thought and feeling that rational persons can adopt within the world. (1971: §87)

This is a slightly perplexing passage since Rawls is both claiming a universal status for the original position, that is, that it is the Archimedean point of moral philosophy, and claiming that it does not constitute a God's-eye view of the sort which is articulated by the ascetic priest. However, in claiming a universal status for the original position and, thus, that all societies – past, present and future – can be properly judged by reference to the principles of justice which derive from it, Rawls is precisely articulating a view from nowhere and his qualifications simply amount to the claim that we can (and should) intelligibly adopt this perspective, that is, it is not beyond our essential capacities as antecedently individuated persons to adopt this perspective. Like the ascetic priest (or, rather, as an ascetic priest), Rawls is concerned to legislate the absolute priority (i.e., truth) of one perspective, to provide an Archimedean point from which to move the moral world. Thus, from Nietzsche's perspective, Rawls' account of justice exhibits the central feature of the ascetic ideal: a commitment to the thesis of *soul atomism*, that is, a commitment to a disembedded and disembodied vision of rational subjectivity. By assigning priority to the making of autonomous choices over the ends chosen, Rawls reveals the anti-erotic core of his theory of justice.[4]

We can see, then, that in *A Theory of Justice* Rawls is committed to the metaphysical account of the self against which Nietzsche's criticisms of the subject/object and appearance/reality distinctions are directed. Consequently, if Nietzsche's philosophical attack on the knowing subject of liberal epistemology is cogent, this critique applies equally to the deployment of this conception of the subject in the domain of moral philosophy and, thus, undermines philosophical (foundational) defences of liberalism. However, although we have already devoted considerable attention to Nietzsche's critique of the presuppositions of the thesis of *soul atomism*, it may be worth briefly drawing out the criticisms of asocial individualism which attend this critique. Let us begin by noting Nietzsche's claim that our capacity for sovereign agency is a product of the long pre-history of man and, in particular, the role of custom and punishment in fabricating a being with the power to make promises, while our conception of the self as antecedantly individuated subject is a product of the slave revolt in morals. Whatever the status of Nietzsche's genealogical reflections in the opening two essays of *On the Genealogy of Morals*, they involve two claims which express his critique of philosophical liberalism: firstly, the claim that our capacities are socially constituted and, secondly, the claim that the idea of the antecedantly individuated subject is not a metaphysical truth but a cultural artefact produced under particular historical conditions to express the practical interests of a specific community. Both of these claims are related to Nietzsche's argument that consciousness is a product of our membership of a cultural/linguistic community and that the character of our consciousness is inseparable from the judgements (including conceptions of the good) which are exhibited in the forms of agency which characterise this community. Thus, for Nietzsche, the individual and, in particular, the individual's self-understanding are the product of a complex history of the entwinement of judgement and agency in the life of a community.

The significance of these criticisms for foundational versions of liberal political theory can be brought out by noting that a consequence of Rawls' view that we are distinct from our interests and, consequently, that our identities are not touched by the fact that we are members of various communities of interest is that our membership of a *cultural* community and a *political* community is in no way constitutive of our subjectivity. By contrast, Nietzsche's emphasis on the constitutive role of community suggests that the questions 'who am I?' and 'what should I do?' is closely related to the interwoven questions 'who are we?' (culture) and 'what should we do?' (politics). Consequently, from Nietzsche's perspective, Rawls' philosophical liberalism is fatally flawed insofar as its reduction of society to a form of civil association between antecedantly individuated persons entails not only that it lacks any account of both culture and politics (and their relationship), but also that this devaluation of community expresses itself in a failure to recognise that the maintenance of our capacities for autonomous reflection and agency is dependent on *communal* practices, and, as such, a liberal polity instantiates an individualism which may undermine the very capacities upon which its cogency depends.

At this juncture, having sketched Nietzsche's critique of philosophical liberalism, let us turn to his critique of political liberalism and liberal politics by way of an introduction to the theme of agonism in Nietzsche's philosophy and, in particular, the relation of agonism to perspectivism and the cultivation of *virtu*.

Perspectivism, Agonism and *Virtu*

In the early essay 'Homer on Competition', Nietzsche explores the agonistic character of Greek culture by focusing initially on Hesiod's comment that there are ' "two Eris-goddesses on earth" ' (HC 189), two types of envy in the vocabulary of Greek ethics, one of which is as praiseworthy as the other is worthy of blame. Focusing on the benevolent form of envy as ambition in Greek society, Nietzsche argues that it is tied to 'the action of *competition*' (HC 190), that is, to the agonal character of Greek culture, and comments:

> Every great Hellene passes on the torch of competition; every great virtues strikes the spark of a new grandeur. If the young Themistocles could not sleep at the thought of Miltiades' laurels, his early-awakened urge found release only in the long contest with Aristides, when he developed that remarkable, purely instinctive genius for political action which Thucydides describes for us. (HC 191)

For the Greeks, Nietzsche argues, it is through contestation that envy is directed towards the cultivation of virtue and the well-being of the state assured. Thus Nietzsche remarks that the original meaning of the institution of *ostracism* is as a stimulant: 'the pre-eminent individual is removed so that a new contest of powers can be awakened' (HC 191).

Similarly Nietzsche argues that Hellenic education was based on the idea that our capacities only develop through struggle, whereby the goal of this agonistic education is the well-being of the *polis*: 'For example, every Athenian was to develop himself, through competition, to the degree that this self was of most use to Athens and would cause least damage' (HC 192). It is not only students who contest with each other, however; educators are also in competition with one another:

> Full of mistrust and jealousy, the great music masters Pindar and Simonides took their places next to eachother; the sophist, the advanced teacher of antiquity, contested with his fellow sophist; even the most general way of teaching, through drama, was only brought to the people in the form of an immense struggle of great musicians and dramatists. (HC 192)

Thus, on Nietzsche's account, the public culture of Greek society cultivated human powers through an institutionalised ethos of contestation in which citizens strove to surpass each other and, ultimately, to set new standards of nobility.

Reflecting on Nietzsche's essay, we can note that it is a prerequisite of an agonistic culture that there can be no determinate judgement as to how, for example, education is to be best conducted; such judgements are necessarily perspectival. For just as the pre-eminent individual – the genius – threatens the contest and must be ostracised to allow the flourishing of our collective powers, so too the pre-eminent perspective – the God's-eye view – undermines the agonistic cultivation of other perspectives.[5] When Nietzsche comments that the Hellenic idea of competition desires 'as *protective measure* against genius – a second genius' (HC 192), the same thought applies to perspectives (including Nietzsche's own). The basic thrust of the essay is clear: through contestation, we develop our human powers, and, as such, an agonistic ethos, as exhibited in the praiseworthy Eris-goddess, is integral to the cultivation of our capacities. However, insofar as Nietzsche is not simply advocating a return to ancient Greek culture, we need to try to grasp the character of Nietzsche's account of virtue and the relations between perspectivism and agonism to which his work commits itself.

In *The Anti-Christ* Nietzsche sketches his understanding of virtue by reference to the Renaissance: '*Not* contentment, but more power; *not* peace at all, but war; *not* virtue, but proficiency (virtue in the Renaissance style, *virtu*, virtue free of moralic acid)' (AC §2). But to what does this concept of *virtu* refer? Hanna Pitkin has pointed out that this Italian term does not simply mean virtue:

> In the Renaissance, it was often used, for instance, to mean something like power or motive force. It appears in Leonardo's notes on dynamics as more or less equivalent to physical motive power. The Italian term derives etymologically from the Latin term *virtus*, on the root *vir*, meaning 'man.' *Virtus* thus meant something like manliness, energetic strength, and was one of the traditionally admired Roman virtues along with *dignitas* and *gravitas* and the others. . . . These earlier uses of the concept of virtue remain only in occasional English forms like 'by virtue of,' which clearly implies not morality but force, or 'virtuousity,' which is a matter of skillfulness and achievement, not of good motives or good behavior. (1972: 309)

If we reflect on Nietzsche's remark in the light of this comment, it seems reasonable to suggest that he is using *virtu* in the sense of virtuousity, insofar as the account of subjectivity explored in the previous chapter connects will to power with our capacity to act to perform actions and is related to both the idea of mastery and that of the self as a work of art. This understanding of *virtu* leads us to a further question, namely, what are virtues within the context of *virtu*?

Let us note to begin with that the concept of virtuousity is related to the concept of a *practice* (recall the examples of *amor fati* offered in the previous chapter) as an activity with publicly constituted criteria of mastery. Thus, for example, lying in the grass may be part of a practice (for example, of meditation) but it is not itself a practice, while playing tennis is an activity to which criteria of mastery are appropriate. A route into this distinction is highlighted by MacIntyre, who has pointed out that practices (such as tennis) are distinct from other activities (such as lying in the grass) in possessing a *history* in which the rules and standards of excellence which characterise the practice are developed and revised (MacIntyre, 1981: 190). However, I want to depart from MacIntyre's account slightly insofar as I think that a more felicitous distinction than that between rules and standards of excellence as the constitutive features of a practice is that between standards of engagement and standards of excellence. My reasons for adopting this latter distinction are twofold. Firstly, it is simply the case that not all practices involve rules in the way that chess or tennis do (consider cooking, art and politics), yet engagement in such practices is still bound by norms which specify what counts as engagement. Secondly, this distinction draws out the relation between the criteria governing engagement and the criteria governing excellence in that it suggests that standards of engagement are the minimal requirements of proficiency to which standards of excellence refer. However, whichever distinction is deployed, it follows from this general account that to learn a practice such as tennis involves the recognition of the authority of not merely the rules or standards of engagement of the practice but also its currently constituted standards of excellence (criteria of mastery):

> To enter into a practice is to accept the authority of those standards [of excellence] and the inadequacy of my own performance as judged by them. It is to subject my own attitudes, choices, preferences and tastes to the standards which currently and partially define the practice. . . . [T]he standards are not themselves immune from criticism, but nonetheless we cannot be initiated into a practice without accepting the authority of the best standards realized so far. (MacIntyre, 1981: 190)[6]

Thus while the activity of lying in the grass makes no reference to either rules or standards unless it is part of a practice, the practice of tennis does entail such reference. But what does this concept of a practice entail with respect to virtues in the context of *virtu*? Using tennis as an example, I want to suggest that we can distinguish three types of virtue: (i) virtues which are specific to the particular practice; (ii) virtues which are non-specific and related to a family of practices; and (iii) virtues which are not specific to any particular practice but are related to engagement in practices *per se*.

The first type of virtues are simply those qualities (by which I mean capacities and abilities) which make up virtuousity in the particular practice in which one is engaged. For example, in playing tennis, such virtues would involve features such the ability to serve, volley, smash, and play backhands and forehands with control and good judgement of shot-selection, as well as the ability to 'disguise' one's shots, to 'read' the opponent's game and to anticipate his or her shots, and to 'know' where one is spatially in relation to the court as a whole. Thus to engage in a practice is to cultivate specific virtues, that is, specific uses of specific human powers.

The second type of virtues refer to features of the qualities which make up virtuousity in playing tennis which are requisite to virtuosity in a family of practices of which tennis is a member (such as racquet sports). For example, integral features of playing tennis shots with control include abilities with respect to hand to eye co-ordination and balance, while the other tennis-specific virtues cited involve features such as cunning, imagination and cognitive mapping. What is noticeable about these powers is that they are integral to virtuousity in all racquet sports. Thus we can suggest practice-specific virtues involve virtues which are related to families of practices, and, indeed, we can suggest that the family of which a given practice is a member is dependent on the non-specific but practice-related virtues which are integral to its specific virtues. Probably a simpler way of putting this point is to say that any practice involves specific uses of particular human powers, while a family of practices is characterised by non-specific uses of particular human powers.

The final type of virtues are not specific to practices or families of practices but relate to engaging in a practice as such. My claim is that there are (at least) two virtues of this type: truthfulness and justice.[7] Let us recall, firstly, that engaging in a practice entails the recognition of the authority of the standards of engagement and standards of excellence which constitute this practice (even if one is involved in contesting what these standards are) and, consequently, submission to standards. Now we can note with respect to standards of engagement that the very idea of such standards involves a commitment to truthfulness, that is, that one does not cheat by abrogating the standards (i.e., rules and/or norms) which govern engagement in a practice. The cheat is not playing the game. Standards of excellence also involve an immanent commitment to truthfulness insofar as they call on us to reflect honestly on the merits (degree of mastery) of our own performance. Indeed, truthfulness with respect to both standards may be integral to conduct; for example, deciding whether or not to let someone 'play through' in golf involves observing the rule that one should let a better player go through and, as part of this reflection, judging one's performance against the other player's by reference to standards of excellence.

The second virtue which I've suggested is tied to engagement in any practice is justice, which refers in this context to the rendering up of one's claim both to be engaged in the activity (standards of engagement) and to exhibit a certain degree of proficiency in the activity (standards of excellence) to the collective judgement of the community constituted by the practice in question. In its simplest form, this virtue involves just the recognition that such standards are constituted and reconstituted by the historical community which attends the practice *and* that this community is characterised by an order of rank in which different voices speak with distinct degrees of authority whereby the degree of authority granted is based on the public recognition of the speaker's mastery of the activity (or relevant aspect of the activity). Thus, this virtue points to the fact that we can deceive ourselves concerning our engagement and excellence and, consequently, denotes the submission of the judgement of the self to the judgement of the other (the community), while it *refers* to our capacity to internalise the other (the standards of the community) in reflecting on our performance and, concomitantly, our ability to overcome our capacity for self-deception. Part of mastery is not deceiving oneself concerning one's degree of mastery by being able to judge one's performance impartially, that is, by reference to standards. Thus, in its simple form wherein the standards are uncontested, the virtue of justice simply refers to the fact that the standards act as an internal other. However, where a practice (such as politics) involves the contestation of standards (in terms of what count as standards and/or how to rank these standards), the virtue of justice refers to our 'enlarged mentality' (to borrow Hannah Arendt's use of Kant's phrase), that is, our capacity to entertain a plurality of competing perspectives within the process of coming to a judgement. We might note in this context the following remark by Nietzsche on human beings:

> This contradictory creature has . . . in his nature a great method of knowing: he feels many fors and againsts – he raises himself up to *justice* – to a comprehension beyond the evaluation of good and evil. The wisest man would be the richest in contradictions, who, as it were, has feelers for all kinds of men: and right among them his great moments of *grandiose harmony*. (cited in Strong, 1988: 301)

Our main point, however, is now clear: to engage in any practice is to cultivate the virtues of truthfulness and justice. Mastery of a practice involves not deceiving oneself about one's performance and being able to entertain the possibly plural perspectives on the standards of the practice which are immanent to the community constituted by this practice.

At this juncture, having outlined what I take to be Nietzsche's position on *virtu* and the virtues, let us tie this position into our discussions of eternal recurrence and perspectivism. The first point to note is that this account helps to reveal why Nietzsche stresses truthfulness as integral to self-mastery, because it points out both that truthfulness is a virtue proper to any practice and that, since it is through one's engagement in certain practices (and not others) that one gives style to one's character, truthfulness is a virtue central to self-mastery (note the implication that whatever one's degree of technical excellence, one cannot be said to have fully mastered a practice unless one has mastered oneself at least when engaged in this practice). But if this account is plausible, it would suggest that integrity (as the virtue relevant to self-mastery) does not consist merely of truthfulness but also of justice, a conclusion supported further by the passage just cited – yet my consideration of Nietzsche's notion of eternal recurrence did not appear to broach this topic. This is not quite accurate since the account of eternal recurrence offered in the previous chapter did note the public character of integrity, but it is certainly true that this account only implicitly touched on justice as an element of integrity.

Perhaps we can approach this topic by noting that to affirm the eternal recurrence of an action immanently involves the affirmation of the eternal recurrence of the belief or perspective according to which *one* acts – but what is involved in such an affirmation? Insofar as will to power denotes the affective structure of reason and eternal recurrence denotes the maximal experience of will to power, it seems to me that to affirm the eternal recurrence of a perspective entails holding that this perspective is rationally justifiable, that is, represents the maximal satisfaction of the interests or, to put it another way, the maximal expression of the virtues which characterise the practice in which the actor is engaged. Thus, the virtue of justice involves the courage to put one's perspective (and thus oneself) to the test by truthfully examining its claim to satisfy our interests or exhibit the virtues of the practice against the claims of other perspectives. In other words, since different perspectives involve different ordered sets of interests (or virtues), that is, highlight different (ordered sets of) features as significant to the practice, to exhibit integrity involves testing these perspectives against each other in coming to an honest judgement concerning the degree to which they satisfy the interests (exhibit the virtues) of the practice; perspectival reason reveals itself as agonistic dialogue. In this context, we can note the immanent relationship between the doctrine of eternal recurrence and the perspective theory of affects by pointing out, firstly, that we need the doctrine of eternal recurrence precisely because we recognise the existence within our practices of a plurality of perspectives between which we must decide in participating in a practice, and, secondly, that the doctrine of eternal recurrence serves as a principle of selection by identifying the rational justifiability of a perspective for oneself with the affective experience of this perspective as necessity. Thus the doctrine of eternal recurrence cultivates both justice as the recognition of, and deliberation on, the agonistic encounter of the plurality of perspectives within a practice and truthfulness as the condition of the rational justifiability of the perspective which governs one's agency within this practice.

The discussion thus far suggests that the person of *virtu* is characterised by integrity which is constituted by the virtues of truthfulness and justice, and that this understanding of *virtu* is immanently related to the doctrine of eternal recurrence and the perspective theory of affects. In this context, we can reasonably claim that integrity is the ruling virtue in that it is the virtue which attends the *becoming* of what we are as opposed to the *what we are* which we become. In this sense, the perfectionist ideal of integrity expressed in the figure of the Overman represents the *formal* standard of excellence against which nobility is judged. However, we should also note three further points which are significant for this discussion. The first two points are concerned with drawing out aspects of the discussion thus far, while the third – which I will treat separately – develops the implications of this discussion with respect to politics.

Firstly, our integrity as persons is tied to our integrity as participants in various practices, where the practices in which one engages (and one's ranking of these practices) denotes the style of one's character. In other words, our self-mastery is constituted by the self-mastery we exhibit in the ordered set of practices in which we participate. Secondly, our practices are agonistic in a twofold sense: firstly, practices are characterised by historical communities in which persons contest with themselves and each other to achieve excellence; and, secondly, practices are characterised by the contestation of plural perspectives concerning the character of excellence. These contests are typically related in public debates concerning who is the greatest exponent of a given practice. Thus, for example, arguments concerning the respective claims of Rod Laver and John McEnroe to be the greatest ever tennis player, for example, typically involve not only disagreements concerning the degree to which they set standards of excellence but also disagreements about the character of excellence, that is, what count as the virtues of tennis and how to rank the virtues of this practice. In this context, it is important to note that our argument can be said to be rational because our debate concerning the virtues and their ranking is neither arbitrary nor abstract but takes place in the context of the history of the practice and in relation to the exemplars of greatness recognised in this history. Thus while we may never agree on who is the best, we can agree that it is in relation to figures such as Laver and McEnroe that claims to greatness in tennis must be adjudicated.[8]

The third and final point to which I want to draw attention concerns the public ranking of practices. The significance of this point is that while integrity as expressed in the figure of the Overman denotes the *formal* standard against which nobility is to be judged, the *substantive* standard against which nobility is judged is dependent on the public ranking of both practices and, more importantly, families of practices within the community and thus of virtues (or human powers) in terms of their cultural value. I think that the point of Nietzsche's argument in this context is simply that any cultural community as a *political* community is necessarily concerned with the question of which cultural practices and virtues should be cultivated and which should be discouraged (i.e., what should *we* do?) as well as related questions such as the degree to which we, as a public, should collectively facilitate or hinder particular cultural practices. This point is of crucial significance since it implies that politics as a practice is concerned with the ranking of cultural practices and virtues, that is, politics is the practice through which the community reflects on and constitutes itself as a community. In other words, in addressing the political question 'what should we do?', we articulate and rearticulate our cultural identities because our response to the cultural question 'who are we?' is expressed through the political practice of collective engagement in the public ranking of the virtues which constitute our cultural standards of nobility. Thus, whereas ethics poses the question 'what should I do?', politics poses the question 'what should we do?', and while these two questions are related insofar as 'I' am part of 'we', they are by no means identical.

To draw out the immense importance of this point for Nietzsche's account, we can begin by recalling that to affirm the eternal recurrence of a perspective entails holding that this perspective is rationally justifiable, that is, represents the maximal satisfaction of the interests (i.e., the maximal expression of the virtues) of the practice in which one is engaged. What does this mean with respect to politics? Insofar as the central interest or virtue of politics is the communal ordering of the virtues, it implies that to affirm the eternal recurrence of one's political perspective entails that honest deliberation on the plurality of political perspectives has led to the judgement that this political perspective exhibits the best ordering of the virtues for the community *and* that one exhibits this ordering of virtues as a citizen, that is, that one's political perspective expresses the ordering of one's soul. The implication of this argument is that Nietzsche, like Aristotle, is committed to the primacy of politics as a form of human practice on two counts. Firstly, it is through being a member of a political community that we acquire standards of nobility (however contested these standards may be). In other words, it is in and through the history of politics as a practice that we become members of a historical community characterised by standards of excellence and the contestation of these standards (both in terms of what count as virtues and in terms of how to rank them) which are constitutive of our cultural and political identities. Secondly, it is in the political arena that we both exhibit and test our claim to excellence *qua* nobility against the claims of others. In other words, politics is the arena in which one's soul is at stake and we exhibit our integrity by having the courage to acknowledge the claim to recognition of others and to test ourselves against them in agonistic dialogues. The claim that our beliefs are rationally justifiable, on Nietzsche's account, *commits* us to dialogue, to agonistic encounters in which we test our claims against the claims of others. Moreover, since Nietzsche regards integrity (i.e., truthfulness and justice) as the ruling virtue, what is important to him is not so much the various outcomes of our political arguments in terms of collective decisions but the process of argumentation, since it is through this process that our capacities for truthfulness and for justice are tested and cultivated. It is through the unending quest for the determination of the best ordering of the soul that we develop what, on Nietzsche's account, are the most important human powers, namely, reason and imagination, which are expressed as truthfulness (the limitation of imagination through reason) and justice (the expansion of reason through imagination).

These political themes will be taken up again in our discussion of political agonism, but I want to conclude by stressing the relation of perspectivism and agonism as an immanent feature of modern culture. The point is simply this: insofar as perspectives are rooted in (and articulate) affects and modern individuals are characterised by different embodied experiences of being-in-the-world and, thus, different ordered sets of affects, the contestation of perspectives is necessarily integral to modern culture and to the communities constituted by our practices. Consequently, the mainten-ance of the communities constituted by our practices entails that these communities are *agonistic* communities in which our shared identities relate not to shared perspectives but to a shared process of contestation. In other words, the perspective theory of affects entails an *agonistic* culture if we are to sustain the communal practices through which we develop our powers. This point further explains why integrity is presented by Nietzsche as the ruling virtue since it is central to the constitution and maintenance of such a cultural community in that the simple virtues of truthfulness and justice are the prerequisites for reconciling contestation and community in a sense of solidarity, of being enaged in a common quest. I will return to this issue in relation to the political features of Nietzsche's philosophy in more detail in exploring his political agonism and agonistic politics. However, before we turn to this topic, it is necessary to consider briefly whether perspectivism need be related to agonism in the way in which Nietzsche's account suggests.

Agonistic Perspectivism *contra* Liberal Perspectivism

In taking up this question, we confront the work of Richard Rorty, who shares Nietzsche's rejection of foundationalism in favour of an anti-foundational perspectivism and his recognition that modern culture is characterised by a plurality of perspectives concerning the good. However, Rorty rejects the relation which Nietzsche proposes between perspectivism and an agonistic culture. There are two distinct moves in this rejection: firstly, Rorty seeks to separate perspectivism from what he takes to be Nietzsche's metaphysics, that is, the concepts of will to power, eternal recurrence and the Overman; and, secondly, he *privatises* perspectivism by tying it to a liberal distinction between public and private spheres, confining the plural perspectives on the good to the private domain.[9]

To begin, let us recall that Nietzsche's commitment to perspectivism is expressed through the perspective theory of *affects* which presents our perspectives as rooted in our affective constitutions: our perspectives are *embodied* perspectives, that is, our ways of knowing are tied to our ways of being-in-the-world. Putting forward this 'theory' requires that Nietzsche provide an ontological account of human beings which specifies the relation between our perspectives and our affective constitution; the account which Nietzsche offers is the thesis of *will to power* in which the affective interest in experiencing ourselves as autonomous agents is presented as the architectonic interest of our affective constitution. The significance of this reminder for our discussion of Rorty is that the first step in Rorty's appropriation of Nietzsche's perspectivism is to divorce perspectivism from the thesis of will to power by offering an alternative social constructionist account of the self. Rorty's claim is that perspectivism needs to be reclaimed from the thesis of will to power in order that its anti-essentialist insights are not compromised by the 'metaphysical essentialism' of this thesis (1989: 106, cf. Conway, 1991 and 1992b). However, if we do not adopt the Heideggerian reading of will to power as a claim about the metaphysical essence of human beings which Rorty mobilises and simply view this thesis as claiming to be a rationally justifiable account of human beings which is open to contestation by other accounts, then the divorce which Rorty initiates presents itself not as a redemption of perspectivism from metaphysics but as a contestation of will to power as an ontological account. This already suggests that the practice of philosophy should be regarded as exhibiting an agonistic character whereby Rorty's rhetorical attempt to win the contest by redescribing it in non-agonistic terms is simply one move amongst others. However, to explore whether or not Rorty does offer us good reasons for disconnecting perspectivism from agonism, we can take up his arguments in more detail.

Integral to Rorty's account is a narrative model of self-creation characterised by social constructionism, voluntarism and a commitment to autonomy. Firstly, Rorty's social constructionism emerges in his acceptance of the idea that 'to change how we talk is to change what, for our own purposes we are' (1989: 20) and, concomitantly, in his commitment to the claim that socialisation 'goes all the way down' (1989: 185). Secondly, this position is linked to voluntarism via the claim that, within the given resources of our culture, we can change how we talk about ourselves (our perspectives or 'final vocabularies') and create ourselves anew more or less at will (if we make the effort). Finally, as Conway comments:

> The goal of this process of narrative re-description is the achievement of autonomy, i.e., the life of the 'strong poet' who deploys a final vocabulary that is neither imposed upon her from without, nor (simply) inherited by her from another. (1992b: 283)

Such strong poets are ironists: they recognise that there is no 'essence' to the self and that their self-descriptions are contingent fabrications.

What is going on in Rorty's account? Let us note, firstly, that this account presents perspectives as articulating more or less enabling narrative descriptions of one's self, wherein the degree to which a given perspective enables or constrains is not related to *what* one is in any extra-linguistic sense but to the social context in which one is embedded. While Nietzsche's perspectives are rooted in the extra-linguistic affective economies of embodied individuals, Rorty's perspectives are disembodied (Conway, 1992b: 285). Secondly, and relatedly, since there are no extra-linguistic constraints on our redescriptions of ourselves, we have no reason to suppose that any given description of ourselves is epistemically more or less adequate than any other description (Conway, 1992b: 286). While Nietzsche's rooting of perspectives in an account of our embodied human interest in will to power allows for an account of perspectival knowing which recognises that the equal right of perspectives to claim epistemic authority does not entail an equal right to epistemic authority, this is not the case with Rorty's disembodied perspectivism, which restricts perspectivism to 'an anti-position that ventures no positive account of perspectival knowing' (Conway, 1992b: 287). The weakness of this position emerges at the point that Rorty seeks to connect his perspectivism to a normative concern with the development of human solidarity, since to make this connection Rorty requires some kind of account of selfhood which expresses an embodied human interest in solidarity. Moreover, Rorty also needs to suggest arrangements such that irony and solidarity can co-exist with each other, since it is not immediately apparent that the commitment to a culture of individual ironists, of which the Romantic genius is the paradigmatic exemplar (Rorty, 1989: 29), can easily be reconciled with an interest in developing human solidarity. Let us turn to these two points.

We can begin by noting Rorty's characterisation of his expression of 'our' interest in solidarity in terms of our common susceptibility to suffering and, more particularly the pain of humiliation:

> Solidarity is not thought of as recognition of a core self, the human essence in all human beings, but rather thought of as the ability to see more and more traditional differences (of tribe, religion, race, customs and the like) as unimportant when compared with their similarity in respect to pain and humiliation – the ability to think of people wildly different from oneself as included in the range of 'us'. (1989: 192)

Rorty's contention that cruelty is the worst thing we do and his concern to minimise human suffering by promoting human solidarity may not entail a metaphysical (i.e., essentialist) account of the self but it certainly does involve a philosophical anthropology, an account of what it is to be a human being, namely, that the self is 'something which can be humiliated' (Rorty, 1989: 91, cf. Haber, 1994: 67–8). However, insofar as Rorty is not making an essentialist claim about the self, why should we regard this feature of human beings as beings characterised by affective interests (i.e., our susceptibility to humiliation) as prior to other features of human beings? Why regard the avoidance of humiliation (through the promotion of solidarity) as our architectonic human interest? Presumably Rorty's response to these queries is to note that, within the liberal cultures of constitutional democracies, we prize autonomy as the highest value (after all, Rorty's narrative model of self-creation is tied to the valuing of autonomy as the highest value) and, consequently, regard humiliation – conceived as the undermining of our autonomy – as the worst thing we can do to each other. Of course, this does not explain or justify why 'we' should regard our liberal description of the self as better than any other description available *either* within our culture *or* in other cultures. Rorty recognises this point when he comments:

> There is no *neutral*, non-circular way to defend the liberal's claim that cruelty is the worst thing we do, anymore than there is a neutral way to back up Nietzsche's claim that this expresses a resentful, slavish, attitude. (1989: 197)

For Rorty, this simply means that we are where we are and we cannot start from anywhere else. This may entail regarding the kind of non-liberal position expressed within our culture by Nietzsche as 'mad' (Rorty, 1991a: 187) and being ethnocentric with regard to other cultures (Rorty, 1991a: 203–10), but this is simply the necessary consequence of abandoning metaphysical essentialism.

Is Rorty justified in his assertion that there are no neutral, non-circular ways of justifying claims about how to rank different features of human beings and/or claims about what count as the features of human beings? If Rorty's claim is justified, then it is hard to see how liberals and Nietzscheans, for example, could engage in meaningful argument at all, and Rorty's justification of liberalism plays on this feature by reintroducing the old argument for the superiority of liberalism, namely that, unlike other ideologies, liberalism allows persons to hold whatever views they wish so long as they don't harm others (i.e., respect the right of others to hold different beliefs), in a slightly new form:

> The advantage of postmodernist liberalism is that it recognizes that in recommending that ideal [of liberal justice] one is not recommending a philosophical outlook, a conception of human nature or of the meaning of human life, to representatives of other cultures. All we should do is point out the practical advantages of liberal institutions in allowing individuals and cultures to get along with each other without intruding on each other's privacy, without meddling with each other's conceptions of the good. (1991a: 209)

In this argument, scepticism about our ability to adjudicate between accounts of selfhood or conceptions of the good is tied to a pragmatic commitment to 'getting along' which establishes the superiority of liberalism by default. Since, on Rorty's account, we cannot adjudicate between perspectives in terms of truth, the obvious thing to do is to privatise perspectives under the aegis of a public liberalism which protects our rights to pursue, revise and reject particular final vocabularies in the private sphere; thus, the most appropriate philosophy to our 'postmodern' age is one which places us as private ironists and public liberals.[10] However, Rorty's new, postmodern version of this argument is no less disingenuous than its old, sceptical modern version since it has the effect of producing a *de facto* justification of liberalism in which the public commitment to individual autonomy has lexical priority over private conceptions of the good and, thus, acts against the pursuit of conceptions of the good which have a communal rather than individual character. Rorty's liberalism is tolerant as long as we accept liberal criteria of tolerance. Of course, if we have no real alternative (and this is the point of the either/or rhetoric deployed by Rorty in which we are presented with the choice between discredited metaphysics and postmodern liberalism), Rorty's position might seem attractive, but it is by no means clear that this is the case. Here Rorty's crucial move is to claim that the attempt to construct debates between, for example, liberals and Nietzscheans is simply meaningless since each side is involved in a circular set of claims. It is not clear to me, however, why attempts at arguments between liberals and Nietzscheans should necessarily be doomed endeavours (if it was, this book would involve a performative contradiction), and I will try to explain why I think Rorty is mistaken on this point.

Let us start by setting out the general character of Rorty's position on this topic in more detail:

> Consider the claim that we liberals can simply dismiss Nietzsche and Loyola as crazy. One imagines these two rejoining that they are quite aware that their views unfit them for citizenship in a constitutional democracy and that the typical inhabitants of such a democracy would regard them as crazy. But they take these facts as further counts against constitutional democracy. They think the kind of person created by such a democracy is not what human beings ought to be. (Rorty, 1991a: 190)

On Rorty's account, this consideration presents the liberal with a dilemma: either he or she must refuse to argue about what human beings should be, that is, be intolerant towards these non-liberal views, or he or she must be thrown back on an account of human nature. Rorty's argument is that we must grasp the first horn of this dilemma and 'insist that not every argument need be met in the terms in which it is presented' (1991a: 190). Consequently, Rorty asserts that the postmodern liberal must cease to accommodate the question 'what kind of human beings are you hoping to produce?' as relevant to an account of the primacy of (liberal) justice and respond thus:

> . . . even if the typical character types of liberal democracies *are* bland, calculating, petty, and unheroic, the prevalence of such people may be a reasonable price to pay for political freedom. (1991a: 190)

Notably this response seems to involve (at least) two dubious assumptions: firstly, that the liberal idea of political freedom is unproblematic (i.e., it fails to recognise the contested character of freedom within our culture) and, secondly, that liberalism is the only way of achieving political freedom. Moreover, it may not be so easy to avoid the second horn of the dilemma as Rorty supposes, even if we admit that accounts of the self do not add to political theories but act as alternative expressions of them. As Mulhall and Swift comment:

> . . . a defender of a given political theory might eschew *articulating* her vision of a given political theory in terms of a theory of the person; but it does not follow (as Rorty claims) that she is free to ignore criticisms of her political blueprint that are couched in terms relating to the nature of the people that blueprint would create. (1992: 236)

Rorty's argument is also somewhat disingenuous since a large part of his reason for advocating liberalism is that it is supposed to allow us to act as private ironists in pursuit of autonomy and to foster human solidarity, and thus an answer to the question of the kind of human beings Rorty wants to produce is 'autonomous beings with a developed sense of human solidarity'. As such it seems reasonable to ask if liberalism accomplishes these aims; Nietzsche, for example (as we'll see in the following sections), argues that liberalism does not, and cannot, deliver the goods which Rorty wants. Can Rorty respond here that an argument between liberal and Nietzschean views is meaningless because there is no neutral, non-circular way to justify either position? Such a response would seem somewhat bizarre since both Rorty and (on my account) Nietzsche are committed *qua* politics to the development of our capacities for autonomy and solidarity (albeit slightly differently conceived). However, Rorty does not appear to offer this response; instead he seems to adjust his position and argues not that argument is effectively impossible but that it is pointless:

> . . . we do not conclude that Nietzsche and Loyola are crazy because they hold unusual views on certain 'fundamental' topics; rather, we conclude this only after extensive attempts at an exchange of political views have made us realize that we are not going to get anywhere. (1991a: 191)

Now since the postmodern liberal recognises that Nietzsche is a person who expresses certain political views and this recognition entails (on Rorty's Davidsonian view) that some degree of translation between their respective positions is possible, Rorty's point looks suspiciously like saying that 'not getting anywhere' means 'not getting agreement' (cf. Rorty, 1991a: 191 fn. 41). But we need to ask both why not getting agreement is a good reason to give up arguing about politics, the self, etc., and why this final refusal to engage in potentially irresolvable arguments on the part of liberals should commit us to liberalism. To the first of these queries Rorty might make the pragmatic claim that 'we' can only be a political community if we share certain common judgements (minimally those about the desirability of 'getting along' and 'respect for each other's privacy'). It is not clear, though, why 'we' might not be able to be a political community characterised by an agreement to argue about the character of politics (particularly if we think that it is through argument that we develop our human powers). To the second query, Rorty might respond that, since arguments between liberals and non-liberals are ultimately pointless, we are better off appealing to Rawls' idea of 'reflective equilibrium', in which we weigh our fundamental moral intuitions against each other and work from the fact that, within the public political cultures of constitutional democracies, our fundamental intuitions are liberal. Quite apart from the questionable assumption that such arguments are pointless, this response seems to involve two further assumptions: firstly, that the only relevant consideration in justifying a political theory (e.g., liberalism) is whether or not it fits the intuitions expressed in our public political culture; and, secondly, that the dominant political intuitions of our current public political culture are liberal. Rorty attempts to justify the former of these assumptions by arguing that, firstly, 'the world' gives us no reasons to accept one political vocabulary rather than another, and, secondly, since this implies that there are no neutral, non-circular ways of justifying political vocabularies, the only thing one can do with respect to other (non-liberal) vocabularies is to ignore them and go about the business of emphasising the attractions of liberalism, that is, cultivating the connection between liberalism and our moral/political intuitions. This links to the second claim, namely, that we have come to accept a liberal vocabulary (though not through any act of will on our part) and thus we can reasonably forget about any other political vocabularies; in a sense, being liberals is simply our fate. There are, however, three fairly serious problems with these arguments.

The first problem, which has been pointed out by Mulhall and Swift, concerns Rorty's contention that postmodern bourgeois liberals should simply ignore other vocabularies and highlight the attractions of liberalism. They comment:

> It seems eminently plausible that one way of persuading someone to adopt a new outlook on life would be to emphasise the scope, sophistication, flexibility, etc., of the concepts that embody it. . . . However, another equally important part of such reasoning must be that of engaging with the old vocabulary, for example, by highlighting its unwieldiness, its failure to mark certain distinctions, its propensity to obscure or play down certain fundamental aspects of human behaviour and experience – and by responding to similar claims that its proponents make about the new vocabulary. . . . Critical engagements that employ terms of criticism of the sort mentioned above no more assume that concepts describe or represent reality than does the positive part of the process that Rorty endorses. (1992: 246)

This criticism points out that, within the practice of political philosophy, there are certain, albeit contested, canons of relevance specifying the properties we want from a political theory which Rorty must admit if the idea of making liberalism attractive to non-liberals is to be intelligible, but which commit Rorty (unless liberalism has no signifiant opponents left) to an agonistic engagement with other political theories. Mulhall and Swift's point gestures towards a second problem with Rorty's idea of the lack of non-circular, neutral ways of adjudicating between his political liberalism and Nietzsche's political agonism since the practice of politics is also characterised by certain contested canons of relevance which are constituted by the history of this practice and specify the properties we want from a politics (such as autonomy and solidarity); thus, Rorty is committed to an agonistic encounter with Nietzsche in which he needs to give reasons why a Rawlsian liberal politics satisfies our interest in autonomy and solidarity better than Nietzsche's agonistic politics. We can press this point further and argue that the considerations which apply to arguments about political theories and arguments about types of politics also apply to arguments about conceptions of the good which would appear to call for such arguments to be part of our public political culture and not rendered into purely private concerns. The final problem attends to Rorty's implicit claim that the dominant intuitions within our public political culture are liberal. The difficulty here is twofold: firstly, as our preceding comments indicate, the dominance of liberal intuitions does not entail refusing to engage with other political theories and types of politics but simply needing good reasons to give up these intuitions; and, secondly, Rorty provides absolutely no evidence whatsoever to support his claim that liberal intuitions are dominant in our public political culture (presumably he thinks this is obvious?).

At this stage, let us try to draw together the relevant considerations with respect to Rorty's attempt to divorce perspectivism and agonism. We can note, firstly, that none of the arguments that Rorty actually offers for liberalism is sufficient because his attempt to establish the priority of liberalism by ruling out its opponents is unconvincing; this does not mean that sufficient arguments cannot be given, only that such arguments need to be made. Secondly, we have seen that, despite himself, Rorty's perspectivism commits him to an agonistic position with respect to arguments about political theory and types of politics, and there seems no particular good reason why this should not also apply to arguments about the good. However, the argument presented in this section is basically a limited one in that it simply seeks to show that Rorty does not provide us with good reasons to disconnect either philosophy and political theory (on the contrary, it looks as though philosophical debates about rationality, selfhood, etc., are thoroughly political) or perspectivism and agonism (if argument is possible and not limited to an instrumental concern with attaining agreement, there seems no reason to rule out political agonism as a theory and agonistic politics as a practice). However, the response offered to Rorty's arguments is not sufficient to explain why we should adopt Nietzsche's agonistic politics, only to explain why it makes sense to engage in an argument about whether or not we should adopt it and to specify the relevant considerations of such an argument. These considerations are twofold: firstly, we need to take up the question of the capacity of liberal and agonistic types of political theory to exhibit the properties we want from a political theory; and, secondly, we need to examine the question of the capacity of liberal and agonistic politics to satisfy the interests we want from a politics (i.e., autonomy and solidarity or community). These tasks are the respective focuses of the next two sections.

Political Agonism *contra* Political Liberalism

The starting point for this discussion is the fact that both Nietzsche and political liberals such as Rawls (and Rorty) are committed both to a recognition that our modernity is characterised by the existence of a plurality of conflicting conceptions of the good *and* a concern with human autonomy and the possibility of a political community. For Nietzsche, our modernity entails that no general *substantive* account of the good can serve as a basis for a modern polity. Thus Nietzsche comments:

> To say it briefly (for a long time people will still keep silent about it): What will not be built any more, is – a society in the old sense of that word; to build that everything is lacking, above all the material. *All of us are no longer material for a society*; this is a truth for which the time has come. (GS §356)

While Rawls argues similarly (but not identically) that the fact of pluralism and of respect for autonomy entails that no *comprehensive* account of the good can serve as the basis of a well-ordered society:

> . . . the hope of political community must indeed be abandoned, if by such a community we mean a political society united in affirming the same comprehensive doctrine. This possibility is excluded by the fact of reasonable pluralism together with the rejection of the oppressive use of state power to overcome it. (1993: 146)

However, despite this similarity, Nietzsche and Rawls part company when it comes to the conceptions of autonomy and, concomitantly, the conceptions of political community compatible with reasonable pluralism which they articulate. In this context, to adjudicate (at least provisionally) between these positions requires that we attempt to determine the degree to which each account expresses the relevant virtues we require from a political theory. But what are these virtues? In this context, following (and slightly adjusting) Hilary Putnam, I suggest that we can identify three virtues which will serve as shared canons of relevance for this imagined argument between Nietzsche and Rawls:

> (1) the desire that one's basic assumptions, at least, should have *wide* appeal; (2) the desire that one's system should be able to withstand rational criticism; (3) the desire that the [politics] recommended should be *liveable*. (Putnam, 1981: 105)

These intellectual virtues – which are not presented as transcendental requirements but as historically constituted interests – seek to specify the sorts of qualities which we might expect a good political theory to exhibit. To take up the capacity of Nietzsche's and Rawls' account to exemplify these virtues, I will begin by addressing Rawls' account before arguing that Nietzsche's political theory offers us a fuller satisfaction of these interests.

In *Political Liberalism* (1993), Rawls abandons the idea of basing a well-ordered society on a comprehensive liberal account because he now regards this possibility as implausible in the context of the pluralism characteristic of modernity. While Rawls maintains the basic idea of justice as fairness articulated through the representative device of the original position, he restricts this conception of justice to the political domain (i.e., the basic social, economic and political institutions of society), that is, it applies to persons only as citizens and not to their non-public identities. He argues: 'Only a political conception of justice that all citizens might reasonably be expected to endorse can serve as a basis of public reason and justification' (1993: 137).[11] Here Rawls' liberalism is fundamental since it is his commitment to the liberal idea of the freedom and equality of persons as citizens which leads him to argue for the basic criterion of public justifiability (Mulhall and Swift, 1992: 190). The purpose of Rawls' argument is to demonstrate that justice as fairness as political is capable of generating the 'overlapping consensus' requisite to a well-ordered society characterised by free and equal citizens because it can be affirmed by persons from within their divergent reasonable comprehensive views of the good by reference to ideas latent within our public political culture. Rawls' argument develops by two stages: firstly, he offers a freestanding account of justice as fairness as the conception of political justice appropriate to free and equal citizens characterised by the moral powers of a capacity for a sense of justice and a capacity for a conception of the good; and, secondly, he argues that this conception of political justice can serve to develop an overlapping consensus between reasonable comprehensive doctrines of the good which is not merely a *modus vivendi* since this conception of political justice can be affirmed as reasonable by persons as citizens from within their reasonable comprehensive conceptions of the good.

How does Rawls' political liberalism compare and contrast with his earlier philosophical liberalism? Firstly, we can note that Rawls still presupposes the value of consensus for the maintenance of a well-ordered society but, in the context of pluralism, limits the consensus he hopes to achieve to political justice (and guidelines for its application) rather than justice *per se*. For Rawls, we require a consensus about the extent of the political domain and the character of justice (and how to apply it) within this domain but no more can be reasonably expected and no more is required. Central to this position is the claim that there are *no* exceptions to the rule that an attempt to unify modern political society in terms of a comprehensive doctrine *necessarily* entails breaching the autonomy of persons as citizens (Rawls, 1993: 37–8, especially fn.39). Secondly, we can note that Rawls' conception of autonomy is still presented in terms of a capacity to revise and replace one's conception of the good. However, this conception of autonomy is no longer connected to either a metaphysical view of the self as antecedentally individuated or a comprehensive view of the self in which autonomy functions as the ruling value in public and non-public spheres alike, but, rather, to a conception of the person as citizen of a constitutional democracy. Rawls is quite prepared now to accept that our non-political identities may be constituted by our conceptions of the good rather than the act of choosing them, and that these conceptions of the good may be communal rather than individualistic. In other words, Rawls can accept the communitarian view of the self in which our identities are not separable from our conceptions of the good. But how does this cohere with his arguments that our political identities should be liberal? Here we return to the fact of pluralism and the criterion of public justifiability since it is because our society is characterised by an irreducible plurality of conceptions of the good that a publicly justifiable account cannot involve a comprehensive account of the good and, as such, must be committed to a conception of political community which recognises this 'fact' by embodying a commitment to the shared goal of political justice in which it is our autonomy as persons able to choose, revise and replace our conceptions of the good which is significant. Rawls' account is consonant with communitarianism because our political identities embody a conception of the political community in which there is a common identification with political justice (albeit in terms of the various reasonable comprehensive doctrines of the good held by citizens). We should also note, however, that this position requires that our political identities have priority over our non-public identities because this priority ensures the possibility of this (weaker form of) political community insofar as the lack of such a priority rule would undermine the overlapping consensus requisite to sustaining the basic institutions of society as a scheme of fair co-operation between citizens.

In the light of these brief reflections, we can see that the criticisms of Rawls' philosophical liberalism do not apply to his political liberalism. Firstly, as already noted, Rawls does not deploy a metaphysical account of the self but a political conception. Secondly, his emphasis on political community structured in terms of an overlapping consensus on political justice absolves him of the charge of asocial individualism. Thirdly, while Rawls may still intelligibly be committed to universalism, this commitment can only be expressed in terms of the recommendation of a political ideal rather than the legislation of a comprehensive ideal. Now, in articulating this shift in his perspective, Rawls introduces two distinctions which are fundamental to his account: firstly, his distinction between political and comprehensive doctrines and, secondly, his distinction between reasonable and unreasonable comprehensive doctrines (which articulates the difference between pluralism and reasonable pluralism). If Rawls' account is to have wide appeal, to be able to be sustained in the face of rational criticism, and to be liveable, it is vital that these distinctions as well as his assumption of the necessity of consensus for maintaining a well-ordered society hold up in terms of these criteria.

The rationale for Rawls' assumption that an 'overlapping consensus' is required concerning the demarcation of the political domain and the character of justice seems to be based on the judgement that disagreement about the character of the political and of justice threatens the basic fabric of society as a fair scheme of co-operation between citizens. However, it is not clear that this is necessarily the case. Since Rawls nows effectively holds a communitarian view of the self, it seems reasonable to ask if he is justified in ignoring the possibility of an agonistic community in which our common political identities are tied to a process of argumentation (including the contestation of the criteria of argumentation) about the domain of the political and the character of justice (wherein the content and form of argument are bounded, at least partially, by our political history). I will return to this topic, but perhaps Rawls' presupposition of the value of consensus about the content of politics and justice is simply an expresson of his liberalism? If so, this presupposition can only be secured by demonstrating the superiority of the liberal position; therefore, let us turn to the other features of Rawls' account.

On the basis of the brief examination of Rawls' position thus far, it seems that his distinction between comprehensive and political accounts involves two claims: firstly, that when we act as citizens we *must* act in terms of the priority of the political account to the (rest of) the comprehensive account; and, secondly, that the distinction between a purely political liberalism and a comprehensive liberalism is sustainable. Addressing the first of these claims, we might wonder how plausible it is, how *liveable* it is, that we, as citizens, assign priority to the virtues and values that sustain political justice when these clash with other virtues and values constitutive of our comprehensive doctrine. This distinction requires that, for example, the Christian fundamentalist bracket off his or her beliefs concerning the desirability of abolishing the separation of church and state when acting as a citizen. As Mulhall and Swift comment:

> [Rawls] posits a split between the political and the personal which seems to require that those holding comprehensive perfectionist doctrines hold them in a rather half-hearted (perhaps even liberal way). (1992: 209)

To this critical query Rawls' response is to emphasise that, in the context of reasonable pluralism, the non-political values that clash with the political conception of justice 'may be normally outweighed because they come into conflict with the very conditions that make fair social cooperation possible on a footing of mutual respect' (1993: 157). There are two notable features of this response: firstly, Rawls appeals to 'reasonable pluralism' rather than pure pluralism and, secondly, he limits his claim to what may be 'normally' expected. How, then, does reasonable pluralism differ from pluralism as such? Commenting on the relation between comprehensive views and his political liberalism, Rawls writes:

> I shall suppose – perhaps too optimistically – that except for certain kinds of fundamentalism, all the main historical religions admit of such an account [of free faith] and thus may be seen as reasonable comprehensive doctrines. (1993: 170)

Thus, a reasonable comprehensive view differs from an unreasonable comprehensive view by virtue of the fact that, while it holds to its own truth, it recognises that persons may reasonably hold other views and, on this basis, respects the freedom to hold other views which is modelled by Rawls' political conception of justice. Effectively it seems that being a political liberal serves as the criterion of reasonableness. However, if we turn to the second feature of Rawls' response, the limited claim that political values will 'normally' outweigh non-political values, we can note that this position appears consonant with a weaker notion of reasonableness articulated by Rawls earlier in his argument when he comments:

> It is left to citizens individually – as part of liberty of conscience – to settle how they think the values of the political domain are related to other values in their comprehensive view. (1993: 140)

I suggest that this claim is weaker because it seems reasonable to suggest that part of fitting political values into the comprehensive scheme of values would be working out their relative priority for oneself as a person, which might well entail that although the political values normally have priority with respect to one's actions as a citizen, they need not always do so. How does Rawls deal with these abnormal instances? He gives two distinct responses to this question. In the first response, he comments:

> If it is said outside the church there is no salvation, and therefore a constitutional regime cannot be accepted unless it is unavoidable, we must make some reply. . . . [W]e say that such a doctrine is unreasonable: it proposes to use the public's political power – a power in which citizens have an equal share – to enforce a view bearing on constitutional essentials about which citizens as reasonable persons are bound to differ uncompromisingly. When there is a plurality of reasonable doctrines, it is unreasonable or worse to want to use the sanctions of state power to correct, or to punish, those who disagree with us. (1993: 138)

The significant point about this defence is that it appeals to the *fact* that citizens 'are bound to differ uncompromisingly'. Rawls' anti-perfectionist defence of state-neutrality is predicated on the assumption that such a position is required because of the fact of disagreement between reasonable comprehensive doctrines, but if such doctrines happen to agree on a particular issue, then, in the face of such social agreement, it is not clear that the state should be neutral; rather, it pushes him to regard 'the anti-perfectionist neutrality of the state as a circumstance-dependent require-ment of justice' (Mulhall and Swift, 1992: 225). The problem with such a move, however, is that Rawls' anti-perfectionism is closely tied to his emphasis on the autonomy of citizens, and it might seem that state intervention, even where publicly justifiable in terms of the social agree-ment, would broach that autonomy by closing down a space for the revision and replacement of our comprehensive doctrines which is compatible with political justice even if it is in disagreement with the existing reasonable comprehensive doctrines. In the light of this problematic position, let us turn to Rawls' second defence:

> . . . in affirming a political conception of justice we may eventually have to assert at least certain aspects of our own comprehensive religious or philosophical doctrine (by no means necessarily fully comprehensive). This will happen whenever someone insists, for example, that certain questions are so fundamental that to insure their being rightly settled justifies civil strife. The religious salvation

of those holding a particular religion, or indeed the salvation of a whole people, may be said to depend on it. At this point we have no alternative but to deny this, or to imply its denial and hence to maintain the kind of thing we had hoped to avoid. (1993: 152)

The obvious problem with this defence is that it surrenders the fundamental distinction between political liberalism and comprehensive liberalism which Rawls' account was designed to overcome. In the face of pluralism, this defence admits the controversy it was designed to avoid. Thus it appears that Rawls must *either* give up the strong connection between anti-perfectionism and autonomy modelled by his political conception of justice *or* recognise the unsustainability of the distinction between political and comprehensive liberalism.

In the light of these problems, let us turn to Rawls' distinction between reasonable and unreasonable comprehensive doctrines. The difficulty with this distinction does not lie so much in the idea of reasonable doctrines as those which recognise the possibility of reasonable pluralism and unreason-able doctrines as those which don't, but in the slippage between a weak notion of reasonableness which includes respect for citizens as autonomous but does not necessarily affirm the priority of this value and a strong notion of reasonableness which assigns priority to political liberalism in clashes with other aspects of the comprehensive doctrine. If Rawls holds to the weak version of this thesis, he is caught in the problems concerning the relationship of the political and the comprehensive which we have just explored, but if he holds to the strong version of this thesis, he is effectively ruling out the problem by definition and presupposing what he is meant to be showing, namely, that political liberalism can generate an overlapping consensus of reasonable comprehensive doctrines. Of course, Rawls might claim that he is justified in making this strong assumption because there is *no* alternative to political liberalism available, but this claim also is assumed and not shown by his argument. Consequently, in reflecting on Rawls' political liberalism in terms of the three criteria which have been specified as appropriate, we may reasonably conclude that while Rawls' basic assumptions may have wide appeal, we can query their capacity to withstand rational criticism and to be liveable. It remains, however, to demonstrate that any better alternative is available.

To introduce Nietzsche's alternative and to explore its capacity to satisfy our interests, we can begin by noting that Nietzsche's position as expressed by the schema of will to power, eternal recurrence, self-overcoming and the Overman is a comprehensive doctrine in Rawls' terms insofar as it specifies a formal hypergood, namely, the perfectionist ideal of the Overman which attends becoming what one is. However, this comprehensive doctrine does not specify any substantive goods, that is, make any demands on what one is. What is going on here? Nietzsche shares Rawls' recognition that modernity is characterised by an irreducible pluralism concerning the character of the good life; however, this recognition leads him to begin with a different question in attempting to work out the best form of polity appropriate to pluralism. Nietzsche's starting point is a simple question: 'what is involved in holding a substantive comprehensive conception of the good to be true?' He then makes two claims which attend respectively to the topics of 'holding' and of 'truth': firstly, to *hold* a substantive doctrine about the character of the good life entails that one's activity exemplifies one's commitment to this doctrine (i.e., if I say I hold a belief and knowingly act against it, I cannot properly be said fully to affirm this belief); and, secondly, to hold a substantive doctrine to be *true* entails that this doctrine on the ordering of the soul manifests the best satisfaction of our human interests. In the context of these claims, Nietzsche proposes a conception of autonomy as self-overcoming which, *qua* holding a doctrine, refers to the activity of working on the self to achieve self-mastery with respect to the exemplification of the doctrine one affirms and, *qua* the truth of a doctrine, refers to the activity of testing (and potentially revising and replacing) this doctrine against the claims of other doctrines to represent the best ordering of the soul. Both of these activities constitutive of self-overcoming involve *public justification* insofar as one's exemplification of the ordered set of values one espouses is subject to public scrutiny and testing, while the claim that this doctrine represents the best ordering of the soul entails engagement in an agonistic dialogue concerning what count as virtues and values as well as how these virtues and values are ranked. Thus, as citizens, we are concerned with the question of the values and the ranking of values which should be cultivated by the community and it is in engaging in argument about these questions that we cultivate both the virtues of truthfulness and justice appropriate to citizens and, concomitantly, the sense of political community as an engagement in a common quest to identify the character of the best (i.e., most noble) ordering of the soul. Politics is revealed on this civic humanist account as the highest form of human activity, the privileged locus of the good life, since it is in the arena of politics that we are concerned with the character of nobility in arguing about which virtues and values should be communally cultivated.

Reflecting on this conception of an agonistic political community, we can begin by noting that it represents a modelling of Nietzsche's perspective theory of affects. It will be recalled that this theory of truth involves the claim that the perspectival character of knowing rules out any claim to offer a non-perspectival perspective which could claim absolute epistemic authority; in other words, this thesis regards perspectives as having an equal right to claim epistemic authority and only rules out the attempt by certain perspectives (e.g., Kant's) to deny this right to all other perspectives. The modelling of this theory of truth as a political theory entails that persons holding particular substantive perspectives on the good have an equal right to claim political authority and that the only position ruled out is that of denying this equal right to those whom we disagree with. In effect, Nietzsche's position might be said to give rise to a similar distinction between reasonable and unreasonable doctrines to that offered by Rawls, albeit from a different direction, since what matters on Nietzsche's account is whether or not a doctrine recognises its own perspectival character. Insofar as we have already noted that this idea of an agonistic community entails the autonomy of citizens, we can reasonably conclude that this political theory models a non-liberal conception of citizens as free and equal, and exhibits its commitment to pluralism by ruling out as unreasonable any demand to impose a given doctrine on others on the grounds that such a demand is based on the contradictory idea of a non-perspectival perspective and would abrogate the freedom and equality of citizens. However, it should be noted that just as the fact that perspectives have an equal right to claim epistemic authority does not entail that they have an equal right to epistemic authority, so too the fact that citizens holding particular substantive doctrines have an equal right to claim political authority does not entail that citizens have an equal right to political authority. There are two relevant considerations which demarcate Nietzsche's position from that of liberalism on this topic, for while Nietzsche's position seems to entail equal access to the arena of political debate, the authority of a citizen's voice within this arena of contest will depend on both the degree to which the citizen is publicly recognised as *recommending* a substantive doctrine (the question of integrity) and the degree to which the recommendation of this *substantive doctrine* can generate public support (the question of truth). For Nietzsche, the criterion of public justifiability attends not only to what is said but also to who is speaking, and reveals a concern with an order of rank in terms of the formal and substantive nobility of citizens.

If both Nietzsche and Rawls model citizens as free and equal, what of the other features claimed by Rawls for his political liberalism? Closely connected to Rawls' political conception of justice is the virtue of tolerance, and it is obvious why a recognition of pluralism should involve the cultivation of this virtue. However, for Rawls, tolerance requires that public reason put aside the question of truth, subordinating this topic to reason-ableness and the priority of the political; however, we have seen that this move produces a series of problems internal to Rawls' account, so can Nietzsche offer a better theory in this regard? Let us note, firstly, that Nietzsche does not divide the self into political and personal components. On the contrary, one's substantive conception of the good is what is revealed in the ordered set of values which one argues for in the political arena; in manifesting the ordered evaluations of one's soul, one reveals the ranked set of values which one recommends to the community. What is important is that the formal conditions of holding one's perspective to be true entail an open-ended agonistic process of dialogue with persons holding other perspectives which cultivates our capacities for truthfulness and justice. To put this point another way, we can say that, for Nietzsche, tolerance for other views, a willingness to enage with them in an open and fair-minded way, is a condition of claiming to hold one's own beliefs to be true. In other words, on this view, one does not tolerate the views of others because this is the condition of reciprocal toleration of our views by them, one tolerates the views of others because this toleration is the condition of one's own integrity. Moreover, precisely because one's integrity is tied to tolerance, this position commits citizens to a form of society which is characterised by the cultivation of the conditions of honest and just argument between free and equal citizens. But perhaps these comments and the ideal of agonistic community they support do not seem plausible? Let me give an example to clarify matters.

In *Reason, Truth and History* (1981), Hilary Putnam reflects on a fundamental argument which he, as a welfare liberal, has with Robert Nozick, as a libertarian, and comments:

> In *my* view, *his* fundamental premises – the absoluteness of the right to property, for example – are counterintuitive and not supported by sufficient argument. On *his* view, I am in the grip of a 'paternalistic' philosophy which he regards as insensitive to individual rights. This is an extreme disagreement. . . . Each of us regards the other as lacking, at this level, a certain kind of sensitivity and perception. To be perfectly honest, there is in each of us something akin to contempt. (1981: 164–5)

However, the fact that such arguments are quite possibly irresolvable and that such disagreements involve feelings of disdain between the participants with respect to the substantive views constitutive of their political identities does not preclude also holding mutual respect on the basis of a common commitment to truth expressed in their mutual participation in an agonistic dialogue and the virtues appropriate to this process. Thus Putnam comments:

> I want to urge that there is all the difference in the world between an opponent who has the fundamental intellectual virtues of open-mindedness, respect for reasons, and self-criticism, and one who does not. . . . [T]he ambivalent attitude of respectful contempt is an honest one: respect for the intellectual virtues in the other; contempt for the intellectual and emotional weaknesses (according to one's own lights of course, for one always starts from them). (1981: 165–6)[12]

The central point about Nietzsche's perspectivism and the agonistic conception of political community which attends it is that, by tying our identities as citizens to the process of argument about the good, it makes the virtues of argument (in Nietzsche's terms, truthfulness and justice) into the fundamental formal virtues of political community. Indeed, one can easily imagine a community in which formal respect for other persons (because they are willing to engage in argument and to exhibit the virtues appropriate to this engagement) is twinned with substantive disdain for them (because we hold that the ordered set of values they recommend is lacking by our lights). At minimum, Putnam's example suggests both that Rawls' argument that political liberalism is the only way to cope with pluralism while maintaining an idea of free and equal citizens whose relations involve mutual respect is ill-founded and, at least implicitly, that Nietzsche's agonistic conception of political community can avoid the problems of Rawls' splitting of the individual into citizen and non-political person while supporting an overlapping consensus of reasonable substantive doctrines (i.e., doctrines which recognise their own perspectival character) because such doctrines acknowledge the agonistic and dialogical character of reason. Far from requiring us to bracket our comprehensive views when acting as citizens, Nietzsche's political agonism makes the dialogical conditions of holding our comprehensive views to be true into the fundamental features of citizenship.

If the claim that Nietzsche's political agonism models an understanding of citizens as free and equal, and cultivates the virtue of toleration, is plausible on the account given, it would seem reasonable to suggest that Rawls' concern with avoiding political controversies is perhaps less adequate in terms of our three criteria than Nietzsche's concern with making political contestation into the basic feature of a modern community. Political agonism seeks to cultivate the virtues appropriate to political argument rather than attempting to elide such argument; it views social co-operation as predicated on a common quest rather than on common agreement. But before we reach such a premature conclusion, we must ask what objections can be raised to Nietzsche's position. Perhaps the most fundamental objection from Rawls' position is that Nietzsche's account involves a comprehensive, albeit formal, conception of the good (i.e., the Overman) which involves controversial views about the character of selfhood (i.e., becoming what you are), of truth (i.e., the perspective theory of affects), and of human beings (i.e., the thesis of will to power). Fundamentally what is at issue here is the relationship of politics and philosophy; whereas Rawls supposes that philosophical controversy must be bracketed out of any plausible political view in order for it to generate overlapping consensus, Nietzsche's position would appear to require the entwinement of politics and philosophy. How might Nietzsche respond to Rawls' charge? Perhaps an appropriate response would be to argue that the philosophical claims which Nietzsche puts forward are open to contestation but that such philosophical contestation involves the same normative features as contestation in any practice (i.e., honesty and justice) which is modelled by Nietzsche's political agonism. For Rawls to deny this claim would require that he maintain that philosophical disputes do not involve a normative commitment to honest and open-minded argument, yet I would suggest that such a commitment is embedded in the history of philosophy as a practice (and, I would claim, reveals itself in the grammar of our concept of reason).[13] Consequently, I think that Nietzsche's position can avoid the critical query which would seem to flow from Rawls' position.

To conclude this section, let us review Nietzsche's position *contra* that of Rawls in terms of the criteria proposed. Firstly, there is the question of the wide appeal of basic assumptions. Since both Nietzsche and Rawls may be taken as modelling a political theory on the idea of free and equal citizens, there may seem little to choose between their appeal in terms of ideas latent within our public political culture; however, Nietzsche's stress on integrity draws on a further element with this culture which Rawls' position lacks. Secondly, there is the question of the capacity of their positions to withstand rational criticism. Here I have suggested that Nietzsche's perspective avoids the dilemmas of Rawls' account and, in particular, avoids the problematic character of the political/comprehensive distinction by deploying a distinction between formal and substantive comprehensive doctrines. Finally, there is the question of liveability. On this topic, I have claimed both that the potentially schizoid split in persons which is an aspect of Rawls' account is avoided by Nietzsche's civic humanism, in which the political arena is the domain within which substantive comprehensive doctrines contest with each other, *and* that Nietzsche's position is capable of cultivating the virtue of toleration requisite to social co-operation in the context of pluralism, which Rawls' account also identifies as central to contemporary political theory. It would be foolhardy to suggest that these claims exhaust the debate between these rich positions, not least since my account of both positions has been highly limited; however, if it has been made plausible that Rawls' claim for political liberalism as the only position appropriate to pluralism is undermined by Nietzsche's political agonism, then perhaps these comments can serve as a starting point for further dialogue.

Agonistic Politics *contra* Liberal Politics

In the preceding section, I have argued that it is at least plausible that Nietzsche's political agonism satisfies our theoretical interests better than Rawls' political liberalism. However, this claim cannot reasonably be divorced from the claim that an agonistic politics satisfies our – no doubt contested – political interests better than a liberal politics as advocated by Rorty and Rawls. It is the task of this section to render this claim plausible by considering Nietzsche's critique of liberal politics and his advocacy of an agonistic conception of politics. Here I want to return to Rorty's comment that we can set aside the question of the types of human being produced by a given form of politics because, even if liberalism produces uninspiring human beings, the fundamental question is that of political freedom which, for Rorty, *only* liberalism provides.[14] This objection to Nietzsche's position sets out the stakes of the contest on Rorty's terms: if, and only if, it is plausible that Nietzsche's agonistic politics can provide both political freedom and more valuable types of human being does it pose a challenge which liberals feel constrained to accept.

To begin our reflections on this topic, I will quote – at length – one of Nietzsche's most sustained contrasts between his position and liberalism from the perspective of freedom before arguing that the explication of these remarks reveals that Nietzsche's agonistic politics can meet the challenge which Rorty poses to it. Nietzsche comments:

> *My conception of freedom.* – The value of a thing lies sometimes not in what one attains with it, but in what one pays for it – what it *costs* us. I give an example. Liberal institutions immediately cease to be liberal as soon as they are attained: subsequently there is nothing more harmful to freedom than liberal institutions.

One knows, indeed, *what* they bring about: they undermine the will to power, they are the levelling of mountain and valley exalted to a moral principle, they make small, cowardly and smug – it is the herd animal which triumphs with them every time. Liberalism: in plain words, *reduction to the herd animal*. . . . As long as they are still being fought for, these same institutions produce quite different effects; they then in fact promote freedom mightily. Viewed more closely, it is war which produces these effects, war *for* liberal institutions which as war permits the *illiberal* instincts to endure. And war is a training in freedom. For what is freedom? That one has the will to self-responsibility. . . . How is freedom measured in individuals as in nations? By the resistance which has to be overcome, by the effort it costs to stay *aloft*. (TI 'Expeditions of an Untimely Man' §38)

In this passage we can see the by now familiar stress on freedom as self-overcoming and on the importance of struggle in Nietzsche's thinking in which the relationship between freedom and agonism marks the site of his critique of liberalism as reduction to the herd animal. To explicate the meaning and significance of this passage, I will focus on the two topics which concern us: firstly, the question of the conceptions of freedom exhibited in agonistic and liberal politics and, secondly, the question of the value of the human types produced by agonistic and liberal politics.

For liberals such as Rorty and Rawls, political freedom is conceptualised in terms of the *opportunity* (i.e., absence of external constraints) to pursue, revise and replace one's conception of the good. It is assumed that human beings as citizens have the capacity to engage in this activity and that all liberal politics need secure is the opportunity to exercise this capacity. By contrast, in the passage just cited, Nietzsche presents political freedom as self-overcoming, which denotes a will to self-responsibility, because only in mastering oneself can one justifiably claim self-responsibility. On this account of freedom, this concept denotes the *exercise* of our capacity to master ourselves and, thus, pursue, revise and replace one's substantive conception of the good *rationally*.[15] Thus, while both positions characterise human beings as having the capacity to pursue, reflect and revise their conceptions of the good, Nietzsche's position stresses that freedom is the *rational exercise* of this capacity and not simply the opportunity to exercise it (rationally or otherwise). Is this further step which Nietzsche takes sustainable or, even perhaps, necessary? Let us consider an example concerning the pursuit of conceptions of the good.

Imagine two persons of similar intellectual capacities at a given university who each desire as a significant good to write a book (and assume the relevant academic resources are equally available). But whereas person A gets down to work, person B is profoundly lazy and, despite his desire to write a book and his experience of his laziness as a constraint, succumbs to indolence. In this case, although they have an equal opportunity to pursue their conception of the good, it would seem odd to describe them as equally free since person B is bound to some significant degree by his laziness whereas person A is not. Of course, it might be objected that this example simply entails that the idea of opportunity to exercise our capacity to pursue our conception of the good needs to be expanded to include internal as well as external constraints, that is, freedom is the opportunity to pursue our conceptions of the good without external or internal constraint. But, unless it makes the implausible assumption that we are all characterised by equal self-mastery, this objection gives the game away since it entails that, other things being equal, an increase in self-mastery is an increase in freedom and, thus, that the exercise-concept of freedom as self-overcoming is prior to the opportunity-concept of freedom as absence of internal as well as external constraints.

There is, however, a second objection to freedom as self-overcoming which might be made, namely, that if freedom is conceptualised as the activity of mastering oneself, this conception seems to have little to say about external constraints. This line of argument connects to a third objection which is concerned with the emphasis on the idea of freedom as the *rational* exercise of one's human powers, worrying that this stress on rationality might lead to a position whereby people are 'forced to be free', and I will address these objections together. Let us note, firstly, that engagement in the activity of self-overcoming means overcoming not only weaknesses such as indolence, greed, etc., but also weaknesses such as self-deception; to master oneself entails not deceiving oneself about what one is. But how can I know if I am deceiving myself? To argue that I can know whether or not I am deceiving myself independently of being *able* to check this with others is analogous to the argument for a private language and similar objections follow, namely, that any standard which I use to check whether or not I am deceiving myself must first be checked for its suitability for that role since I might be deceiving myself about its appropriateness, but the only standard I have to check it against is itself and this is to make the incoherent demand that the standard adjudicate on its own suitability as a standard.[16] If this argument is cogent, it entails that self-overcoming requires a public standard against which one's claim to integrity can be judged and, concomitantly, a public characterised by unconstrained dialogue to engage in the activity of coming to this judgement. The second – and probably more obvious – point to note is that self-overcoming takes the form of rational engagement in practices and, consequently, requires that we are not constrained from such rational engagement. Finally, we can note that self-overcoming as the pursuit of both the formal *telos* of self-mastery and one's substantive conception of the good implies that one is committed to the claim that one can rationally hold one's substantive conception of the good. As we have noted in earlier discussions, this does not entail that it is legitimate for those persons who disagree with one's substantive conception of the good to force one to act according to a different conception, but it does imply that one must be willing to engage in open and fair-minded discussion about one's conception of the good, and this agonistic engagement also requires a public characterised by free and unconstrained dialogue.

While the purpose of these observations has been to argue that Nietzsche's agonistic politics involves a conception of political freedom which is reasonable (i.e., can do all the work that liberals require in terms of political freedom) and thus that the first aspect of Rorty's charge can be responded to, it seems plausible to claim that this argument also suggests that the liberal understanding of political freedom as an opportunity-concept is incoherent, and I will return to the significance of this point shortly. At this stage, though, let us turn to the other question which we need to address, that of the value of the human types produced by agonistic and liberal politics.

Isn't the very idea of more or less valuable types of human being deeply objectionable? We can note, firstly, that to talk in this way does not entail that some types of human being are without value; on the contrary, just as Nietzsche's perspectivism recognises the equal right of perspectives to claim epistemic authority without necessarily granting them equal authority, so – by analogy – I would suggest that Nietzsche's agonistic politics recognises the equal right of persons to claim political authority without necessarily granting them equal authority. If correct, this position entails that all persons have an equal right of recognition which implies that all persons are valuable and, as such, deserving of respect, even if it does not imply that all persons are of the same value and deserving of equal respect. Secondly, we can note that the phrasing of Rorty's remark admits – albeit perhaps unwittingly – the possibility of distinguishing more and less valuable human types since it only makes sense to say that political freedom is a price worth paying even if liberal politics produces petty, bland, and unheroic human types if there is some reason for regarding such types as less valuable than other types who are magnanimous, interesting and heroic. Nietzsche's position would no doubt seem less objectionable if we spoke of the ranking of human qualities rather than human types, but the point is essentially the same, namely, that both individually and collectively we value certain types of human being (i.e., those who exhibit the qualities we value) more than others (which is certainly not to say that we don't argue about what those qualities are and how to rank them; Nietzsche's point is precisely that such arguments are integral to politics). In this context, we need to ask why Nietzsche despises liberal politics and why he thinks an agonistic politics can better deliver noble human beings.

There are two central issues with respect to both of these questions: firstly, that of an *order of rank*, that is standards of value (i.e., excellence) whereby qualities, practices and types are ordered in terms of publicly recognised criteria; and, secondly, that of the relationship between an order of rank and agonistic politics. Let us begin with the thrust of Nietzsche's critical argument *contra* liberalism. In the lengthy passage cited above, Nietzsche makes it clear that he does not object to the struggle for liberalism precisely because it is the struggle over values which is important, but that he regards liberal institutions as disastrous for freedom – why? I think that the crucial issue is one already touched on in our discussion of Rorty and Rawls, namely, that liberalism depoliticises politics by introducing both a distinc-tion between the public (or political) and the private (or non-political) spheres and an anti-perfectionist defence of state neutrality. What is objectionable, on Nietzsche's account, about these features is that they entail the absence of a publicly constituted order of rank (either formal or substantive) because they privatise (or depoliticise) the pursuit of conceptions of the good and refuse to intervene in such non-political issues (except when necessary to prevent or repair breaches of rights). But perhaps this is to beg the question and we need to ask why we require an order of rank (however contested it may be).

In the essay 'Homer on Competition' touched on earlier, Nietzsche argues that, in an agonistic culture, an order of rank directs the activity of self-overcoming towards the development of the human powers valued by the community. Now if we reflect on Nietzsche's account of freedom as self-overcoming, we can note that both the formal standards of excellence constituted by the distance between the utopian figure of the Overman and the dystopian figure of the Last Man *and* the substantive standards of excellence constituted by the community in public dialogue direct the activity of the citizen towards integrity and the highest values of the community because it is the degree to which one attains these goals which governs both the value, respect and authority with which one is publicly endowed and, concomitantly, the feeling of power one experiences.[17] In this context, the significance of an agonistic politics is that it provides the conditions appropriate to self-overcoming in an age of pluralism by recognising that the features of integrity in this condition are truthfulness and justice, and establishing these features as the formal criteria of good citizenship and the pursuit of nobility. However, where a public political order of rank is lacking, that is, where either there is no order of rank or it is depoliticised (i.e., social), the activity of self-overcoming lacks either direction (a *telos*) or the conditions of its public significance (i.e., the recognition of politics as the highest form of human activity, that activity concerned with the public ordering of the virtues). Thus, since we have noted that if liberals are committed to the incoherent idea of freedom as an opportunity-concept and fail to recognise the priority of freedom as self-overcoming, Nietzsche's point that liberal politics (as expressed in its institutions) undermines either the possibility of self-overcoming by leaving it without direction or the significance of self-overcoming by depoliticising it (i.e., undermining the public *agon*) seems to construct a serious dilemma for liberal thought.

In reply to this critique, Rorty and Rawls might argue that political liberalism does provide a public order of rank by specifying the conditions of good citizenship in terms of tolerance and fair-mindedness, that is, a concern with political justice. However, two replies are available to Nietzsche. Firstly, he can argue that the liberal assumes a capacity for reasonableness on the part of persons which exhibits itself as support for political justice but does not provide the conditions appropriate to the cultivation of this capacity by attempting to impose closure on the question of the domain of the political and the character of justice. Secondly, Nietzsche can admit the political liberal's claim and argue that while liberalism may – just possibly –

be capable of cultivating tolerance and fair-mindedness, it does nothing to cultivate other virtues because it renders all other virtues non-political, whereas his account can facilitate the cultivation of a wide range of human powers precisely because even in arguing about the character of the substantive order of rank, citizens are concerned to exemplify the order of rank which they seek to recommend.

To conclude this section, let us sum up the main points of this discussion. The purpose of this section has been to argue that Nietzsche's agonistic politics can satisfy Rorty's implicit demand for both political freedom and noble human beings because it provides both a more adequate account of freedom and a concern with an order of rank which in the context of an agonistic political community leads to the cultivation of the human powers valued by the community. Thus, it is my contention that Nietzsche's agonistic politics is more conducive to human flourishing than liberal politics, whose emphasis on state neutrality and the public/private (or political/non-political) distinction undermines the conditions requisite to the production of a noble humanity.

Conclusion

Although this is the concluding chapter, the claims developed herein represent the central thesis of this book, namely, that it is at the very least plausible to argue that Nietzsche's political thinking offers a significant critique of liberalism and articulates an alternative vision of politics which has much to give. By attending to philosophical and political versions of liberal political theory, I hope to have shown that Nietzsche can reasonably claim that both are deeply flawed and that an emphasis on the construction of an agonistic politics, a form of civic humanism compatible with pluralism, presents us with greater resources for facing the challenge of modernity.

Notes

1 In this discussion, I am indebted to (and draw on) Mulhall and Swift's *Liberals and Communitarians* (1992) for its clear presentation of the issues at stake.

2 For consideration of this issue and related questions, see Daniels, ed., *Reading Rawls* (1975) and Kymlicka, *Contemporary Political Philosophy* (1990).

3 Kymlicka (1990: 206–15) argues that Rawls' setting up of the original position does not entail the metaphysical thesis which Sandel argues is implicit in Rawls' account, and I think Kymlicka is right in suggesting that the comprehensive position articulated by Rawls need not be a metaphysical thesis, but I agree with Sandel that there are enough remarks in Rawls' work to suggest that he is committed to a metaphysical thesis in *A Theory of Justice*.

4 For an interesting albeit implicit discussion of Rawls' commitment to rationality *contra* affectivity, see Bonnie Honig's *Political Theory and the Displacement of Politics* (1993).

5 Nietzsche's criticisms of Socrates can be readily grasped when set in this context. For a discussion of this topic, see Strong (1988).

6 Richard Bernstein (1986: 126) has pointed out that MacIntyre's position is quite consonant with Nietzsche's on this idea of a practice.

7 MacIntyre (1981: 178) argues for justice, truthfulness and courage, but I think that courage is immanent to the combination of truthfulness and justice (could one honestly subject one's deepest beliefs to the test of other views without courage? surely to do this is to exhibit courage as truthfulness and justice?), and consequently do not think it needs separate specification.

8 I draw this point from Mulhall and Swift (1992: 84), who use chess as their example.

9 In this section, I am drawing on Daniel Conway's articles 'Thus Spoke Rorty: The Perils of Narrative Self-Creation' (1991) and 'Disembodied Perspectives: Nietzsche *contra* Rorty' (1992b). I am grateful to Dan for our discussions on this topic.

10 Honi Fern Haber (1994: 41–71) points out that Rorty does not arrive immediately at this position, but after viewing liberalism and irony as complementary and then as antithetical eventually concludes that only through a public/private distinction can the advantages of both be combined.

11 For a general discussion of Rawls' reasons for advancing this claim, see Lecture I in *Political Liberalism* (1993: 3–46).

12 For an insightful and fun discussion of Putnam and others on reason as dialogue, see George Myerson's *Rhetoric, Reason and Society* (1994).

13 To refer to a dishonest argument or an argument which refuses to consider criticisms as reasonable would surely be to misuse the concept as we understand it.

14 Rorty must be committed to the claim that only liberalism can secure political freedom because otherwise this objection to non-liberal positions does no work in his argument.

15 I borrow the distinction between freedom as opportunity and as exercise from Charles Taylor's essay 'What is Wrong with Negative Liberty?' (1985b: 211–29). A similar concern with freedom as exercise can be found in Foucault and Deleuze, although with a more fluid notion of the subject of freedom. For a comparison of Taylor's position with that of the post-structuralist, see Paul Patton's essay 'Freedom, Power and Subjectivity' (1994).

16 For a concise discussion of the private language argument, see Stephen Mulhall's *On Being in the World* (1990: 55–60).

17 In other words, since self-mastery denotes the maximal experience of the feeling of power and is governed by public criteria, the degree to which one achieves self-mastery by reference to these public criteria is the degree to which one experiences the feeling of power and can have reverence for oneself.

Bibliography

Allison, H.E. (1983) *Kant's Transcendental Idealism*, New Haven: Yale University Press.

Allison, H.E. (1990) *Kant's Theory of Freedom*, Cambridge: Cambridge University Press.

Ansell-Pearson, K. (1991) *Nietzsche contra Rousseau*, Cambridge: Cambridge University Press.

Ansell-Pearson, K. (1994) *An Introduction to Nietzsche as a Political Thinker*, Cambridge: Cambridge University Press.

Ascheim, S.E. (1992) *The Nietzsche Legacy in Germany, 1890–1990*, Berkeley: University of California Press.

Babich, B.E. (1994) *Nietzsche's Philosophy of Science*, Albany: SUNY Press.

Beiner, R. (1983) *Political Judgement*, London: Methuen.

Bergmann, F. (1988) 'Nietzsche's Critique of Morality' in R.C. Solomon, and K.M. Higgins, eds, *Reading Nietzsche*, Oxford: Oxford University Press, pp. 29–45.

Bernstein, R.J. (1986) *Philosophical Profiles*, Oxford: Polity.

Blondel, E. (1991) *Nietzsche: The Body and Culture*, trans. S. Hand, London: Athlone Press.

Caygill, H. (1991) 'Affirmation and Eternal Return in the Free-Spirit Trilogy' in K. Ansell-Pearson, ed., *Nietzsche and Modern German Thought*, London: Routledge, pp. 216–39.

Clark, M. (1990) *Nietzsche on Truth and Philosophy*, Cambridge: Cambridge University Press.

Connolly, W.E. (1993) *The Augustinian Imperative*, London: Sage.

Conway, D. (1991) 'Thus Spoke Rorty: The Perils of Narrative Self-Creation', *Philosophy and Literature*, vol. 15, pp. 103–10.

Conway, D. (1992a) 'Heidegger, Nietzsche and the Origins of Nihilism', *Journal of Nietzsche Studies*, vol. 3, pp. 11–44.

Conway, D. (1992b) 'Disembodied Perspectives: Nietzsche *contra* Rorty', *Nietzsche Studien*, vol. 21, pp. 281–9.

Conway, D. (1993) 'Nietzsche's *Doppelgänger*: Affirmation and Resentment in *Ecce Homo*' in K. Ansell-Pearson and H. Caygill, eds, *The Fate of the New Nietzsche*, Aldershot: Avebury Press, pp. 55–78.

Daniels, N. ed. (1975) *Reading Rawls*, Oxford: Basil Blackwell.

Danto, A.C. (1988) 'Some Remarks on *The Genealogy of Morals*' in R.C. Solomon and K.M. Higgins, eds, *Reading Nietzsche*, Oxford: Oxford University Press, pp. 13–28.

Deleuze, G. (1983) *Nietzsche and Philosophy*, trans. H. Tomlinson, London: Athlone Press.

Descartes, R. (1968) *Discourse on Method and The Meditations*, trans. F.E. Sutcliffe, London: Penguin.

Dunn, J. (1985) *Rethinking Modern Political Theory*, Cambridge: Cambridge University Press.

Foucault, M. (1981) 'Is it Useless to Revolt?', *Philosophy and Social Criticism*, 8: 3–9.

Foucault, M. (1985) *The Use of Pleasure*, trans. R. Hurley, New York: Pantheon Press.

Gadamer, H.-G. (1976) *Philosophical Hermeneutics*, Berkeley: University of California Press.

Guyer, P. (1987) *Kant and the Problem of Knowledge*, Cambridge: Cambridge University Press.

Haber, H.F. (1994) *Beyond Postmodern Politics*, London: Routledge.

Habermas, J. (1987) *The Philosophical Discourse of Modernity*, trans. F. Lawrence, Cambridge, Mass.: MIT Press.

Hacking, I. (1982) 'Language, Truth, and Reason' in M. Hollis and S. Lukes, eds, *Rationality and Relativism*, Oxford: Basil Blackwell, pp. 48–66.

Conclusion

The argument of this book has been twofold: firstly, that Nietzsche can be appropriately read as a significant political thinker and, secondly, that in offering a sustained critique of liberalism from an agonistic perspective, Nietzsche elaborates a political theory which restates the case for civic humanism without eliding the fact of pluralism and without abrogating the autonomy of citizens. It is not claimed that Nietzsche 'finishes off' liberalism but simply that it is not sufficient for liberals either to ignore the agonistic position (Rawls) or to recognise but refuse to engage with this position (Rorty). Similarly, it is not claimed that this political theory is the only one which could be drawn from Nietzsche's work, it is simply the position which I think offers most of interest in terms of Nietzsche's ongoing relevance to contemporary debates. The hope of this argument is that it opens up a space for an encounter between agonistic and liberal forms of political theory in which a concern with the development of human capacities may flourish.

Hart, H.L.A. (1961) *The Concept of Law*, Oxford: Oxford University Press.

Hegel, G.W.F. (1952) *Philosophy of Right*, trans. T.M. Knox, Oxford: Oxford University Press.

Heller, E. (1988) *The Importance of Nietzsche*, Chicago: University of Chicago Press.

Hennis, W. (1983) 'Max Weber's "Central Question"', *Economy and Society*, vol. 12(2), pp. 135–80.

Honig, B. (1993) *Political Theory and the Displacement of Politics*, Ithaca: Cornell University Press.

Houlgate, S. (1991) *Freedom, Truth and History*. London: Routledge.

Hume, D. (1975) *Enquiries concerning Human Understanding and concerning the Principles of Morals*, Oxford: Oxford University Press.

Kant, I. (1957) *Critique of Judgement*, trans. J.C. Meredith, Oxford: Oxford University Press.

Kant, I. (1966) *The Critique of Pure Reason*, trans. N. Kemp-Smith, New York: St Martin's Press.

Kuhn, T. (1970) *The Structure of Scientific Revolutions*, 2nd edition, Chicago: University of Chicago Press.

Kymlicka, W. (1990) *Contemporary Political Philosophy*, Oxford: Clarendon Press.

Lampert, L. (1986) *Nietzsche's Teaching*, New Haven: Yale University Press.

Loewith, K. (1989) 'Max Weber's Position on Science' in P. Lassman and I. Velody, eds, *Max Weber's 'Science as a Vocation'*, London: Unwin Hyman, pp. 138–56.

Love, N.S. (1986) *Marx, Nietzsche, and Modernity*, New York: Columbia University Press.

McFall, L. (1987) 'Integrity', *Ethics*, vol. 98, pp. 5–20.

MacIntyre, A. (1977) 'Epistemological Crises, Dramatic Narrative and the Philosophy of Science', *The Monist*, vol. 60, pp. 453–72.

MacIntyre, A. (1981) *After Virtue*, London: Duckworth.

MacLean, A. (1993) *The Elimination of Morality*, London: Routledge.

Magnus, B. (1988) 'The Use and Abuse of *The Will to Power*' in R.C. Solomon and K.M. Higgins, eds, *Reading Nietzsche*, Oxford: Oxford University Press, pp. 218–36.

Magnus, B., Stewart, S. and Mileur, J.-P. (1993) *Nietzsche's Case: Philosophy as/and Literature*, London: Routledge.

Mendus, S. (1989) *Toleration and the Limits of Liberalism*, London: Macmillan.

Mulhall, S. (1990) *On Being in the World*, London: Routledge.

Mulhall, S. and Swift, A. (1992) *Liberals and Communitarians*, Oxford: Basil Blackwell.

Myerson, G. (1994) *Rhetoric, Reason and Society*, London: Sage.

Nagel, T. (1986) *The View from Nowhere*, Oxford: Oxford University Press.

Nehamas, A. (1985) *Nietzsche: Life as Literature*, Cambridge, Mass.: Harvard University Press.

Nishitani, K. (1990) *The Self-Overcoming of Nihilism*, trans. G. Parkes with S. Aihara, Albany: SUNY Press.

O'Neill, O. (1989) *Constructions of Reason*, Cambridge: Cambridge University Press.

Owen, D. (1991) 'Autonomy and "Inner Distance": A Trace of Nietzsche in Weber', *History of the Human Sciences*, vol. 4(1), pp. 79–91.

Owen, D. (1994) *Maturity and Modernity: Nietzsche, Weber, Foucault and the Ambivalence of Reason*, London: Routledge.

Patton, P. (1993) 'Politics and the Concept of Power in Hobbes and Nietzsche' in P. Patton, ed., *Nietzsche, Feminism and Political Theory*, London: Routledge, pp. 144–61.

Patton, P. (1994) 'Freedom, Power and Subjectivity', unpublished manuscript.

Pitkin, H. (1972) *Wittgenstein and Justice*, Berkeley: University of California Press.

Putnam, H. (1981) *Reason, Truth and History*, Cambridge: Cambridge University Press.

Quine, W.V.O. (1961) *From a Logical Point of View*, New York: Harper and Row.

Rawls, J. (1971) *A Theory of Justice*, Oxford: Oxford University Press.

Rawls, J. (1987) 'The Idea of Overlapping Consensus', *Oxford Journal of Legal Studies*, vol. 7(1), pp. 1–25.

Rawls, J. (1993) *Political Liberalism*, New York: Columbia University Press.

Rorty, R. (1980) *Philosophy and the Mirror of Nature*, Oxford: Basil Blackwell.

Rorty, R. (1989) *Contingency, Irony and Solidarity*, Cambridge: Cambridge University Press.

Rorty, R. (1991a) *Philosophical Papers, Vol. 1: Objectivity, Relativism and Truth*, Cambridge: Cambridge University Press.

Rorty, R. (1991b) *Philosophical Papers, Vol. 2: Essays on Heidegger and Others*, Cambridge: Cambridge University Press.

Sandel, M. (1982) *Liberalism and the Limits of Justice*, Cambridge: Cambridge University Press.

Staten, H. (1990) *Nietzsche's Voice*, Ithaca: Cornell University Press.

Strong, T.B. (1988) *Friedrich Nietzsche and the Politics of the Soul*, expanded 2nd edition, Berkeley: University of California Press.

Taylor, C. (1985a) *Philosophical Papers, Vol. 1: Human Agency and Language*, Cambridge: Cambridge University Press.

Taylor, C. (1985b) *Philosophical Papers, Vol. 2: Philosophy and the Human Sciences*, Cambridge: Cambridge University Press.

Taylor, C. (1989) *Sources of the Self*, Cambridge: Cambridge University Press.

Thiele, L.P. (1990) *Friedrich Nietzsche and the Politics of the Soul*, Princeton: Princeton University Press.

Tully, J. (1989) 'Wittgenstein and Political Philosophy', *Political Theory*, vol. 17(2), pp. 172–204.

Warren, M. (1988) *Nietzsche and Political Thought*, Cambridge, Mass.: MIT Press.

Weber, M. (1989) 'Science as a Vocation' in P. Lassman and I. Velody, eds, *Max Weber's 'Science as a Vocation'*, London: Unwin Hyman, pp. 3–22.

Weber, M. (1994) *Political Writings*, ed. P. Lassman, Cambridge: Cambridge University Press.

Williams, B. (1978) *Descartes*, London: Penguin.

Williams, B. (1985) *Ethics and The Limits of Philosophy*, London: Fontana/Collins.

Williams, B. (1993) *Shame and Necessity*, Berkeley: University of California Press.

Wittgenstein, L. (1958) *Philosophical Investigations*, trans. G.E.M. Anscombe, Oxford: Basil Blackwell.

Wittgenstein, L. (1969) *On Certainty*, trans. D. Paul and G.E.M. Anscombe, Oxford: Basil Blackwell.

Yovel, Y. (1980) *Kant and the Philosophy of History*, Princeton: Princeton University Press.

Index